Such Great Heights

Such Great Heights

THE COMPLETE CULTURAL HISTORY of the INDIE ROCK EXPLOSION

Chris DeVille

ST. MARTIN'S
PRESS
NEW YORK

First published in the United States by St. Martin's Press,
an imprint of St. Martin's Publishing Group

EU Representative: Macmillan Publishers Ireland Ltd, 1st Floor, The Liffey Trust Centre, 117–126 Sheriff Street Upper, Dublin 1, DO1 YC43

SUCH GREAT HEIGHTS. Copyright © 2025 by Christopher T. DeVille. All rights reserved. Printed in the United States of America. For information, address St. Martin's Publishing Group, 120 Broadway, New York, NY 10271.

www.stmartins.com

Designed by Steven Seighman

The Library of Congress Cataloging-in-Publication Data is available upon request.

ISBN 978-1-250-36338-1 (hardcover)
ISBN 978-1-250-36339-8 (ebook)

The publisher of this book does not authorize the use or reproduction of any part of this book in any manner for the purpose of training artificial intelligence technologies or systems. The publisher of this book expressly reserves this book from the Text and Data Mining exception in accordance with Article 4(3) of the European Union Digital Single Market Directive 2019/790.

Our books may be purchased in bulk for specialty retail/wholesale, literacy, corporate/premium, educational, and subscription box use. Please contact MacmillanSpecialMarkets@macmillan.com.

First Edition: 2025

10 9 8 7 6 5 4 3 2 1

For Amy, Nora, Naomi, and Isaiah

Contents

1. Slanted and Enchanted 3
2. Take Me Out 25
3. This Song Will Change Your Life 47
4. Best New Music 75
5. Music Is My Boyfriend 103
6. D.A.N.C.E. 133
7. Upward over the Mountain 153
8. Fake Empire 179
9. Terminally Chill 205
10. Late Registration 235
11. Art Angels 269
12. Love It If We Made It 303

    Acknowledgments 337
    Notes 339
    Index 345

Such Great Heights

Chapter 1 Soundtrack

R.E.M., "Radio Free Europe" (1983)

The Cure, "Boys Don't Cry" (1979)

The Replacements, "Left of the Dial" (1985)

The Smiths, "There Is a Light That Never Goes Out" (1986)

Pixies, "Where Is My Mind?" (1987)

Sonic Youth, "Teen Age Riot" (1988)

Beat Happening, "Indian Summer" (1989)

Dinosaur Jr., "Freak Scene" (1989)

Superchunk, "Slack Motherfucker" (1990)

The Breeders, "Divine Hammer" (1993)

Liz Phair, "Fuck and Run" (1993)

Pavement, "Cut Your Hair" (1994)

Guided by Voices, "Game of Pricks" (1995)

Belle and Sebastian, "Get Me Away From Here, I'm Dying" (1996)

Elliott Smith, "Between the Bars" (1997)

Yo La Tengo, "Sugarcube" (1997)

Neutral Milk Hotel, "Holland, 1945" (1998)

Cat Power, "Metal Heart" (1998)

The Flaming Lips, "Race for the Prize" (1999)

Built to Spill, "Carry the Zero" (1999)

1

Slanted and Enchanted

What do we mean when we say "indie"?

On the bus to high school my freshman year, everyone chose a side. We weren't literally split down the aisle like Congress, but the debate was polarized, largely along gender lines: The girls swore allegiance to teen pop, the boys to nu metal. There were factions within the two parties—Britney vs. Christina, Korn vs. Limp Bizkit, Backstreet Boys vs. NSYNC—but the coalitions generally held together, even as chaos agents like Eminem swung in to complicate the picture. (None of us knew who Stephen Malkmus was, but this *is* a book about indie rock, so I promise we'll get there eventually.)

This was the 1998–1999 school year. As we approached the new millennium, we were witnessing the rise of our own generation's pop culture, aligning ourselves with avatars for our raging hormones. In one corner were pristine ballads and dance-pop tracks about fairy-tale romance, manufactured with a meticulous craftsmanship surpassed only by what the boy band stylists were doing with hair gel. In the other corner were hulking, aggressive rap-rock war cries targeting parents, nemeses, and "bitch" ex-girlfriends, rendered in transgressive outbursts that made you feel like you were getting away with something by listening.

I liked some of the pop songs—and not just because the "... Baby One More Time" video left my mouth agape—but as an aspiring guitar hero in suburban Ohio who desperately wanted to impress girls, I wasn't about to define myself as a fan of that scene. As in politics, so much of this discourse was about posturing. Popular music was a way to figure out who we were, but also how we wanted to present ourselves to the world. And as with the two-party system, the nu metal vs. teen pop binary was an extremely reductive lens for identity—like attempting to boil down an eclectic student body to jocks and cheerleaders.

The theater for this pageantry was *Total Request Live*, colloquially known as *TRL*, the fan-voted music video countdown that aired weekday afternoons on MTV. On rides home from school, my neighbors and I bantered about the relative worth of tracks from Kid Rock and 98 Degrees. At home, before doing homework or logging on to AOL Instant Messenger (AIM), we'd tune in to see where they charted on the daily Top 10. For a while I was very invested in "Freak on a Leash" disrupting the endless back-and-forth between "All I Have to Give" and "(God Must Have Spent) A Little More Time on You."

But *TRL* viewership wasn't *just* about the countdown. The show was also a stop on the promotional circuit. Between videos, enlightened bro Carson Daly welcomed a parade of the biggest names in music to MTV's studios overlooking Times Square, where hordes of screaming kids gathered outside the windows hoping to get into the room where the magic happened. For lots of people my age, *TRL* became ground zero for pop culture. I loved the feeling of connecting to that shared experience, in part because it felt like social currency. The music featured on *TRL* was a lingua franca that allowed even socially awkward wimps like me to dialogue with the actual jocks and cheerleaders in my vicinity. (For what it's worth, I lettered in cross-country, but only because I wasn't good enough at soccer to make the team.)

Part of *TRL*'s appeal was the viewer's ability to dictate which videos would be shown that day. This was long before the emergence of the streaming-era pop stan—Eminem hadn't even released "Stan," the song about an obsessive fan that named the phenomenon—but the impulse was similar to the one that later had BTS and Ariana Grande supporters rallying to send their favorites up the charts. "Girls were able to see themselves as the authors of culture," Gayle Wald, a professor of English and American Studies at George Washington University, told Vulture in 2018. "They were pulling all the strings. The show became this really fun excuse for them to display their consumer power."

It's true that the frenzy around *TRL* marked the arrival of millennials as a marketing demo with purchasing power, distinct from our boomer parents and Gen X older cousins. The historic CD sales figures circa Y2K are proof of that. But *TRL* offered only the illusion of control. It was hard for artists beyond the show's main cast of characters to break into the mix. MTV carefully selected new videos to premiere on *TRL*—sometimes clips from established stars like Usher or Ricky Martin, but also sometimes as trial balloons for new artists aspiring to join the *TRL* universe. The show was at least as much about what MTV wanted teens to see as what teens wanted MTV to play, contributing to what eminent critic Ann Powers called "an intense caste system."

Still, as a child building my music fandom from scratch, FM radio and music videos felt like portals into vast worlds ripe for exploration. For me, early '90s youth phenomena like New Kids On The Block, Kris Kross, and Vanilla Ice were like items glimpsed in a store window yet not taken home. I encountered them through friends and their older siblings, but they weren't a part of our household like my dad's Beatles records, my mom's Whitney Houston cassettes, or the many Christian pop albums—from Amy Grant to DC Talk—that dominated our listening. The alternative rock explosion was even more foreign to me, though I recognized a lot of the album covers from ads for mail-order music clubs like Columbia House and BMG.

Toward the end of elementary school, pop radio and VH1 (but not the more scurrilous MTV) entered the picture. I came home from the library with stacks of CDs. I heard Top 40 hits like TLC's "Waterfalls," Blues Traveler's "Run Around," and Real McCoy's Eurodance cheese-fest "Run Away" so often that obtaining the albums seemed unnecessary. The enduring memory of my short-lived country music phase is attempting to tape Garth Brooks's "Friends in Low Places" off the radio (the live version with the extra verse that ends with "And you can kiss my ass!").

By the time I got clearance to watch MTV in middle school, Kurt Cobain was dead. Billy Corgan had shaved his head. Pearl Jam were at war with Ticketmaster and the concept of fame itself. The first wave of grunge-era stars was giving way to less, um, vigorously canonized fare like Bush, Live, and Everclear.

Alternative rock was no longer the vanguard, and its blockbuster status was slipping away.

The fact that rock was going through a weird in-between phase did not stop it from becoming the bedrock of my personal taste. My peer group adopted Weezer and Foo Fighters as perennial favorites. I started watching *Saturday Night Live* and was stunned by performances from Soundgarden and Rage Against The Machine. Through my pal across the street, I got into Metallica and Pantera, then spent hours hacking away at their guitar tablature. And thanks in part to the new world order established by *TRL*, for a while nu metal was my central focus.

Despite my appreciation for Korn and Bizkit, I never identified with the nu-metal lifestyle to the extent of wearing gargantuan JNCO jeans, growing my hair into dreadlocks, or starting a riot at Woodstock '99. Instead, I began to gravitate toward the artsier side of the scene. Deftones swirled goth, new wave, and shoegaze influences into glamorous, dreamy alt-metal sleaze. System Of A Down combined zany madcap energy and jarring emotional intensity into some of the most explosive music I'd ever heard. Incubus moved fearlessly between genres, toggling from crunchy power-chord riffs to wacky funk-rap to jazzy party grooves and beyond.

By the summer of '99, I'd anointed Incubus as my new favorite band. The day I got my driver's license, *S.C.I.E.N.C.E.* was the first CD I blasted in my '88 Camry. I loved their dynamism and their fearless collision of styles. I also liked that they were a little more obscure than your average Ozzfest performer, a secret I could share with less knowledgeable listeners for clout. "Incubus fan" became my personality. But within a year, I'd replaced it with one that struck me as far more sophisticated: "Radiohead fan."

David, a friend from school with a similar hunger for music, had started tracking down every title from *SPIN*'s list of the 100 best albums of the '90s and sharing his favorites with me. He reserved his most evangelical fervor for *OK Computer*. At first, I was resistant. In middle school I'd been scared off by the jagged, queasy "Paranoid Android" and its disturbing cartoon video. But David was insistent, so I borrowed his CD and kept waiting to be walloped. On a sunny day in the spring of 2000, something clicked. Driving home from track practice, I had a religious experience with "Exit Music (for a Film)," and suddenly the whole album opened up to me. Thom Yorke's powerhouse falsetto, Jonny Greenwood's elastic lead guitar, a futuristic grandeur informed by the classics: This music moved me, and based on the way Radiohead was framed in the media, liking them made me feel both cool and smart. I'd found my new obsession.

I spent the summer cruising around the suburbs basking in *The Bends*, then coming home and downloading every Radiohead rarity I could find on Napster, the file sharing service that had revealed vast new galaxies of sound to anyone with broadband internet. (For those on a dial-up connection, it was more like vast new solar systems of sound.) In the fall I lined up outside Sour Records to buy *Kid A* at midnight, then stayed up even later dissecting it with David on AIM. I don't remember anything about my junior year homecoming dance, but I acutely recall returning home in the early morning hours, rewinding my VHS tape, and watching a manic, transcendent performance of "The National Anthem" on *SNL*.

By then, the internet was becoming a hub for music discovery and fan communities. For me, that network included an array of Radiohead fan sites like Green Plastic Radiohead and At Ease. As winter set in, those sites began linking to every year-end best-albums list that included *Kid A*. Most of them presented a mix of the same few names—OutKast, U2, D'Angelo, PJ Harvey—but one countdown stood out. An obscure website called Pitchfork Media had ranked Radiohead No. 1, and I knew virtually none of the other artists mentioned.

There were quirky band names like Modest Mouse and Yo La Tengo and Grandaddy and Godspeed You! Black Emperor. There was a mysterious group from Iceland with an alien baby on their album cover. The one other record I'd heard, by Badly Drawn Boy, had mesmerized me almost as much as *Kid A*. So I figured a bunch of these albums must be worth picking up.

I didn't realize it then, but this was a paradigm shift. I'd drilled down into a world that existed just beneath the mainstream, into a subculture that would transform the way I approached music for better and for worse. Life would never be the same again. I had discovered indie rock.

* * *

What does "indie" mean? I'm not sure anyone could have given me a clear answer in the year 2000, when I started to construct my self-image around bands like Pavement and Pixies. I'm even less sure it can be coherently explained a quarter century later, even after building my career around it as an editor for the indie-centric music blog *Stereogum*. What I *can* say with certainty is that the indie culture I stumbled into at the turn of the millennium has transformed in radical ways since then.

In what ways has it changed? How and why did those changes happen? What about them stands out as good or bad? My aim in this book is to explore those questions while revisiting how indie music blew up, became the soundtrack to many millennials' coming of age, morphed into a kind of prestige pop music, flew too close to the sun trying to become actual pop music, and returned underground in the streaming era, even as its influence rippled through the upper echelons of the music industry. In some ways, it is the story of how hipsters—those urban-dwelling, trend-conscious early adopters often closely linked with indie rock—moved from worshiping Built to Spill to Beyoncé to boygenius.

Maybe you feel like you know that story intuitively because you've lived it. Or maybe you're like I was at seventeen, newly entranced by this world and eager to learn as much about it as possible. If you're reading this book, there's a decent chance the word "indie" is already loaded with significance for you. But defining your terms is important, and this one is slippery, so let's get pedantic.

In the most literal sense, "indie" refers to music released on independent record labels—i.e., companies not associated with the "big three" major labels Warner, Sony, and Universal—or self-released without label support at all. Due to economies of scale, these kinds of records don't tend to reach a very large audience compared with music backed by massive corporations, so "indie rock" is sometimes synonymous with "underground rock." But an artist on an indie label can become a household name, and artists on majors can toil in obscurity, so indie and underground aren't perfectly congruent terms.

And anyhow, this isn't simply a matter of corporate taxonomy. Independent labels have always been part of the music industry, yet no one really threw around the phrase "indie rock" until a whole ecosystem had sprung up around some of those records. By the time Sebadoh released their *Gimme Indie Rock* EP in 1991, "indie" implied a vast network of bands, labels, concert venues, record stores, radio stations, and homemade zines, which largely existed apart from the major-label system. In that sense, it was less a genre than a culture: a loose coalition of outsiders, idealists, elitists, critics, creatives, college students, and so forth.

Because that culture gravitated toward certain strains of guitar-based rock, "indie rock" became shorthand for a family tree of musical aesthetics, too—a lineage tracing back to artsy, noisy late '60s pioneers like the Velvet Underground and the Stooges, with stops at punk, hardcore, and new wave but also power-pop, shoegaze, twee, and a parade of other hip subgenres you could discuss with the clerk at your local record store if you dared strike up a conversation.

During the alternative rock explosion set off by Nirvana in the early '90s—a movement that mainstreamed loud, angsty, aggressive hard rock, especially the punk-metal hybrid known as grunge—a lot of underground bands ended up on major labels and, by extension, on MTV and the radio. They often did not soften their sounds in the process of crossing over, which is to say they became popular without really "going pop." Suddenly, you could be on a major label but still be an indie band in essence. Things got blurry. But really, when *hadn't* they been?

* * *

To understand how indie rock has changed in the early twenty-first century, we have to understand what it was circa Y2K. So, in search of a painfully abbreviated indie-rock genealogy, let's go way back—past Pitchfork, Pixies, and Pere Ubu, to the cultural upheaval of the 1960s. (Warning: I'm leaving out a zillion important bands. Just sketching an outline here.)

As rock rose up from the underground to become the driving force of global youth culture, subcultures emerged. Some bands got rawer and more unruly, inventing garage rock—an ancestry that eventually led to proto-punk acts like Detroit's Stooges and their bloodied, bare-chested singer, Iggy Pop. Avant-garde classical types in New York brought droning experiments to bear on rock 'n' roll, most famously the Velvet Underground, with their sensory-overload art-stunt live shows and noise-strewn songs about sex and drugs. Iconoclasts like LA's Captain Beefheart seemed to delight in confusing and alienating potential listeners.

In their moment, these bands were cult favorites at best. By the time I discovered them, they were pillars of a hipster history starter pack. That glow-up was partially the result of these acts taking on a your-favorite-band's-favorite-band status and exerting an outsized influence over cutting-edge music. In an oft-recycled quote, Brian Eno told the *Los Angeles Times* in 1982, "I was talking to Lou Reed the other day, and he said that the first Velvet Underground record sold only 30,000 copies in its first five years. Yet, that was an enormously important record for so many people. I think everyone who bought one of those 30,000 copies started a band!"

This class of artists owed some of their reputation to writers like Lester Bangs and Lenny Kaye, who were beginning to shape rock-snob conventional wisdom. As magazines like *Crawdaddy*, *Creem*, and *Rolling Stone* and alternative newspapers like *The Village Voice* began to take rock seriously, a canon of critically acclaimed releases emerged, often diverging from the popular consensus. "[Led] Zeppelin's enormous commercial success, in spite of critical opposition, revealed the deep division in what was once thought to be a homogenous audience," critic Jon Landau wrote in 1971. "The division has now evolved into a clearly defined mass taste and a clearly defined elitist taste."

When punk came along in the '70s, it was branded as a reaction against the bloated rock establishment and a return to the raw simplicity of early rock 'n' roll. "Branded," I say, because impresarios like Malcolm McLaren and Vivienne Westwood—who assembled and managed the Sex Pistols out of their London boutique, Sex—were creatures of fashion, marketing, and show business. Still, punk counted some true idealists among its ranks, from bleeding-hearted icons the Clash to radical anarchists Crass.

One of punk's tenets was that anyone could create great art, regardless of ability, resources, or training. This philosophy is one reason why the movement birthed a new class of underground media: the DIY fanzine. Magazines like NYC's *Punk* and cut-and-pasted, photocopied zines like London's *Sniffin' Glue* (named for a Ramones song) chronicled the burgeoning punk subculture with an irreverent bent and a conversational tone that matched the scene's subversive, safety-pinned fashion sense.

As the look and sound of punk became codified in the public imagination, many of the genre's pioneers moved on. Punk was always more than loud, fast three-chord diatribes performed by amateurs (see: Television's *Marquee Moon*), and by the end of the '70s the scene was splintering into umpteen subgenres, including "post-punk" acts that steered the genre in arty, experimental directions. Groups like New Order and Throbbing Gristle incorporated elements of synth pop and electronic dance music. Post-punk's more accessible cousin, new wave, leaned even harder into those sounds and spawned a whole generation of hits from Human League, Tears For Fears, Blondie, and more, helping to define the look and feel of early MTV.

Meanwhile, another wave of alternative bands was percolating, thanks to . . . the federal government? In 1978, responding to complaints from more professionalized public radio stations that low-wattage college stations were interfering with their signals, the FCC forced them all to make the leap to 100 watts or shut down. Many upgraded their signals, putting a megaphone to communities that had not been represented on commercial radio. The following year *College Media Journal* (*CMJ*), a trade magazine aimed at college broadcasters, launched with a debut issue that resembled a photocopied punk zine.

As college radio expanded its reach and developed a nationwide network, a new platonic ideal known as "college rock" took shape. The foundation of the scene became the jangly guitars, nervy rhythms, and melodious poetry of Athens, Georgia's R.E.M. They found British counterparts in the Smiths, who paired Morrissey's dour, depressive croon with Johnny Marr's brightly chiming guitar, and the Cure, who emerged from post-punk's goth wing to craft stadium-scale sadboi anthems decades before the term "sadboi" was invented.

Back in the US, hardcore punk sprouted up in parallel with college rock. A circuit of VFW halls and all-ages clubs connected scenes in locales like Southern California (most notably Black Flag and SST Records) and Washington, DC (where members of straightedge pioneers Minor Threat launched the fiercely idealistic Dischord Records). Zines like *Maximumrocknroll* chronicled it all, providing nationwide exposure for bands too abrasive or DIY to be covered in *Rolling Stone* (or even the alternative-leaning *Spin*).

Soon bands started merging poppy college rock with the hard-hitting distortion of hardcore, at which point we arrived at the music we now think of as indie rock. Minnesota yielded both the howling, rocket-fueled Hüsker Dü and the Replacements, self-sabotaging rock 'n' rollers whose "Left of the Dial" became a theme song for college radio. Sonic Youth arose out of New

York's "no wave" scene with an exhilarating sound that made the experimental feel accessible. In Western Massachusetts, Dinosaur Jr. turned up to deafening volumes and piled sludge onto the classic rock template. Over in Boston, explosive pop weirdos Pixies perfected a loud-quiet-loud dynamic that would soon become standard practice in alternative rock. A slew of feminist bands, zines, and labels in Olympia, Washington, cohered into the riot grrrl movement, while bands in nearby Seattle landed on a heavy new style known as grunge.

Most people who were involved in underground rock back then remember Nirvana's *Nevermind* as a B.C./A.D. moment. Climbing to the top of the *Billboard* album chart by early 1992, Nirvana's major-label debut sent stylistic shockwaves through MTV and rock radio and incited a feeding frenzy in which record labels threw money at any artist who could feasibly be sold as "alternative." But even before "Smells like Teen Spirit," alternative rock was becoming big business. R.E.M. and the Cure were headlining arenas by the end of the '80s. The first Lollapalooza, a touring festival centered on alternative rock, swept across America in the summer of 1991, months before *Nevermind*.

As flannel-clad slackers became a pervasive cultural archetype, heavy Seattle bands like Pearl Jam, Soundgarden, and Alice in Chains rose to superstardom by cranking out Generation X's version of arena rock. So did Chicago's ambitious, perfectionist Smashing Pumpkins, whose Billy Corgan worshiped hard-rockers like KISS and Black Sabbath rather than the gods of punk, and Hole, a Los Angeles combo led by Courtney Love that evolved from guttural noise-rock to crystalline power-pop. Despite the popular half-truth that grunge killed hair metal, many of the biggest alt-rock bands—with their chunky power chords, thunderous drum fills, and ripping guitar solos—sounded just fine on the radio alongside macho monsters of rock like Van Halen or Guns N' Roses.

That resemblance didn't sit well with Kurt Cobain, who'd emerged from the underground with a strong critique of the mainstream, then watched the mainstream become a funhouse-mirror reflection of himself. After complaining that the glossy production of *Nevermind* made it sound like Mötley Crüe, Cobain recruited indie celebrity Steve Albini to record the pointedly abrasive follow-up *In Utero*. When Nirvana appeared on the cover of *Rolling Stone*, faithful zine reader Cobain wore a T-shirt with the hand-scrawled message "CORPORATE MAGAZINES STILL SUCK."

Everyone underground was wrestling with the same tensions. One core ethic of independent music was an aversion to "selling out"—compromising your moral integrity, creative purity, et al., in exchange for fame and fortune. To sign with a major label rather than remain staunchly independent was to sell out. To water down your music in pursuit of more listeners was to sell out. To license your song for use in an advertisement was especially egregious. Yet many musicians struck while the iron was hot, including some who attempted to maintain their principles (or at least the appearance of principles).

Some of the greatest artists in the underground cashed in on the alternative gold rush and went on to have long, fruitful careers in the major-label system. But many had ethical concerns about aligning with a major-label machine that encouraged homogeneous music and was funded by giant, shady corporations. Others feared the loss of control that could come along with corporate support—or, worse, corporate neglect—and exploitative contracts that left bands in debt to their labels. (This is where I refer you to Albini's legendary *The Baffler* article "The

Problem with Music," which ends with the sentence, "Some of your friends are probably already this fucked.")

Some from the indie scene attempted to keep one foot in both worlds. In the early '90s, Matador Records emerged as one of the hottest new labels in indie rock thanks to artists like Teenage Fanclub, Superchunk, Pavement, and Liz Phair. Matador's bands weren't just college radio sensations, they got coverage in the mainstream music press—especially Phair, whose debut, *Exile in Guyville*, shared frank perspectives on life as a woman in a male-dominated rock scene (often by singing about Chicago alt-rock bros in scathing, scandalous ways). In 1993, Matador's success led to a partnership with Atlantic Records, part of the Warner Bros. media empire, which created headaches related to the optics of indie rock.

Quirky, lackadaisical geniuses Pavement's 1992 debut *Slanted and Enchanted*—which mixed arty British post-punk with shambolic pop songwriting, above-it-all California cool, and copious stoner absurdity—had been a massive critical and commercial success for Matador. In 1994, Pavement released their follow-up, *Crooked Rain, Crooked Rain*. It lifted Pavement out of lo-fi static and into a graceful, slipshod West Coast classic rock vibe, and it upped the band's pop appeal with radio-friendly singles like "Cut Your Hair." Matador and Atlantic co-released *Crooked Rain*, but Matador feared indie fans wouldn't approve of a major-label Pavement album, and Pavement weren't comfortable with the Atlantic staff following hip exec Danny Goldberg's departure. So Atlantic's name wasn't on the sleeve, and Atlantic didn't help promote the record.

"We ended up with the worst of both worlds," Matador co-owner Gerard Cosloy told me in a 2014 *Stereogum* feature, referring to hurt feelings within the Atlantic staff and suspicion from indie record buyers who wondered what Matador was trying to hide. "We've essentially shot ourselves—we don't have enough feet to count how many times we shot ourselves in the foot with this entire setup." Pavement were on their way to becoming an iconic, deeply influential band—to this day, the simplest explanation of indie rock is "music that sounds like Pavement"—but let's just say "Cut Your Hair" did not become the next "Smells like Teen Spirit."

Some indie bands opted out of the major-label circus. Superchunk, tuneful and hyperactive rockers from North Carolina, scored an underground smash with 1990's "Slack Motherfucker" and were one of the earliest bands signed to Matador. They took a meeting with Goldberg at Atlantic but decided not to sign, preferring to maintain greater autonomy. When Matador partnered with Atlantic months later, it contributed to Superchunk's decision to leave for their own upstart label, Merge. As the '90s wore on, Superchunk's Mac McCaughan and Laura Ballance built Merge from a plucky passion project into an indie powerhouse, releasing landmark albums like Neutral Milk Hotel's *In the Aeroplane Over the Sea* and Magnetic Fields' *69 Love Songs*.

Even within "alternative rock," an alternate canon was forming, situated somewhere below ubiquitous MTV-grade rock stardom. The kinds of loud, abrasive bands that spearheaded alt-rock's mainstream breakthrough started to seem gauche in indie-rock circles, especially as the aggression from grunge's big bang filtered out into dunderheaded nu metal like Limp Bizkit and painfully earnest butt rock like Creed. As indie musicians scrambled to distance themselves from corporate rock radio playlists haunted by the ghost of grunge, a new landscape coalesced around the softer, prettier remnants of college rock.

Within this universe, there were singer-songwriters like Cat

Power and Elliott Smith who channeled intense feelings into hauntingly intimate music. There were Belle & Sebastian, whose pastoral folk pop borrowed from the droll melodrama of the Smiths and the twee preciousness of indie-pop. There were psych-pop revivalists like Oklahoma freaks the Flaming Lips, and the Elephant 6 collective, a sprawling friend group loosely centered on Athens, Georgia, headlined by Neutral Milk Hotel's surreal, nasal bombast. The Pacific Northwest, once known as the hotbed of grunge, yielded a more sensitive, less sludgy generation of guitar bands like Built to Spill, Modest Mouse, and Death Cab for Cutie.

In his 2009 Pitchfork article "The Decade in Indie," the brilliant critic Nitsuh Abebe summed up indie rock's late '90s baseline:

> This music was pleasant, accessible, and aesthetically interesting, but without making a whole lot of noise or sudden moves about it. There were things about the songs that were comfortable and traditional, which was how consensus got built around them: They were easy to like. But there were also things about them that, in the context of their time, seemed rare and special and worth getting behind. Some acts were soft-spoken and wry, which was a big contrast not only from pop but from buzzy, earnest alternative. Some, like Belle & Sebastian or Cat Power, had a sense of privacy and withdrawal to them, like they lived in your bedroom instead of blaring everywhere—like there was something precious about them. There was a level of fantasy and whimsy around a lot of records, a light psychedelia, that hadn't been heard in a while and couldn't be gotten elsewhere—this sense, when listening to the Lips or Stereolab or Elephant 6 bands, that the artists

were picking up different aspects of pop music and painting swoony little dreams out of them. It felt *thoughtful*, a quality that's hard to define but a very big part of what made it appeal. Thoughtful and, of course, different. Music your parents could like, but probably found strange: This could feel subversive, somehow, in a world where youth culture was presumed to be aggressively loud. This stuff wanted to be *nice*; it wanted—rather unusually—to be subtle, maybe even a bit quaint.

Indie had evolved into a strange tension. On the one hand, the culture was mostly walled off from the mainstream, and after witnessing what happened in the early '90s, both artists and fans were ambivalent about the idea of crossing over. On the other hand, in lieu of "the next Nirvana," this was a scene full of would-be R.E.M.s—bands with clean-cut pop appeal to go along with indie cred, who might be stable and savvy enough to build long, legendary careers. Plenty of esoteric music was being championed by tastemakers, but the artists who were gaining traction were approachable and charming in a way that made it easy for outsiders to buy in. Buying in was certainly easy for me.

At age seventeen, it didn't take long for indie rock to colonize my brain. I started piecing together the genre's history by poking around the internet (All Music Guide was an invaluable pre-Wikipedia database) and any CD store within driving distance. By the end of high school, I was faithfully loading up Pitchfork every day and reading each review—or at least checking the scores, eager to be told whether to feel excited, disgusted, or meh.

I truly loved the music, but I also liked the sense that I'd discovered something special, something secret, something *su-*

perior. It didn't bother me that three of the best "indie" albums of 1999—the Flaming Lips' *The Soft Bulletin*, Built to Spill's *Keep It Like a Secret*, and Wilco's *Summerteeth*—were all released under the Warner Bros. umbrella. I didn't mind that a lot of my new favorite bands were all over MTV2 or that I could find their albums on the wall at Virgin Megastore. Julian Casablancas's silver-spoon childhood in no way complicated my love for RCA recording artists the Strokes.

For me, indie wasn't about DIY ethics, avant-garde disruption, or any kind of radical worldview. It was about albums I could spin incessantly and organize into lists in place of a personality, songs I could burn onto mix CDs for my friends and family to show off my good taste, and bands that doubled as a secret handshake with people cooler than me. As someone with average-or-worse charisma, looks, and athletic ability, who'd never had much to brag about besides my grades, I bought into the snobbery that often seemed inextricable from indie-rock fandom. "Hipster" was an aspirational status for me, albeit one I always felt too sheepish and basic to fully achieve.

By the time I showed up at Ohio University in 2002, indie rock had so monopolized my listening that I was oblivious to what was happening in mainstream music. I'd encounter a pop song here and there, but *TRL* and the *Billboard* charts meant nothing to me. I barely even had time for *Rolling Stone*, *Spin*, or alt-rock radio. It was all about whatever was being hyped on Pitchfork and the burgeoning network of websites, blogs, and message boards that cohered into an online media ecosystem. Within this alternate universe, Matador was the most important label in the world, talented nobodies like Menomena could become low-key celebrities by virtue of a Best New Music designation, and a pop-rap dynasty as dominant as Murder Inc. did not exist except as a punch line in a review of some experimental Def Jux release.

My secret world would not stay secret for long. In the years ahead, indie rock reached an exponentially larger audience and was utterly transformed in the process. Looking back on it, there's a lot to consider: about who gets to define what's hip and how those same things become passé when the "wrong" people get involved; about how reckoning with prejudices can alter your worldview and broaden your horizons; about how new technologies can build up, shake up, and destroy; about the nobility of trying something new and the folly of pretending to be something you're not; about how the meaning of one word can drift and mutate over the course of a quarter century; about how, for good and for ill, an insular subculture can become something else entirely.

Chapter 2 Soundtrack

The Dismemberment Plan, "The Ice of Boston" (1997)
The Faint, "Agenda Suicide" (2001)
The Hives, "Hate to Say I Told You So" (2000)
The Strokes, "Hard to Explain" (2001)
The White Stripes, "Fell In Love With a Girl" (2001)
Liars, "Mr Your On Fire Mr" (2001)
Interpol, "PDA" (2002)
Hot Hot Heat, "Talk to Me, Dance with Me" (2002)
The Rapture, "House of Jealous Lovers" (2002)
Yeah Yeah Yeahs, "Maps" (2003)
!!!, "Me and Giuliani Down by the Schoolyard-A True Story" (2003)
The Postal Service, "Such Great Heights" (2003)
LCD Soundsystem, "Losing My Edge" (2002)
TV On The Radio, "Staring at the Sun" (2003)
Les Savy Fav, "The Sweat Descends" (2004)
Franz Ferdinand, "Take Me Out" (2004)
The Killers, "Somebody Told Me" (2004)
Bloc Party, "Banquet" (2005)
The Bravery, "An Honest Mistake" (2005)
Kelly Clarkson, "Since U Been Gone" (2004)

2

Take Me Out

The indie kids learn to dance.

Many of indie rock's true believers turned to the genre because it stirred their soul; much of the broader world bought into indie because it moved their body.

In the late '90s, most indie music was not yet suited to the dance floor. You could jump up and down to some of it, but—give or take a Stereolab track—you couldn't build a DJ set out of it and expect the general public to cut loose. Even much of the electronic music touted by indie tastemakers was abstract fare more suited to headphones than giant club speakers. So although the Dismemberment Plan would have been weird in any era, in the late '90s indie scene they *really* stood out.

The Plan did things other bands just didn't do. Their show-closing renditions of "OK Joke's Over" found Travis Morrison un-ironically crooning portions of Top 40 hits before the chaotic finish kicked in. They covered one of those hits, Jennifer Paige's

"Crush," on the same EP that included their maniacal tongue-in-cheek story-song "The Dismemberment Plan Gets Rich." Years before anyone ever heard of Girl Talk, when the default posture at an indie show was to stand still with your arms crossed, the Plan were welcoming fans onstage to dance with them every night during their neurotic masterpiece "The Ice of Boston."

The dancing was what stood out most. Within the pointedly quaint environs of late '90s indie, not a lot of bands were inspiring listeners to throw ass. Not even a dance-centric band like the Plan achieved that goal all the time. Their 1997 sophomore album *The Dismemberment Plan Is Terrified* included a song called "Do the Standing Still," on which Morrison joked about the dance craze sweeping the nation, "a brand new step that everybody isn't moving to." Morrison's sarcastic lyrics critiqued chin-stroking indie audiences who refused to let their guard down: "In Fargo, six or seven kids watched the Plan in a strip mall/ Well, I thought they were bored out of their skulls, but it turns out they were having a ball!"

The Plan formed in 1993 in Washington, DC, where rhythm is king. The city has long been proud of go-go, its localized strain of funky party music. "It's foundational, really," Morrison told the *Vinyl Emergency* podcast in 2023. "It's one of those things where it's always there. Like, you can't really imagine a world without it." Per Morrison, daily go-go blocks on DC radio taught him to think of every instrument as a percussive instrument. On top of that, the most influential act in DC punk was Fugazi, whose rhythmically complex version of post-hardcore ensured you could dance rather than mosh to songs like "Repeater."

Whatever you wanted to call the Plan's rambunctious, often asymmetrical form of indie rock, it was impossible to miss the DC in it. Critics constantly compared them to brainy, jittery post-punk/new wave legends Talking Heads. They also shared some DNA with art-school marauders Les Savy Fav and, if we're being honest, funky and unhip modern rock mainstays like Red Hot Chili Peppers, Primus, and Incubus. "I remember a show in Baltimore," bassist Eric Axelson once told NPR, "where I think one of us had a Grateful Dead T-shirt on, one of us had a Fishbone shirt on, and Travis came from work in khakis and a button-down."

The Plan were not without peer in the '90s, but they were clearly on their own wavelength. The guitars poked and prodded at a herky-jerky rhythm section that sometimes moved like a Slinky flopping down the stairs. Occasionally, everything exploded into a humongous pop chorus or an unhinged noise spree, or both of those pitted against each other. You'd think their steadfast commitment to such outbursts would be the most confrontational thing about them, but they also liberally incorporated keyboards and cozied up to pop, rap, and R&B when those were still radical gestures for an indie band. Then there was Morrison, a charismatic human cartoon whose personality—a mix of gleeful mischief and sardonic bile, manifested in screams, whimpers, blared nasal melodies, and spoken passages that sometimes veered into quasi-rapping—could be as polarizing as the music itself. I once described him as "Jim Carrey fronting Devo."

1999's near-perfect *Emergency & I* turned the Plan's twitchy, explosive dance-punk into outright pop music, pumping it full of sonic color and emotional depth. *E&I* was a classic quarter-life crisis record. Morrison sang about the messy uncertainty of twentysomething life in wry outbursts and heart-on-sleeve hooks—"a confetti cannon of words," as he once described it. His band mirrored that tumult in a way that felt cinematic, all without discarding the shrieking, the petulance, the weird time signatures, the discordant noise. As a high school senior, the album became crucial to my own indie-rock awakening—so much so that, in my first year of college, I attended seven Dismemberment Plan shows in four different cities. By then, the end was near.

Emergency & I sealed the Plan's legend, but it didn't make them famous, and by 2001's equally great *Change*, the band was settling down in every sense. Their idiosyncrasies remained—the surprising chord changes; an uncommon focus on fidgety grooves; lyrics that render everyday drama in vivid, fantastical imagery—but they were reined in and smoothed out in service of prettier, more contemplative songs. Morrison sang of giving up on dreams, flaking on deals with himself, and visions of a couple from the music scene who disappeared into domestic life. In hindsight, it's unsurprising the band called it quits after that record.

The Dismemberment Plan never enjoyed the kind of breakthrough that buoyed 2002 tourmates Death Cab for Cutie, but history was bending their way even before they were gone. In the early 2000s, the indie rock scene entered its dance-party era. Catchy garage bands revived rock 'n' roll's sock-hop salad days. Jagged disco-punk acts echoed the '70s post-punk era in ever more accessible forms. Sub Pop Records scored its biggest hit since Nirvana with a synth-pop album partially inspired by '80s new wave. By the time the Plan broke up in 2003, their entire approach seemed prophetic.

* * *

When I showed up at college in 2002, my hair had grown into a big, wavy poof. At some point during senior year of high school I'd decided to stop cutting it regularly so that I'd look more like the Strokes. *Is This It*, the band's 2001 debut, had taken over my life. It had also launched a wave of stylishly rumpled retro garage bands, like *Nevermind* with Converse instead of flannel.

Granted, in America, the Strokes were never anywhere near as popular as Nirvana. *Is This It* took years to sell a million copies; *Nevermind* did it within months. "Smells like Teen Spirit" soared to No. 6 on *Billboard*'s main pop singles chart, the Hot 100, whereas the Strokes only managed one meager No. 98 hit with "Juicebox," and not until 2005—an aftereffect of a bygone moment. But the moment was real, and it sent shock waves through pop culture.

The Strokes emerged from a corner of New York that had nothing to do with Times Square and *TRL*. As detailed in Lizzy Goodman's meticulous scene history *Meet Me in the Bathroom*, a revival of hedonist retro rock 'n' roll coalesced in Lower East Side bars in the late '90s. Bands like Jonathan Fire*Eater and the Mooney Suzuki exuded a raw, theatrical swagger. The Sunday-night Shout! party, where hip kids in skinny ties and mini dresses danced to throwback mod and soul records, created an audience for new groups mining the same aesthetic.

The burgeoning garage-rock movement was at odds with not only everything on *TRL* but also the introverted effect of the era's reigning indie rock. The louche, combustible Yeah Yeah Yeahs, for instance, were a reaction against soft, introspective late-'90s indie. In a 2002 *New York* magazine profile, guitarist Nick Zinner complained that his prior project "was more like psychotherapy than a band" and writer Ethan Brown declared, "The Yeah Yeah Yeahs' live show—in which Karen [O] strikes cartoonish rock-star poses and drowns herself in can after can of cheap beer—drives a stake into the heart of shy, retiring indie-rock bands everywhere."

Karen O honed that rock 'n' roll superhero persona on the

dance floor at Shout!, where so many young New Yorkers were rediscovering the power of sweaty, physical rock 'n' roll. At a time when hip-hop and electronic music were gaining new mainstream footholds, the ancient notion of dancing to rock music suddenly started to feel fresh and fashionable again. For years, bands like the Jon Spencer Blues Explosion had kept garage rock alive in the underground. But this new generation of artists exuded youthful, sexy glamour, and some of them knew how to write pop songs without forgoing grit and scuzz.

Nobody struck that balance better than Karen O's fellow Shout! denizens the Strokes, whose music perfectly matched their thrifted sport coats, tousled haircuts (not as easy to replicate as I'd hoped), and sloshed antics. On *Is This It* and their prior EP *The Modern Age*, the band channeled decades of critically adored New York music—especially Television's interlocking guitars and the Velvet Underground's droning, deadpan chug—into easily digestible nuggets like "Someday" and "Barely Legal." Julian Casablancas, son of high-powered modeling agent John Casablancas, sang oblique lyrics about downtown misadventures with a rare mix of fire and nonchalance. The vocal production made his crooning, growling bellow sound intentionally tinny, and the band played his arrangements like miniature machines brimming with energy—none better than the torrent of buzzing eighth notes that coheres into a tidal wave on "Hard to Explain." Essentially, they were turning the building blocks of indie rock into low-fidelity pop music and releasing it through a Sony subsidiary.

Anyone who's heard the Tom Petty guitar octaves the Strokes borrowed for "Last Nite" knows they weren't *only* pulling from the annals of hipster NYC. The band was more likely to cite Ohio lo-fi legends Guided by Voices as a crucial influence than anyone from CBGB. But those Lower Manhattan touchstones made the band irresistible to British critics, who were eager to herald the return of the mythic rough-and-tumble New York of their imaginations. Before *Is This It* even dropped, in a summer 2001 feature that began with the Strokes getting into a fistfight with passersby on the streets of New York, *NME* anointed them as "the most talked-about rock band since Oasis."

That hype boomeranged back to America just as 9/11 fixated the world's attention on New York. (After the attacks, the Strokes removed "New York City Cops" from the US version of *Is This It*, but if you're listening to *Is This It* without "New York City Cops," you aren't *really* listening to *Is This It*.) American journalists, ready to move on from nu metal, were happy to grab the baton from their UK counterparts, granting the Strokes magazine covers and album reviews with opening lines like, "This is the stuff of which legends are made." The skeptics who pushed back against the trendy new band with the nepo-baby lead singer only made the discourse louder.

The haters were unconvincing. From the moment I downloaded "Trying Your Luck" off Napster, I embraced the idea of Casablancas and friends as leaders of a media-anointed New Rock Revolution. I bought the hype, bought the album, and even defied my parents by secretly driving to Cleveland through heavy November fog to see the Strokes' first US tour, an act of disobedience that now feels validated by history. Being there seemed important at the time, too; because they were so young, so new, and so clearly gifted, I felt like I was getting in on the ground floor of something significant. My reverence for this band ran so deep that I enjoyed waking up early on a Saturday and driving down to Ohio State to take the SAT because I got to blast *Is This It* the whole way.

As with grunge, the media frenzy around old-school garage rock wasn't limited to one band. In this case it wasn't centered on one city or even one country. From Sweden came the Hives, howling showmen who hit like a sledgehammer. Australia yielded the Vines, whose music blended garage rock and grunge. In the UK, the Libertines built their legend on not just raucous, catchy music but tabloid-friendly hijinks and hard living. More importantly, there were a slew of Detroit bands headlined by the peculiar, electrifying White Stripes.

Jack and Meg White were ex-spouses who briefly pretended to be siblings. They adhered to a strict red-and-white dress code and used only retro analog equipment, but they put no such restrictions on their songwriting. The duo's 2001 breakthrough *White Blood Cells* veered haphazardly across the twentieth century songbook, from Zeppelin-worthy blues-rock bluster on "Dead Leaves and the Dirty Ground" to hootin', hollerin' country on "Hotel Yorba" to balls-out punk on "Fell in Love with a Girl" to cutesy twee balladry on "We're Going to Be Friends." Jack was an obvious talent whose previous band the Go had signed to Sub Pop. But he didn't pop off until he recruited Meg, a steadfast and unshowy drummer, to counterbalance his madcap energy and ideas. Their 2003 hit "Seven Nation Army," later immortalized as a stadium chant, owed almost as much to Meg's steady thud as to Jack's monster riff.

So much of this music was foisted upon me by major labels. *Is This It* came out on RCA. Unlike the Strokes, the White Stripes built an audience methodically via several albums released by Olympia garage-punk hub Sympathy for the Record Industry, but to me, they seemed to come out of nowhere when Virgin offshoot V2 reissued *White Blood Cells* in 2002. Yeah Yeah Yeahs released their 2001 debut EP through the great Chicago indie

Touch and Go, but by the time their debut album, *Fever To Tell*, dropped in 2003, they were on Interscope. Still, like the grunge bands did for Gen-X listeners a decade earlier, these major-label New Rock Revolution bands provided breadcrumb trails to the indie world.

For one thing, the people accusing these groups of ripping off '70s artists inevitably sent me scurrying back in time to investigate the source material. Critics who waved off the Strokes as a *Muppet Babies* version of the Velvet Underground caused me to listen much more closely to *The Velvet Underground & Nico*, which led to a vast ecosystem of bands also influenced by Lou Reed and friends. This effect was even more acute with Interpol, fellow New Yorkers in sharp black suits who signed to Matador and benefitted from a Strokes-grade media orgy in 2002. It's nearly impossible to find a review of the band's masterful debut *Turn On the Bright Lights* that doesn't mention Joy Division, the gloomy British post-punk icons whose music Interpol transmuted into radio-friendly rock. As someone who found "PDA" exhilarating, of course I was curious to hear "Love Will Tear Us Apart."

Beyond games of spot-the-influence, all the attention on New York stars like Yeah Yeah Yeahs put me onto the less famous acts in their proximity. Members of Jonathan Fire*Eater, a key influence on YYYs, later formed the Walkmen, whose singer, Hamilton Leithauser, screeched and roared like Bob Dylan doing an impression of a cat (complimentary) and whose ramshackle post-punk moved with drunken grace. In Brooklyn, TV On The Radio, whose Dave Sitek produced YYYs' debut album, built towering squalls of noise around soulful, melodious, genre-defiant songs, always guided by Tunde Adebimpe's powerhouse voice. And fellow Brooklynites Liars—fronted by a giant Australian named

Angus Andrew, who was dating Karen O at the time—played a volatile strain of dance-punk.

In that post-Strokes moment, dance-punk (or disco-punk) became *such* a big deal in indie circles, especially as the Strokes and their peers ballooned into actual rock stars, leaving early-adopter types to seek new frontiers. "It's possible 2002 will be looked back on as the Year the Indie Kids Started Dancing Again," Pitchfork's Rob Mitchum wrote in a blurb celebrating Hot Hot Heat's *Make Up the Breakdown*, one of the poppier albums threading dance beats into indie rock. "It might not have been fitting source material for DJs mixing at velvet-rope clubs," he continued, "but it fit nicely into the playlist at every repression-shedding indie sockhop this year."

Within the underground, dance-punk functioned as a middle ground between garage rock and electroclash, a transgressive synth-pop/techno hybrid typified by tracks like Peaches' "Fuck the Pain Away." Within a few years, proudly trashy, nylon-clad pop, rap, and dance music that played out like the soundtrack to a skeezy Terry Richardson photoshoot would become a staple of the indie ecosystem. But in 2002, watching Peaches open for Queens of the Stone Age, my sheltered Midwestern ass was mystified.

Dance-punk made a lot more sense to me. It wasn't just Liars. It was the Faint, who helped foment this craze with the aggro synth-rock of 2001's *Danse Macabre*. It was the Rapture, whose shrieking, throbbing, bass-blasted masterpiece "House of Jealous Lovers" became dance-punk's definitive single. It was DFA, the production duo of James Murphy and Tim Goldsworthy, who shepherded "House of Jealous Lovers" into blown-out transcendence. It was LCD Soundsystem, Murphy's solo project, whose throttling debut single "Losing My Edge" spelled out the record-nerd insecurity driving his aesthetic. It was !!! (pronounced Chk Chk Chk), whose ten-minute disco-punk epic "Me and Giuliani Down by the School Yard (A True Story)" foretold a move away from the more abrasive post-punk template toward something like actual dance music.

Thanks in part to the introduction of high-speed internet that allowed trends to proliferate more rapidly than ever, the music was evolving quickly and spreading broadly. So was the fashion. This was the era when the hipster entered the popular imagination—a caricature at least partially based in truth, exemplified by *Vice*, which evolved from a Montréal punk magazine into an ascendent global media empire with roots in New York and London. Lest they be reduced to a cliché, hipsters consistently refused to self-identify as hipsters in the 2000s, especially once the public became familiar with this archetype. Refusing to acknowledge you are a hipster was an essential part of being a hipster, as illustrated by the 2006 *The Onion* headline, "Two Hipsters Angrily Call Each Other 'Hipster.'"

Many viewed the term as cringe and oversimplified, and to an extent, it was both. But it got at something real that was happening at the time and being co-opted into a marketable package. "The hipster is that person . . . who in fact aligns himself both with rebel subculture and with the dominant class, and thus opens up a poisonous conduit between the two," wrote Mark Greif in his 2010 *New York* magazine article, "What Was the Hipster?"

Vice-style hipsterdom took elements from pre-internet indie culture: a delight in zine-style provocation, a disdain for normie monoculture, a relentless pursuit of authenticity. It was also deeply hedonistic, egocentric, and fashion-forward in ways that clashed with, say, Fugazi's progressive politics and ethically driven business model. Maybe the *Vice*-era move toward excess and artifice can be attributed to a nationwide tonal shift following 9/11, when shellshocked patriotism papered over a lot of foul government activity and people coped with their trauma by cutting loose. But given that one of *Vice*'s founders went on to lead the neo-fascist Proud Boys organization, perhaps it's not surprising that the company helped steer indie culture away from its professed ideals.

On that note, gentrification was a huge aspect of the post-Y2K hipster experience. By now it's a familiar cycle: Artist types flocked to warehouses in blighted neighborhoods like Williamsburg, Brooklyn, in search of cheap rent and bleeding-edge authenticity, then made the formerly undesirable areas so trendy that the original residents were priced out. Eventually, so were many of the creatives who remade the area in their own image. That process of co-opting the working class extended beyond renovating their real estate. As the irony that coursed through 1990s pop culture metastasized, college-educated hipsters began to adopt aspects of so-called low culture—Pabst Blue Ribbon, trucker hats, and so on. Such preferences didn't seem quirky and unique for long. By 2003, trucker hats were so pervasive in the mainstream that they were the subject of a trend piece in *The New York Times*, in which a disgruntled hipster dismissed them as "so six months ago."

The role of the internet in spreading this stuff beyond cutting-edge urban enclaves can't be understated—not only the rise of indie-centric music sites like Pitchfork, which became the ultimate arbiter of hipster music taste in the aughts, but also the overwhelming emphasis on party photography. In a 2015 postmortem titled "How Did the Hipster Become Mainstream?," *Vice*'s Drew Millard made a prescient point: "This nascent movement was obsessed with documenting itself in ways that would help establish a template for the hipsters that came after them, through sites like Cobrasnake, *Vice*, Last Night's Party, and even music like LCD Soundsystem, whose first album largely served as an opportunity for James Murphy to take stock of the hipness all around him."

Even if you weren't actually in New York, you could get a sense of the scene in LimeWire downloads and nightlife photo dumps, especially as early blogging platforms like Xanga and social networks like MySpace became hubs for music discovery. This process turned a lot of people on to what was happening in major urban locales, which sparked widespread imitation that ultimately had a flattening effect. As the savvy critic Keith Harris pointed out in his 2012 article "Did New York Kill Indie Rock?," the internet "diluted the influence of local press outlets, allowing cultural coverage to re-consolidate in metropolitan hubs." Whereas indie rock had always comprised a network of local scenes, burbling out of second-tier cities and cultural backwaters, it began to seem like a phenomenon centered in New York, to be replicated far and wide. As Harris wrote, "In mid-sized towns, facsimiles of the Brooklyn 'hipster' became as common as Yankee caps, and as universally disparaged."

We'd get around to identical "local" microbreweries soon enough, but in the meantime, dancing remained a central element of the hipster zeitgeist. By 2002, Shout! had expanded beyond NYC into Toronto, Miami, Boston, Philadelphia, Atlanta, and Denver. Similar rock-oriented parties popped up in other cities. By 2004, when the Clampdown party began catering to Interpol fans in my hometown of Columbus, a flashier, poppier generation of danceable indie bands was on the rise.

Out of Glasgow came Franz Ferdinand, who turned loose Alex Kapranos's arched-eyebrow art-pop narration over big, dumb guitar riffs and even bigger, even dumber drumbeats. (Kanye West, whose debut *The College Dropout* came out on the same day as *Franz Ferdinand*, called it "white crunk.") Franz Ferdinand's brilliant shout-along single "Take Me Out" soared to No. 2 in Scotland and made it to No. 66 on America's Hot 100—impressive for a release on the indie Domino Records. Coming up fast behind them were London's Bloc Party, who infused their own danceable rock with a hard-hitting dynamism and U2-style stadium-rock yearning. Their 2005 debut album *Silent Alarm* had the sparkle and heft of a major-label production—and indeed, producer Paul Epworth later worked with Adele.

Not all artists riding this wave were so critically acclaimed, especially as every band with "The" in its name enjoyed its fifteen minutes of fame and Strokes-influenced rock started to feel passé in the indie world. Yet the least esteemed bands seemed to blow up the biggest. Bolstered by an appearance in an iTunes ad, Australia's Jet made it all the way to No. 29 on the Hot 100 with their Iggy-Pop-mimicking "Are You Gonna Be My Girl"—then Pitchfork reviewed their sophomore album with a video of a monkey peeing in its own mouth. New York's the Bravery scraped the lower reaches of the chart with "An Honest Mistake," a song that reimagined the Strokes as a dance-punk act, and Pitchfork condemned them as obvious trend-hoppers.

Also hating on the Bravery were the Killers, who took dance-punk to glitzy, theatrical heights worthy of their Las Vegas origins. "They're signed because we're a band," Killers singer Brandon Flowers told MTV. "I think people will see through them." But Flowers didn't need to pick fights with lesser peers to get famous. Released on the Universal-owned Island Records, his band's 2004 debut *Hot Fuss* spiked the sound of the moment with new wave glamour and arena-rock pomposity. In turn, the Killers achieved the pop success that eluded the Strokes: Their bombastic future karaoke fixture "Mr. Brightside" made it all the way to the US Top 10.

Another way the New Rock Revolution impacted the upper reaches of the charts: After Yeah Yeah Yeahs cracked the Hot 100 with "Maps," a simmering breakup ballad likely written about Liars' Angus Andrew, rising superproducers Max Martin and Dr. Luke attempted to rewrite it with a supercharged chorus. The thrilling result was "Since U Been Gone," a signature hit for *American Idol* winner Kelly Clarkson. Pitchfork eventually named it the fourth-best single of 2005—an acknowledgement of the song's indie-rock roots, but also a symptom of a sea change within hipster ideas about pop music.

Perhaps no one did more to change those ideas than the Postal Service, the pairing of Death Cab for Cutie singer Ben Gibbard and Jimmy Tamborello, aka Dntel. The duo's 2003 album *Give Up* didn't come out of nowhere, but it felt revolutionary in its time: An indie rock frontman teaming with an experimental electronic producer? For a whole album of skittering synth-pop tracks? Released via Sub Pop, the label synonymous with grunge?

Let's be clear: Underground rock had morphed into dance-pop before. There's a reason that in LCD Soundsystem's "Losing My Edge," James Murphy quips, "I hear that you and your band have sold your guitars and bought turntables/ I hear that you and your band have sold your turntables and bought guitars." These things move in cycles. But in the twentieth century, alt-rock-to-dance-pop transformations were mostly confined to the UK, where the two genres have always maintained much closer kinship than in the States, from club-friendly '80s new wave bands to rave-adjacent early '90s rockers all the way up to late-'90s big beat acts like the Prodigy and the Chemical Brothers, who ushered in a future in which stadium-scale DJ-producers could be rock stars.

By the time maximalist electronica made it to MTV, the indie world had recoiled from that kind of bombast. But the pendulum that swung away from synthesizers and programmed beats would soon swing back. Created under the influence of Björk's left-field pop and avant-garde producers like Aphex Twin, Radiohead's 2000 game-changer *Kid A*—a chart-topping album that wielded incomparable influence on indie music—climaxed with "Idioteque," a glitchy electronic track that had Thom Yorke dancing like no one was watching. The Flaming Lips, another major-label band popular with indie listeners, laced their quirky and depressive 2002 album *Yoshimi Battles the Pink Robots* with electronic beats inspired by hip-hop producers like Timbaland. The dance-punk wave was Trojan-horsing DJ culture into the indie world, but so many of those bands were still guitar-centric—whereas the Postal Service stood out as an American indie band built on beats and synths who also eliminated all vestiges of punk aggression. What they brought to the table was more like artisanal pop.

In those days, there was some listener spillover between indie rock and the experimental electronic fare known as IDM—"intelligent dance music," in case you wondered how that audience saw itself. LA-based Tamborello recognized this overlap, partially because he was living it; his roommate Pedro Bonito played in indie band the Jealous Sound. Though Tamborello had released only instrumentals, he had the bright idea to invite various indie rockers to sing on Dntel's 2001 album *Life Is Full of Possibilities*. This led to Seattle-based Gibbard jumping on a track while visiting Bonito in LA.

Gibbard was not the most obvious candidate for an electropop makeover. Death Cab's music was the kind of introspective indie rock that bands like Yeah Yeah Yeahs were reacting against—music for feeling, not moving. Nor did Dntel's downtempo productions brim with obvious pop appeal. Yet on a song called "(This Is) The Dream of Evan and Chan," the two artists achieved surprising alchemy. Over Tamborello's rumbling, static-laden instrumental, Gibbard's sensitive vocals sounded like glowing neon in the fog. Among the small circle of listeners who heard it, "Evan and Chan" became a sensation: "not only one of the best songs of 2001, but perhaps the perfect synthesis of IDM production and indie pop songwriting," per Pitchfork's Matt LeMay.

Gibbard liked working with Tamborello enough to suggest they make an EP—a fun, low-stakes side project. When Tamborello mentioned the partnership to his college pal Tony Kiewel, who'd started working in the artists and repertoire (A&R) department at Sub Pop, Kiewel encouraged him to think bigger. "If you're going to do it, do a full album," Kiewel told *Entertainment Weekly*, recalling the moment in a 2013 oral history. "People will review it, and you can sell it for three times as much." With the promise of Sub Pop's support, the duo began collaborating long-distance, recording separately and shipping CD-Rs back and forth, hence the band name the Postal Service (though they actually used UPS). Gibbard invited his friend Jen Wood to sing on a couple songs. And when he returned to LA to mix the album with Tamborello, they added vocals from Jenny Lewis, a former-child-actress-turned-singer for the indie band Rilo Kiley.

The resulting album strikes an ideal balance between indie singer-songwriter confessionals and glitchy electronic pop, leaning into tendencies that would appeal to a far bigger tent than either artist's main project. Gibbard wrote lyrics like an undergrad who was pouring his emotions into a notebook but also trying to impress his poetry professor—most famously "I am thinking it's a sign/ That the freckles in our eyes are mirror images/ And when we kiss, they're perfectly aligned." He channeled his big feelings and big words into big hooks, enunciated politely even when he was fired up. Tamborello steered his production toward a verse-chorus-verse format without losing the textural depth and rhythmic complexity of his Dntel records, and he laced even his hardest beats with unexpected bursts of melody. Opener "The District Sleeps Alone Tonight" molds a moody post-rock slow build into something big, bright, and catchy. The cheery "Nothing Better" foregrounds cute interplay between Gibbard's lovestruck character and Wood as the skeptical recipient of his affection, but the song *moves,* too, gracefully navigating a minefield of floating computer sounds and intersecting vocal lines.

"There was little struggle," Gibbard told *EW* of the uncommonly smooth recording process. "Everything we tried worked." Still, the Postal Service had minimal expectations for their album. "I feel like it's a really homemade, lo-fi-sounding record," Tamborello told The Ringer in 2023. "I didn't ever expect it to translate to a bigger audience or be able to get played on the radio." Upon its release in February 2003, *Give Up* quickly surpassed Sub Pop's estimate of 20,000 in sales. Songs from the album began to circulate widely on the popular new social media network MySpace. When the Postal Service hit the road that spring, the crowds kept getting bigger; the tour-closing show in LA had to be upgraded from 130-capacity DIY space The Smell to the Palace Theater, a venue ten times that size.

Much of the momentum stemmed from "Such Great Heights," the last song written and recorded for *Give Up*. From its pinging, headphone-friendly intro onward, the melodies are indelible. The groove whisks you away, magic-carpet style; when Gibbard professes his intent to stay airborne with his lover indefinitely, you really do feel like you're riding on the clouds. Yet the production is just jagged enough to keep it all from going down too smoothly, be it Gibbard's spiky guitar riff in the middle eight or the jarring cracks of Tamborello's crisp drumbeat. It's a perfect little gem of a song, and the world noticed.

In no time, "Such Great Heights" became a small-scale sensation. "Every coffee shop I walked into, it was playing," Gibbard said on the *Life of the Record* podcast in 2023. "Every bar, at some point it came on. Every store I walked into, it was playing." Eventually the tune found its way into rotation at LA's influential KROQ and other alternative radio stations across America. Then it was featured in the trailer for Zach Braff's *Garden State*. Then Iron & Wine's acoustic cover from the *Garden State* soundtrack appeared in an M&M's ad. By 2007, when the original Postal Service track was licensed for a UPS commercial (poetic!), "Such Great Heights" already felt like a modern classic.

Give Up kept growing. Eventually it went Platinum and became the second best-selling album in Sub Pop history behind Nirvana's *Bleach*. But the record hadn't only been a hit for the Postal Service—it opened up a whole new lane within indie music. Soon that lane would be populated by arty eccentrics like the Knife and of Montreal, dreamy nostalgists like M83, and clubby synth bands like Hot Chip and Cut Copy. By the time the ultra-hooky world-conquerors Passion Pit and MGMT came along in 2008, indie synth-pop bands were normal, not novel.

The Postal Service were not around to take advantage of the zeitgeist they started. The band members stayed busy with their other projects, and the Gibbard-Tamborello duo never regained that initial spark. After several aborted attempts to record a follow-up, in 2007 they followed the advice of their first album and gave up. But don't cry for Gibbard. His other band was enjoying its own glow-up in those years, with help from a primetime soap opera about hot, rich, angsty teens on the California coast.

Chapter 3 Soundtrack

Phantom Planet, "California (Tchad Blake Mix)" (2002)
Spoon, "The Way We Get By" (2002)
Death Cab for Cutie, "A Movie Script Ending" (2001)
Modest Mouse, "Float On" (2004)
The Killers, "Mr. Brightside" (2003)
The Shins, "New Slang" (2001)
The Walkmen, "The Rat" (2004)
Rooney, "I'm a Terrible Person" (2003)
Iron & Wine, "Such Great Heights" (2003)
Peter Bjorn and John, "Young Folks" (2006)
Band of Horses, "The Funeral" (2006)
The Whitest Boy Alive, "Burning" (2006)
Imogen Heap, "Hide and Seek" (2005)
The National, "About Today" (2004)
Michael Cera & Elliot Page, "Anyone Else but You" (2007)
Bishop Allen, "Middle Management" (2007)
She & Him, "Why Do You Let Me Stay Here?" (2008)
Broken Social Scene, "Anthems for a Seventeen-Year-Old Girl" (2002)
Black Lips, "O Katrina!" (2007)
St. Vincent & Bon Iver, "Roslyn" (2009)

3

This Song Will Change Your Life

Hollywood goes indie.

Here are five words that forever changed the trajectory of indie rock: "Welcome to the O.C., bitch."

On August 3, 2003, Fox premiered a new teen soap opera called *The O.C.* The show was set in glamorous Newport Beach, California, where Ryan Atwood—a delinquent teen from the far less ritzy Chino—found himself informally adopted by the wealthy and benevolent Cohen family after his latest brush with the law. Ryan, a brooding James Dean type played by Ben McKenzie, was ostensibly the main character and audience proxy, an interloper getting an inside look at the lavish world of Newport. But *The O.C.*'s most iconic character was a Newport native: Ryan's friend and foil, the Cohens' geeky-cute son Seth.

Series creator Josh Schwartz saw Seth Cohen as his own avatar within the show. As played by Adam Brody, Seth was nerdy and neurotic but also clever, culture-savvy, and even charismatic under the right circumstances. Comic-Con was an annual highlight of his calendar, and he kept a toy horse named Captain Oats at his bedside well into adolescence—facts he sought to hide from his peers, lest they beat him up or ruthlessly ridicule him. In some ways, Seth didn't fit in any better than Ryan, which was the point. As Schwartz explained to Uproxx in 2013, "We were going to take you inside the most exclusive new money place in the country, and the dirty little secret of that is that everybody who's there doesn't feel like they belong. And I think nobody in life really feels like they belong. Everybody feels like an outsider."

As someone who didn't gravitate to teen soaps like *Dawson's Creek* but started watching *The O.C.* because of buzz around its use of indie music, I saw a lot of myself in Seth. He dressed like me—remember the long-sleeved tee under the short-sleeved tee look? He maintained unrequited crushes on seemingly unattainable girls—also a defining trait of my teenage years. Most importantly, and most unexpectedly, he shared my taste in music. On a car trip to Tijuana, he blared Death Cab for Cutie's "A Movie Script Ending" and warned his passengers, "Do not insult Death Cab." ("It's like one guitar and a whole lot of complaining!" his love interest Summer Roberts retorted, with a scorn rarely witnessed since Alicia Silverstone scoffed at Radiohead in *Clueless*.) As gifts for Chrismukkah, the holiday he invented to bridge his dual Jewish-Protestant heritage, Seth prepared "Seth Cohen Starter Packs" featuring Death Cab, Bright Eyes, and the Shins. The show made his love of indie rock a defining trait of his personality.

For Death Cab, this was extremely bizarre. The Bellingham, Washington, band had spent half a decade carving out a solid career in the underground, playing an erudite and moody strain of indie that shared biting, confessional qualities with emo. At both their best and their worst, Ben Gibbard's lyrics were pointedly poetic English-major fare, and he sang those fifty-cent words in a lightweight tenor that made him sound like a plucky underdog. He came off as the kind of smart, sensitive protagonist the Seth Cohens of the world imagined themselves becoming, and despite the meek personal affect, his band could really rip.

But even after quitting their day jobs and selling a healthy-by-underground-standards 50,000 copies of 2001's *The Photo Album*, Death Cab were barely scraping by. They didn't have a manager when *The O.C.* premiered, and they didn't even launch a website until the following year. Gibbard's synth-pop side project the Postal Service was blowing up at the time, threatening to render his main band a footnote. Death Cab for Cutie was not a name anyone expected to hear uttered on TV, least of all the band members themselves.

"We were all sitting on the couch when the character says, 'Do not insult Death Cab,' and we're looking at each other like, 'Oh, no—this isn't what we signed up for,'" bassist Nick Harmer said in Greg Kot's book *Ripped: How the Wired Generation Revolutionized Music*. Speaking to *Stereogum* in 2022, Gibbard said, "We'd never seen a TV show where a fictional character is talking about a real band that is not a household name. It'd be like, 'I love the Beatles.' Yeah, of course, we all love the Beatles. Or like, 'Led Zeppelin rules.' But the idea that a TV show on one of the four major networks would have this character on one of their shows that was name-checking a band that for all intents and purposes was pretty underground at that point?"

This was incredible exposure for such an obscure act. *The O.C.* was a breakout hit, averaging 9.7 million viewers a week in its first season and outpacing all other new dramas in the 18-to-34 demographic. But the band wasn't sure how to feel about it. "As the show continued on, they kind of started really leaning into the, you know, 'Seth Cohen loves Death Cab and Bright Eyes' and whomever else," Gibbard told *Stereogum*. "There was a moment where it started to feel like, 'Oh, it's just gonna be—it's gonna be bad,' you know? It felt like it got a little out of control."

The name-drops were pandering to people like me, and they marked a generational shift. It's not like pop culture was bereft of alt-leaning music geeks in the years leading up to *The O.C.*; 2000 yielded both *High Fidelity* and *Gilmore Girls* (which gave Brody his big break playing Dave Rygalski, a more self-assured version of Seth Cohen). But the characters in those stories mostly celebrated the sounds of a previous generation. They occasionally mentioned contemporary artists like the Beta Band or Belle & Sebastian, but more often the conversation shifted toward decades-old works by the likes of David Bowie, Marvin Gaye, the Bangles, and Jimmy Cliff. John Cusack's Rob Gordon and Lauren Graham's Lorelai Gilmore were hip, but they could have been my babysitters or even my parents. Even the music-obsessed youths of Stars Hollow seemed more fascinated by the canon than the here and now.

For better and worse, Seth Cohen felt like a peer, a product of my era. Hearing someone speak my language on a hit TV series was a thrill, and seeing some of my favorite bands get such a prominent spotlight was surreal. Part of the appeal was that Seth was reflecting back the characteristics of the bands he touted, taking to extremes the music-fan impulse to define yourself by the records you love. As Sharon Steel pointed out in a 2012 essay for *Stereogum*, "Seth continuously mentioned how intrinsic Death Cab were to understanding who he was as a human being,

SUCH GREAT HEIGHTS

a misanthrope, and a lover of unconventionally cool, under-the-radar things." She continued:

> I watched the show religiously. Mostly because I had a stupid crush on Brody, but also because I thought the Seth Cohen character was brilliantly drawn. Even when he was happy, Seth Cohen was never actually happy. He saw the world through a neurotic, overly analytical prism in which the best things that happened to him were merely a precursor to some larger emotional disaster. Before *The O.C.* ever aired, I came to my own set of conclusions that this is what Gibbard was projecting as well, in his music. People labeled it "emo," but to me, it was a gorgeous soundtrack to an inner life that was always more dramatic and engaging than the actual one I led. In my early twenties, I, like Seth (and surely, most definitely, exactly like Gibbard), was a person who felt happiest when I was most miserable. It was just so much more interesting to be sad.

You could just as easily see glimmers of Bright Eyes' emotionally volatile Conor Oberst or the Shins' timid James Mercer in Seth. Long before "sadboi" and "sadgirl" entered the popular lexicon, he crystallized a millennial version of a well-worn trope: the artsy, sensitive soul who romanticizes their own depression. (Maybe in another life he would've been a beatnik.) Partially because he embodied the music in that way—and partially because he wouldn't shut up about his favorite bands—Seth became one of pop culture's first avatars of "indie." For many viewers, he was the public face of the genre: a conventionally attractive hipster-nerd whose good looks and relative charm mirrored indie rock's move toward poppier, more approachable sounds. Seth was the genesis of an archetype within Hollywood, a new kind of beta male sex symbol for those who prefer the virgin in the Virgin vs. Chad meme. He was "adorkable" before the word was even a twinkle in a Fox executive's eye.

Even many who knew nothing about indie rock identified with Seth, and Schwartz—a 26-year-old wunderkind who soundtracked the first six or seven episodes with songs off his own iPod—used the character to shine a much brighter spotlight on a bunch of artists that had been building up steam underground.

From the beginning, *The O.C.* embraced indie music—or at least music with an indie sensibility. (Its opening theme song "California" was by Phantom Planet, a major-label band whose drummer, Jason Schwartzman, was a Coppola family scion already known for starring in Wes Anderson's *Rushmore* as a teen—so, more "indie" than indie.) Besides Schwartz's personal taste, licensing indie music was more affordable than synching major-label hits, and Schwartz found that many indie bands were game, despite some initial hesitation about featuring their music in a high school melodrama.

"This was a time where there was no iTunes and satellite radio I don't really think was in existence, and MTV was not playing music videos, and terrestrial FM radio was like the same eight songs per hour, and 'Hey Ya!' every hour on the hour," Schwartz told Uproxx. "Some of the bands that we reached out to were these indie rock bands, and that was all we could afford. But a lot of these bands probably would have had deeper reservations about having their music debut on a Fox teen soap, but there was no other way to get their music out." In a 2006 *New York Times* feature about television's increased use of popular music, Jen Czeisler of Sub Pop Records affirmed Schwartz's sentiment: "If it weren't for TV, indie bands would never reach audiences this big. Our bands don't get on commercial radio and they don't get on MTV, so these shows are a huge opportunity for them."

The O.C. didn't result in many indie bands crashing the pop charts, but it did nudge several of them into sustainable careers and an alternative rock radio landscape overrun by acts like Linkin Park and Hoobastank. Beyond what it did for any one artist, *The O.C.*'s use of indie rock normalized the aesthetic of the genre's most user-friendly acts in ways that would seep into pop culture in the years to come. Essentially, the show laid the groundwork for indie rock as a lifestyle brand, creating a context for bands like these to be packaged and sold to a mass audience and incentivizing them to soften and brighten their sound.

I didn't fully grasp it at the time, but this raised longstanding questions about exploitation vs. exposure, cultural tourism, and allowing the "wrong" kinds of fans into the club. I was partially blind to these questions because, like Seth, I latched onto this music due to how it sounded, felt, and made me see myself, not because I cared what it stood for. To someone who got into indie rock primarily for the DIY ideals, I was probably the "wrong" kind of fan, too. That didn't stop me from feeling superior to the many, many people who discovered Death Cab for Cutie through *The O.C.*

Coincidentally, three weeks after Seth Cohen first namechecked Death Cab, the band released *Transatlanticism*, the most vivid and dynamic album of their career. With gargantuan vocal melodies buoyed by hard-crashing drums and guitars, songs like "The New Year," "Soul Meets Body," and the eight-minute power ballad "Transatlanticism" made indie rock hit like arena rock while retaining the melancholy essence that defined Death Cab's earliest records. The band used that newfound power to broadcast a wide-eyed yearning that resonated with legions of young people (and occasionally their parents, too).

Given Death Cab's upward momentum, their album likely would have been a hit at some scale. The band had busted their asses to get to this point, and they'd seized their moment by delivering their finest album yet. But *The O.C.* amplified *Transatlanticism*'s reach exponentially, in a way they never could have achieved without a runway out of the indie circuit—a subject the members of Death Cab grew increasingly tired of discussing as their band became unwittingly, inextricably linked with the TV show. "The more I talk about it, the more it devalues all the work we put into the band over the years," Gibbard said in a contentious interview with Kansas City's *The Pitch* in 2005, before conceding that he was "a little crotchety and hungover" at the time of the chat.

Whatever anxieties the band had about the *O.C.* situation, they undoubtedly benefited from it commercially. *Transatlanticism* outpaced first-week sales projections and kept building from there, moving 325,000 copies within its first two years and ultimately going Gold with more than half a million in sales—huge numbers for an album on an independent label, especially one like Barsuk Records, a homespun operation that hadn't even been around as long as Death Cab. By the time the band released their next album, *Plans*, in 2005, they were signed to major label Atlantic and in regular rotation on alt-rock radio; their hit "Soul Meets Body" even climbed to No. 60 on *Billboard*'s main pop singles chart, the Hot 100. By 2006, they were headlining Lollapalooza in Chicago, listed after only Red Hot Chili Peppers and Kanye West on the poster.

The idea of Schwartz making stars out of his favorite bands by funneling them directly from his MP3 library into his hit TV series is nice, but it wasn't long before the boy-wonder showrunner ran out of tracks. As he said in *Interview* in 2012, "There was a moment where I was literally scouring the aisles of Amoeba [record store in California] back when I used to buy CDs: 'I think I've used up all the songs that I like right now, where else do you find new music?' And then Alex Patsavas was brought into my world."

Alexandra Patsavas was thirty-five when she got the call to work on *The O.C.* Patsavas is a Hollywood music supervisor, a person charged with picking songs to soundtrack TV shows and movies, and her work on this show made her arguably the most prominent name within that profession. In the late '80s, Patsavas attended the University of Illinois, where she was on the concert board, helping the school book acts like *Joshua Tree*–era U2. Eventually she became a promoter in her own right, bringing bands like Jane's Addiction, Camper Van Beethoven, and a pre-fame Smashing Pumpkins to Urbana. "In my last two years," she once told IGN, "I probably went to a show every night."

Patsavas quickly applied her experience and taste to *The O.C.*'s soundtrack. "We're all interested in indie music, and have an opportunity to use a lot of music, so why not use the good stuff?" she told *The Seattle Times* in 2005. Schwartz and Patsavas favored the kinds of indie music that could pass for pop—folky singer-songwriter types, rock bands that were more catchy than chaotic—and viewers took to it as such, checking the show's website after each episode to see which songs were featured that week. When a January 2004 episode was built around the gang's trip to see a concert by the indie-presenting major-label rock band Rooney—fronted by Jason Schwartzman's actor-musician brother, Robert—it played like product placement, and it worked: The group's sales spiked.

The *O.C.* brain trust recognized the show's position as a musical tastemaker early on, and they capitalized on it quickly. In March 2004, before the end of the first season, Warner Bros. Records released a soundtrack album called *Music from The O.C.: Mix 1*. Functionally it was simply a compilation of songs that had been featured on the show, and *The O.C.* was hardly the first series to feature indie music on its soundtrack. But by branding them as "mixes," an allusion to the handcrafted mixtapes and CD-Rs that had long been a staple of music fandom, the show was framing these albums as the kind of intimate, personally curated artifact you might receive from a cool older sibling or prospective lover—your very own Seth Cohen Starter Pack.

Death Cab for Cutie weren't on that first volume of *Music from The O.C.*, but the tracklist included one of their critically acclaimed peers from the indie trenches. Spoon, from Austin, had spent the better part of a decade evolving into a gritty and swaggering rock band that expertly balanced accessibility and experimentation. After finding their groove by infusing their wiry indie rock with retro pop and R&B influences on 2001's *Girls Can Tell*, Spoon went minimal on their 2002 masterpiece *Kill the Moonlight*, stripping back their sound to the studs until they sounded like the Rolling Stones gone musique concrète.

The obvious single on *Kill the Moonlight* was a jaunty piano-rocker called "The Way We Get By," which scored Spoon their first TV appearances and landed them in MTV2 rotation. More than a year after the album dropped, "The Way We Get By" enjoyed an even better bit of promo. "They put it on *The O.C.*," frontman Britt Daniel said in a 2023 episode of *The Matador Revisionist History Podcast*. "And to this day people come up to me and say, 'I've been into you ever since I heard you on *The O.C.*'

And no other movie or TV show does that ever happen. And we've been in a few of them."

By the time the second *Music from The O.C.* compilation dropped in October 2004, the show was in its sophomore season and had ramped up the music component even further. Seth was now working at a fictional music venue called The Bait Shop, where real-life bands would take the stage. One episode spotlighted the Walkmen, who by then had released their rip-snorting rock 'n' roll tidal wave "The Rat." Another episode featured Modest Mouse, self-proclaimed trailer trash from Issaquah, Washington, who, over the course of a decade, built up a cult following in the indie scene, signed to Epic, and scored a freak Hot 100 hit with the unusually peppy "Float On." Still another episode turned the stage over to the Killers, who harnessed the momentum from their appearance to send "Mr. Brightside" all the way to the Top 10.

Morphing into an *American Bandstand* for aspiring alt-rock radio stars was unprecedented territory for a network prime-time drama, but especially for a teen soap opera. When psych-pop weirdo-geniuses the Flaming Lips played the Peach Pit on a 1995 episode of *Beverly Hills, 90210*, it was a one-off oddity. *The O.C.* shared *90210*'s melodramatic ethos, but elevating semi-obscure rock bands was baked into its DNA—intuitively at first, and then quite indelicately. "We drove a lot of story through [The Bait Shop]," Schwartz told Uproxx. "It was probably a less organic way of bringing music into the show. It was a little more in-your-face."

Inevitably, the music industry noticed *The O.C.*'s influence. Soon, known quantities like Coldplay, U2, Beastie Boys, and Gwen Stefani—all brand-name superstars with some connection to alternative rock—were using the series to premiere new music. On March 10, 2005, Beck, another celebrity with indie roots, debuted five songs from his new album *Guero* in a single episode (or, ahem, "Beckisode"). By that point, the novelty of a hit TV show centering indie rock was wearing off, and the backlash was setting in. A November 2005 *New York Times* profile of Matt Pond PA, whose cover of Oasis's "Champagne Supernova" was prominently featured on *The O.C.*, suggested that indie bands viewed association with the show as "tantamount to a sellout." It didn't help that the show's third season took a nosedive creatively and ratings were trailing off.

But if *The O.C.* was losing its cred, Hollywood's fascination with the friendly side of indie rock was only ramping up. In January 2004, just months after *The O.C.* premiered, *Scrubs* star Zach Braff screened his directorial debut, *Garden State*, at Utah's esteemed Sundance Film Festival. In the movie's most (in)famous scene, Braff's character, Andrew, meets Natalie Portman's Sam in a waiting room and asks her what's playing in her headphones. She responds that it's the Shins, forces her headphones over his ears, and insists, "You gotta hear this one song. It'll change your life, I swear." The track in question is "New Slang," a dreamy acoustic number at the center of the Shins' 2001 debut album *Oh, Inverted World*. After half a minute staring back at Portman's expectant smile, Braff renders his verdict: "It's good. I like it." He clearly is much more interested in the girl than the song, but as a Shins fan, Portman's enthusiasm for the music was my main takeaway.

Like Death Cab, the Shins were doing pretty well for themselves before being endorsed by a fictional character onscreen. Despite hailing from the indie-rock backwater of Albuquerque and lacking in star power, the group had built up a sterling reputation among those in the know. Frontman James Mercer was a master of punchy yet understated guitar-pop songcraft, and his singing voice carried an almost supernatural melodic power, somehow juiced-up and tame and eccentric and straightforward all at once. *Oh, Inverted World* had been a slow-burn success, and the band's 2003 follow-up, *Chutes Too Narrow*—which snapped their debut's mirage-like sound into crisp clarity—posted the best first-week sales in the history of Sub Pop Records at the time. "New Slang" was even featured in a McDonald's ad in 2002, despite a lyric about "dirt in your fries." The band was out there.

Still, a lot of people learned about the Shins through *Garden State*. Upon its theatrical release in the summer of 2004, the movie became a sleeper hit, its soundtrack even more so. The album went Platinum, won a Grammy for Best Compilation Soundtrack Album for Motion Pictures, Television, or Other Visual Media, and was the subject of a *Saturday Night Live* sketch when Braff hosted the show. Braff had personally selected the tunes in the movie, and his taste overlapped significantly with *The O.C.*'s Schwartz and Patsavas, so much so that Alexi Murdoch's "Orange Sky," which appeared in *Garden State*, was not included on its soundtrack album because *The O.C.* had its rights. Braff framed the *Garden State* soundtrack in the same intimate, personal terms implied by *The O.C.*'s compilations: "Essentially, I made a mix CD with all of the music that I felt was scoring my life at the time I was writing the screenplay," he wrote in promo materials for the album.

In that *SNL* sketch, the *Garden State* soundtrack is dismissed as "a Pitchfork mix CD," a reference to the ascendant webzine that was shaping the taste of hipsters everywhere. But for the most part, the lite folk pop in *Garden State* did not overlap with the music Pitchfork was heralding at the time. The tracklist featured legends like Nick Drake and Simon & Garfunkel, chic electronic pop acts like Frou Frou and Zero 7, and established figures like Coldplay and Colin Hay. "Such Great Heights," the breakthrough hit from Death Cab singer Ben Gibbard's synth-pop side project the Postal Service, was reinterpreted in lullaby-esque fashion by rising indie-folk project Iron & Wine. Still, the act most people associate with the movie is Braff's favorite band, the Shins, who had two songs on the soundtrack and got that notorious shout-out in the screenplay.

For the Shins, all this attention was a mixed blessing. *Garden State* elevated them to a new tier of the music industry and won them gobs of new fans. But Portman's dialogue about the life-changing power of "New Slang" quickly evolved into a meme and then an albatross for the group. The Shins had been the closest thing to an actual Pitchfork darling in *Garden State*, but once the movie made its impact, they also became scapegoats for people's gripes about the softening state of indie.

In 2006, my future coworker Tom Breihan wrote a *Village Voice* article headlined "The Shins Ruined Indie-Rock," in which he lamented the low-stakes nature of a scene that now counted the Shins as its standard-bearers. While acknowledging the band's charms and talents, Breihan observed that indie "was once desperate music made and consumed by awkward and obsessive types who often had to comb through zines and mail-order catalogues to find shit." Whereas in the mid-aughts, easy accessibility had turned indie into a less obsessive pursuit defined by less aggressive bands: "Indie-rock's center, if such a thing can even be said to exist, has moved more toward the sort of stuff you listen to as background music for when you're on the internet."

Not everyone had such a nuanced critique, but even some of

us who loved the Shins felt them losing cool points when they were no longer our little secret. Mercer sensed this change in perception. "When you get big early in your career, the hipsters who liked you before all that don't like you anymore," he told the *Dallas Observer* in 2022. "They think you've jumped the shark. It's a strange feeling because you feel like you've lost a certain part of the audience that was critical to your success before. We were successful, but we weren't getting the buzz kind of talk anymore, and we were too big for the hipsters. It's a funny situation."

The hipsters had reason to be suspicious—not of the Shins, necessarily, but of the emerging Hollywood soundtrack machine presenting a shiny, easy-listening version of indie rock to the masses. Perhaps not maliciously, what had begun as an underground subculture was being broadcast to the world at large. It's a classic scenario: When people who weren't previously familiar with indie rock adopted hipsters' old favorites as their own, it compromised the sense of ownership many early adopters felt toward those bands. Inevitably, the people whose fandom was intertwined with a superiority complex were irked to now be grouped in with normies who lacked their knowledge, taste, and sophistication. Still worse, artists from outside the indie bubble—that were not embraced by the existing infrastructure of record labels, media outlets, booking agencies and the like—were being swept into marketing campaigns alongside the canonical indie favorites.

The first kind of gatekeeping, aimed at boxing out the "wrong" kind of fan, is egotistical, divisive, and silly. The second kind of gatekeeping, geared toward preventing your favorite genre from becoming overrun by lame bullshit and watered down to the point of meaninglessness, is necessary in order for categories to be practically useful. But you're bound to have a bit of the former along with the latter. The only way to maintain an undisturbed ecosystem with unthreatened traditions is to remain completely underground, insulated from outside influence, which—as countless movies have taught us—seems counterproductive if the goal is to maintain a vital creative community rather than an ingrown preservation society. Still, maybe a certain wariness made sense when the Hollywood version of indie music progressed from *The O.C.* to *Garden State* to *Grey's Anatomy* in under two years, as if the industry was racing to see how quickly they could turn this trendy scene into a new kind of adult contemporary.

In 2005, Patsavas began supervising the music for *Grey's*, a new ABC medical drama that became an even bigger (and soapier) breakout hit than *The O.C.* The show's truncated first season featured music from pop-leaning indie acts like Rilo Kiley, Tegan and Sara, and the Postal Service. Its second season mixed in indie bands like Metric and Gomez but also famously made hits out of Snow Patrol's "Chasing Cars," an alt-rock ballad a few degrees softer than Death Cab, and the Fray's "How to Save a Life," a midtempo piano-driven track so pop that it charted at No. 3 on the Hot 100. That kind of sentimental white-bread soft rock came to define the show's aesthetic, even though Patsavas and the *Grey's* team sometimes branched out beyond it. Subsequent seasons featured blogger favorites like Feist, the National, and the Whitest Boy Alive, but it was hard to shake the sense that the show's milquetoast point of view would have some contaminating effect on indie rock as a whole.

In those days, indie's more severe or abrasive artists remained underground, cultivating cult stardom while their poppier contemporaries came to define indie rock in the public imagination. Indie rock was exploding in all directions at the time, but even as the genre became a dominant force in pop culture, there were limits to the kinds of indie acts that could gain a foothold in the world at large. Bands like Constantines were too noisy and aggressive to cross over, at least not without some "Smells like Teen Spirit"–style lightning bolt of a single. The late, great Jason Molina of Songs: Ohia made music too raw and depressing to be marketed alongside Iron & Wine's warm fuzzy sweater music. Quirky, labyrinthine art music by the likes of Joanna Newsom and Fiery Furnaces felt like counterprogramming to the user-friendly bands in the Seth Cohen Starter Pack. It's not like the whole underground was excavated by Hollywood's hippest music supervisors, but there was now a pathway to a payday for those willing and able to play the game.

By the fall of 2007, *The O.C.* had already wrapped up its abbreviated final season, and Schwartz was at work on his next zeitgeist-defining teen soap. He and fellow *O.C.* producer Stephanie Savage launched *Gossip Girl*, a glitzy adaptation of Cecily von Ziegesar's young adult novel series about the exploits of disgustingly wealthy New York City teenagers. Patsavas was once again on board as music supervisor, and although the express focus of the soundtrack was pop music, she put her signature accessible-indie spin on the show from its very first scene: The pilot episode began with "Young Folks," a brisk, whistling ditty that had been a sleeper hit for Swedish indie rockers Peter Bjorn and John. In some ways, *Gossip Girl* picked up where *The O.C.* left off, but music was never a plot point on *Gossip Girl* the way it had been on *The O.C.* As the latter half of the decade rolled on, the indie-rock teen-entertainment industrial complex would continue on even bigger screens.

* * *

At the end of the 2000s, Michael Cera was the Seth Cohen of the silver screen. Cera's ascendance marked a noteworthy shift in Hollywood's embrace of indie music: Whereas *The O.C.* had allowed indie bands to capitalize on their newfound mainstream status, Cera pictures like *Nick & Norah's Infinite Playlist* and *Scott Pilgrim vs. the World* heralded a moment when corporate overlords tried to capitalize on the now-ascendant indie scene. Indie rock was no longer just a genre; it was a lifestyle to be sold, a demographic to pander to, a craze to cash in on. And like Adam Brody before him, Cera was uniquely suited to be its avatar.

Unlike the many suave twentysomethings who have attempted to pass for high schoolers in Hollywood productions, Cera was an actual gawky teenager who honestly looked young for his age. The Toronto-area native had risen to fame as the endearingly pitiful George Michael Bluth on the Fox sitcom *Arrested Development*, a series with an arc that mirrored many great indie bands: critically acclaimed but lacking an audience, building a fervent following only after it ended, returning years later in diminished form to cash in on all that goodwill. (Call it the Pixies model.)

Between the end of *Arrested Development*'s network TV run in 2006 and the start of the show's Netflix revival in 2013, Cera became a movie star. His breakout role was alongside Jonah Hill in 2007's summer blockbuster *Superbad*, the defining teen comedy of its generation, about two high school seniors attempting to lose their virginity before graduating. It wasn't a music-centric movie, but the raunchy coming-of-age film cemented Cera's type as a fainthearted yet fundamentally decent underdog dweeb. "The actor has become something of a go-to performer when it comes to playing the almost painfully earnest hero," wrote the *San Jose Mercury News*.

Just months after *Superbad*, Cera starred in the first of several films in which indie rock would serve as a throughline. In *Juno*—another independent film that became a mainstream hit—he played a geeky suburban teen named Paulie Bleeker, who accidentally impregnates his longtime crush Juno MacGuff, played by Elliot Page. It was the screenwriting debut of Diablo Cody, a stripper-turned-blogger-turned-bestselling author who favored attention-grabbing "weird stylized dialogue," as she described it to *Vanity Fair* in 2017. (Rainn Wilson, as a convenience store clerk watching Juno shake her pregnancy test: "That ain't no Etch A Sketch. This is one doodle that can't be undid, homeskillet.")

Like Amy Sherman-Palladino of *Gilmore Girls* and Aaron Sorkin of *The West Wing*, Cody wasn't afraid to make her characters speak in flowery prose with a twist. But hers wasn't the only distinctive voice shaping the movie. When director Jason Reitman asked Page what kind of music Juno would listen to, the response was "The Moldy Peaches," whose Kimya Dawson became the spine of the soundtrack also featuring Cat Power, Belle & Sebastian, and Sonic Youth.

The Moldy Peaches, a primitive and provocative "anti-folk" band led by Dawson and Adam Green, were peers and tourmates with the Strokes in the Y2K era, even though their twee, childlike affect didn't much jibe with the Strokes' image as a stylish gang of privileged ruffians. Never more than a cult concern, the Peaches had been on hiatus since 2004, but the success of *Juno* brought them briefly back together under a much brighter spotlight. Per Page's advice, Reitman filled the movie with Dawson's music; it ended with Page and Cera grabbing guitars and singing the Peaches' love song "Anyone Else but You" to each other on a front stoop. When the movie took off, the soundtrack shot to No. 1—a first for a Fox Searchlight film—and Rough Trade Records issued the seven-year-old "Anyone Else but You" as a single.

Page and Cera's version of the song from the movie even cracked the *Billboard* Hot 100.

The following year, Cera starred opposite Kat Dennings in *Nick & Norah's Infinite Playlist*. Cera's character, Nick, is the bassist and only straight member of the Jerk-Offs, a band in the punk subgenre queercore. He meets Norah, the daughter of a music industry bigwig, at a Jerk-Offs show in the (real) NYC music club Arlene's Grocery—where, in a bit of social posturing, she asks him to pretend to be her boyfriend. The two teens set off across the city's music scene in search of a secret show by the (fictional) band Where's Fluffy?

Nick & Norah was adapted from a novel by Rachel Cohn and David Levithan, who'd laced their book with references to Gen X alternative rock. The movie's soundtrack incorporated more current indie fare from the likes of Vampire Weekend, Band of Horses, and Shout Out Louds—as well as freak-folk luminary Devendra Banhart, who has a funny cameo in the film, and pop-rockers Bishop Allen, who share a bill with the Jerk-Offs at Arlene's. Nick wears what appears to be one of those zip-up hoodies from American Apparel that were ubiquitous at the time, but the era's other big hipster-chic boutique Urban Outfitters becomes the butt of a joke when Nick's bandmate scoffs at poseurs who buy Ramones T-shirts there. I guess at this point these movies were selling not just indie music but indie elitism, too.

The film was a mild commercial success, but its existence suggested Hollywood execs were all-in on the idea of indie rock as millennial youth culture—or at least as a product to be marketed to young millennials. One of the more negative reviews came from *The Village Voice*'s Robert Wilonsky, who said *Nick & Norah* was "crafted in a lab by 54-year-old hucksters trying to sell shit to the kids under the cheerless guise of 'alternative.'" Boardrooms apparently remained enthusiastic about indie rock youth movies in the years following *Nick & Norah*, but they may have misjudged the hunger for yet another movie starring Michael Cera as a shy musician. Or maybe the next one was so unique and high-concept that people didn't know what to make of it at first.

The conclusion in Cera's trilogy of indie rock rom-coms was 2010's *Scott Pilgrim vs. the World*. Adapted by *Shaun of the Dead* and *Hot Fuzz* director Edgar Wright from Bryan Lee O'Malley's graphic novels, it's more of an action comedy that plays out like a video game, but with a story deeply rooted in music. Wright is a voracious listener whose later works like *Baby Driver* would continue to revolve around tunes. Nigel Godrich, the producer best known as an unofficial member of Radiohead, scored the movie and oversaw its soundtrack. Cera stars as Pilgrim, the bassist (again) for a garage band called Sex Bob-Omb; he must defeat seven evil exes of love interest Ramona Flowers in order to date her. Much of the movie is set at a battle of the bands in Cera's native Toronto, with a number of local talents among the real-life musicians contributing to the soundtrack.

Plans to hire the raucous and sleazy Nashville garage band Be Your Own Pet fell through due to their breakup. Wright rebuffed *Scott Pilgrim* comic author Bryan Lee O'Malley's desire to hire lo-fi greats Times New Viking because their intensely abrasive production style would not fly in Hollywood. "They're mastered too loud," Wright told the *Los Angeles Times*. "They're designed to screw up a playlist." So Godrich recruited his longtime collaborator Beck, a notorious genre chameleon, to write suitably grimy songs for Sex Bob-Omb. (Per O'Malley, Beck's first input was, "I think they should sound like Times New Viking.")

Cornelius, sometimes known as "the Japanese Beck," wrote music for the electronic duo Katayanagi Twins. Two of the movie's other main bands were brought to life by a pair of the biggest indie acts in Toronto. The synth-tinged Metric did the tunes for the Clash at Demonhead, fronted by a young Brie Larson. And Broken Social Scene, the sprawling collective that became one of the most beloved groups in the underground, switched gears to crank out short blasts of goth-punk for Crash and the Boys (including one memorable track that barely lasts four seconds).

Beyond the involvement of actual Toronto bands, there were many more references to specific local rock clubs and hipster hangouts embedded in *Scott Pilgrim*. I'd speculate that these Easter eggs went over a lot of people's heads, except not that many people saw *Scott Pilgrim* to begin with. The movie bobombed at the box office and was only later embraced as a cult classic. It also marked the end of Cera's run as the face of indie rock in Hollywood, which was probably for the best; as *Variety*'s Peter Debruge wrote at the time, "while his comic timing is impeccable, he's finally played the wilty wallflower one too many times."

Cera would, however, continue to exist in the real-life indierock world. Just after *Scott Pilgrim* came out, he took a gig as the touring bassist for Mister Heavenly, an indie supergroup featuring members of Man Man, Islands, the Shins, and Modest Mouse. Around the same time, he contributed backing vocals and mandolin to the Weezer song "Hang On." He even surprise-released a solo album called *True That* in 2014 and collaborated with indie singer-songwriter Sharon Van Etten on a song for 2017's *Dina*.

Cera wasn't the only movie star to moonlight as an indie-rocker. In 2006, the buzzy young actress Zooey Deschanel met indie-folk star M. Ward on the set of her movie *The Go-Getter* when the director asked them to collaborate on a song for the soundtrack. The resulting cover of British folk legends Richard and Linda Thompson's "When I Get to the Border" marked the beginning of a long and fruitful partnership. Deschanel had sung beautifully in 2003's *Elf* and had been recording home demos for years. But she never knew how to proceed with them until meeting Matthew Ward—who, after hearing her demos, expressed a desire to properly record her songs.

Deschanel and Ward's duo, She & Him, signed to Merge Records, home of big-name indie acts like Arcade Fire and Spoon as well as Ward's solo work. Their solid 2008 debut album *Volume One* pulled inspiration from the Beach Boys—an increasingly common indie-world touchstone in the late aughts—and other forms of retro music like classic jazz and country, Phil Spector–produced R&B girl groups, and 1970s AM Gold. That dinner party–friendly sonic palette, plus the band's prim and proper presentation, made She & Him key players in the smoothing out and softening of mainstream indie rock, that ceaseless progression toward the Starbucks CD rack. It was almost too on-the-nose when Deschanel married Death Cab for Cutie's Ben Gibbard in 2009: the king and queen of Hollywood indie rock, if only for a few fleeting years before their divorce.

She & Him positioned Deschanel as the obvious choice to star in 2009's *(500) Days of Summer*, a movie that—even more than Michael Cera's post-*Juno* flicks—now feels like the culmination of the film industry's indie music movement. The main characters are not students but professionals: Deschanel as Summer Finn and Joseph Gordon-Levitt as Tom Hansen, the coworker who becomes enamored with her. Their meet-cute involves a shared admiration for the Smiths. Both of them dress like they're on a Belle & Sebastian album cover (neckties, sweaters, vintage skirts, et al.) except for Tom's collection of band T-shirts worn under blazers, featuring album covers from critic-bait basics like Joy Division's *Unknown Pleasures* and the Clash's *London Calling*. He sings Pixies at karaoke; she does Nancy Sinatra. While roaming an Ikea store (a reference to Pavement's "Date with IKEA"?) they playact as a boring married couple; Summer mockingly quips, "Our place really is lovely, isn't it? Ooh! *Idol*'s on."

(500) Days of Summer seemed to be pitched directly at millennials who'd been in school when *The O.C.* premiered and were now moving into their careers, never mind that the 2008 recession had made jobs much harder to come by. If affording chic apartments while working for a greeting card company seemed unrealistic, an even less believable fantasy being sold was the beautiful woman who'll look directly at you and affirm, "You have good taste in music." In spirit, *(500) Days of Summer*'s elevator scene was perfectly in step with *Nick & Norah* moments like Norah scrolling through Nick's iPod and declaring, "This is amazing. You are literally, like, my musical soulmate," or the early scene where she judges Nick's ex for failing to appreciate all the expertly curated, elaborately packaged mix CDs he made for her. It was as if she was validating my own belief that there is no greater expression of love than sharing my own exquisite taste.

This idea of finding your doting musical soulmate was threaded all throughout the decade's indie-rock cinema. Though Natalie Portman's Sam from *Garden State* offers music recommendations rather than receiving them, she has long been cited as a core example of the Manic Pixie Dream Girl, described by critic Nathan Rabin as a type of stock character who "exists solely in the fevered imaginations of sensitive writer-directors to teach broodingly soulful young men to embrace life and its infinite mysteries and adventures." So much of this subgenre played like wish fulfillment for dudes like myself who came to think of ourselves as protagonists and our well-curated media libraries as some kind of virtue.

To be fair to *(500) Days of Summer*, if the movie is happy to lure you in with lots of stylish, aspirational shots of Tom and Summer together, it also seems invested in puncturing the myth of the nice-guy indie rocker who connects with a girl out of his league. Summer might seem like a Manic Pixie Dream Girl at first, but rather than complete Tom, she holds him at a distance, then ultimately loses interest and moves on. Late in their relationship, he views it as a personal affront that she's never heard of Spoon. "They were on the mix I made for you," he utters in disbelief. "They were track one." We're clearly supposed to see him as pathetic in that moment. Ditto to the part where his young half sister Rachel, played by Chloë Grace Moretz, gives it to him straight: "Just 'cause some cute girl likes the same bizarro crap you do, that doesn't make her your soulmate, Tom." The movie essentially does for millennials what *High Fidelity* had done for Gen X a decade earlier, demonstrating that good taste in music is neither a winsome personality unto itself nor a sufficient foundation for long-term romance.

But was it a sufficient basis for a marketing scheme? More or less, yeah. In a 2004 article headlined "The Seth Effect" in Portland's *Willamette Week*, future Pitchfork editor Amy Phillips wrote about the changes percolating in culture thanks to *The O.C.* and Seth Cohen:

Imagine if half of *The O.C.*'s audience bought a copy of *Transatlanticism*. We'd have a new Nirvana on our hands. That probably won't happen, as Gibbard is attractive in a lost-puppy sort of way but lacks charisma and star power, and the fluff-pop "The Sound of Settling" is no galvanizing, "Smells like Teen Spirit"-style anthem. But the potential is there for a mass teen culture revolution, the likes of which we haven't seen since Kurt Cobain made it hip for boys to wear dresses. For the first time since the grunge years, wimpy dudes have got a big-time role model, a soundtrack and some serious cred. What they do with that power remains to be seen.

It's true: Death Cab did not become the next Nirvana, but they and their peers did break through in a huge way. By 2009, Gibbard could honestly tell Greg Kot that "this type of music has really started to mold pop culture." That same year, even the most mainstream of youth movie franchises bought into the indie rock phenomenon. As curated by one Alexandra Patsavas, *Twilight: New Moon*—a record-setting box-office smash about the soapy exploits of mopey vampires—packed its chart-topping soundtrack with indie stars like Grizzly Bear, St. Vincent, and Lykke Li, artists that might have gotten *O.C.* needle drops if they'd emerged in the show's prime. Naturally, the tracklist began with Death Cab for Cutie.

Chapter 4 Soundtrack

Broken Social Scene, "KC Accidental" (2002)
Menomena, "The Late Great Libido" (2003)
The New Pornographers, "The Laws Have Changed" (2003)
The Unicorns, "I Was Born (A Unicorn)" (2003)
Fiery Furnaces, "Blueberry Boat" (2004)
Arcade Fire, "Wake Up" (2004)
Clap Your Hands Say Yeah, "In This Home on Ice" (2005)
Sufjan Stevens, "Chicago" (2005)
Architecture In Helsinki, "Do the Whirlwind" (2005)
Sleater-Kinney, "Jumpers" (2005)
Wolf Parade, "I'll Believe in Anything" (2005)
The Boy Least Likely To, "Be Gentle With Me" (2005)
Animal Collective, "The Purple Bottle" (2005)
Tapes 'n Tapes, "Just Drums" (2005)
The Hold Steady, "Stuck Between Stations" (2006)
Grizzly Bear, "Knife" (2006)
TV On The Radio, "Wolf Like Me" (2006)
Spoon, "The Underdog" (2007)
Deerhunter, "Nothing Ever Happened" (2008)
Vampire Weekend, "Oxford Comma" (2008)

4

Best New Music

Pitchfork, blog rock, & the indie media pipeline

"All right. We're the flavor of the month," the towering man at the microphone joked. "Let's go."

In the early hours of October 14, 2004, Arcade Fire were onstage at Mercury Lounge in New York City. Exactly a month after the release of their debut album, *Funeral*, the buzzy young Montréal band was headlining the Merge Records showcase at CMJ Music Marathon, the conference and festival affiliated with the college radio magazine *CMJ*. There were amazing gigs happening all over town, including CMJ's official opening night party with Sonic Youth and RJD2 at Irving Plaza. But of all the clubs in the city, this tiny Lower East Side enclave was the place to be. No band's hype was burning as hot as Arcade Fire's.

When I heard about CMJ as a college student in Ohio, I couldn't believe it: four days and nights of concerts across NYC, featuring some of my most beloved bands, and because I worked at my college radio station I could get a free ticket? In a trance, I trekked to the Big Apple in 2003 and 2004 with my fellow volunteers at our little online-only campus station, ready to have my mind blown by indie rock.

At my first CMJ in 2003, that's exactly what happened. I saw Death Cab for Cutie play an intimate, low-key daytime set at the Museum of Television & Radio for KCRW's *Morning Becomes Eclectic*. I watched lit-geek folk-rockers the Decemberists play a small Brooklyn electroclash club called Luxx on its last night in business. I cackled in disbelief at Les Savy Fav's wide-eyed, dad-bodded Tim Harrington, who thrust his microphone into his pants so an audience member could scream into his crotch and leapt from the Knitting Factory balcony. I commiserated with anyone in earshot about the death of Elliott Smith, who died by suicide during the festival.

When I returned in 2004, my objective was clear: see Arcade Fire, no matter what. *Funeral* had become my latest obsession. Centered on the songwriting partnership of spouses Win Butler (the bellowing 6'5" Texan frontman) and Régine Chassagne (a petite, theatrical Montréal native born to Haitians of French-African descent), the album combined bits of hip indie touchstones like Neutral Milk Hotel, Modest Mouse, and Bright Eyes into raw and overpowering songs sparked by genuine grief. Arcade Fire took that relatively lo-fi sound—marked by howling vocals, soaring strings, throttling drums, and even an accordion sometimes—and infused it with the searching earnestness of U2 and Bruce Springsteen, inflating song after song to anthem scale. It was the closest indie rock had ever come to feeling like arena rock, and Arcade Fire were about to unleash that explosive energy within the confines of a very small nightclub.

The band gave a legendary performance that night. From the

moment those slowly chugging guitar chords introduced "Wake Up" and the whole group joined together in resounding wordless cries, I was enraptured. The feeling turned to giddiness when, during "Neighborhood #2 (Laika)," Richard Reed Parry and Win's brother Will donned helmets and pounded each other's heads with drumsticks. It was overwhelming: the songs, thunderous and wild, but also the sheer mass of people onstage together in old-timey garb bringing that racket to life.

Mercury Lounge's capacity is only 250. Demand was intense; industry people who paid hundreds of dollars for their badges waited forever in line only to be turned away at the door. My solution was to enter before the music began at 8:00 P.M. and camp out up front for all five opening acts, the kind of plan that now seems insane as a dad with back pain but felt completely reasonable as a music-obsessed undergrad.

Being young and foolish also accounts for my indifference about how much talent cycled onto the stage that night, including influential figures like Lou Barlow (Dinosaur Jr., Sebadoh, the Folk Implosion) and the Clean's David Kilgour (backed by all three members of Yo La Tengo!). Merge had curated a killer lineup, but like everyone else, I was there to see the band that got a 9.7 on Pitchfork.

* * *

Win Butler was probably legitimately worried that Arcade Fire would be the flavor of the month and nothing more. The online critical apparatus that built up around indie rock in the 2000s was powerful enough to mint new superstars instantaneously and fickle enough to dispose of them just as quickly. In those days, bands emerging from that world often seemed to have been shot from a cannon. Arcade Fire achieved escape velocity and maintained a career even after indie tastemakers lost interest, but many of their contemporaries crashed and burned.

The early internet was a new frontier outside the control of traditional media gatekeepers, which made it much easier not only to discover indie rock but to immerse yourself in it. Broader access to the music, combined with the hipster impulse to stay ahead of the curve and the internet attention economy's constant demand for the new, sped up many artists' arcs from obscurity to the spotlight to history's trash bin.

At the center of that world was Pitchfork, a webzine that began as a scrappy underdog but grew into the most prominent music publication of its generation. Pitchfork succeeded in part by becoming one of the first journalistic enterprises to put down roots in the indie music world online. But just as important to the site's success was a distinctive approach—including a credibility-conferring willingness to trash even indie rock's sacred cows—that inspired intense loyalty in its core readers and just as intense a revulsion in haters. (It wouldn't be Pitchfork if it wasn't pissing people off.)

Though it would one day move to offices in the World Trade Center, at first Pitchfork was run out of basements, bedrooms, and closets. A freshly twenty-year-old Ryan Schreiber started the site at his parents' house in the Minneapolis suburbs in early 1996, on a Mac with a dial-up connection, publishing to pitchforkmedia.com (the name was a reference to Al Pacino's pitchfork tattoo in *Scarface*) after learning his original name, Turntable, was already trademarked.

As a teenager, Schreiber fell in love with indie rock via Twin Cities college radio. He read music magazines voraciously and eventually became smitten with zine culture—not only the focus on underground artists but the snarky, irreverent tone. He felt like he could do something similar but without the endless trips to Kinko's to use the Xerox machine, one of the built-in expenses that caused many zines to cease publication after a few issues.

Schreiber recognized online publishing's limitless reach and lack of overhead. And as he told the *New York Times Popcast* in 2024, he saw a wide-open lane to cover the subculture beneath the alternative rock mainstream, which "felt to me like the main story." In that interview, Schreiber elaborated on his vision: "I really wanted to create something that was very outspoken, that was very tough from a critical standpoint on what sort of deserved to be part of this culture? Who's making music that's truly innovative and progressive? And really try and center that for people as the centerpiece of what's happening in music."

That plan involved interviews and news, but Pitchfork's driving force quickly became reviews. This was a time when music was not readily available to stream, when reviews could be the difference between spending $16 on a CD or not. A daily website could distribute critiques much faster than print publications, especially the monthly magazines that ruled music journalism at the time. "I was already an obsessive consumer of record reviews," Schreiber said in a 2021 Pitchfork feature. "I just loved the debates, the conversation about music, even if it was a one-way conversation. I knew I wasn't a good writer, and I had no pretenses about that, but my perspective was, I have strong convictions about music, I care about it immensely, and I'm just going to write like I talk."

Pitchfork's writers focused on under-the-radar music, and they staked out strong opinions on it, translated into ratings on a ten-point scale that went down to the first decimal point. Those numbers, displayed prominently at the top of every review, would become crucial to the site's power and influence—fodder for infinite arguments, but also marching orders for a legion of loyal readers who came to take Pitchfork's word as gospel.

It didn't happen overnight. At first, Pitchfork amounted to Schreiber and his friends getting their takes off and trying to crack each other up. The perspective was distinctly Midwestern and guided by youthful ardor, so Schreiber's beloved Minneapolis bands 12 Rods and Walt Mink both got perfect 10s, while the Flaming Lips' gambit *Zaireeka*—four discs designed to be played simultaneously—got a 0.0 because tracking down four CD players was expensive and inconvenient. It was also distinctly male and white, a reality that remained baked into the site's point of view for decades, even as Pitchfork grew into a behemoth and the staff took pains to reflect a broader range of perspectives.

Schreiber moved to Chicago in 2000, just as Pitchfork published its most famous review. Brent DiCrescenzo's perfect-10 rave about Radiohead's *Kid A* is a work of criticism so notorious and impactful that it got its own oral history in *Billboard* twenty years later. DiCrescenzo filled the review with radical hyperbole, like "Comparing this to other albums is like comparing an aquarium to blue construction paper"; in its most-quoted line, he proclaimed, "The experience and emotions tied to listening to *Kid A* are like witnessing the stillborn birth of a child while simultaneously having the opportunity to see her play in the afterlife on Imax."

This kind of praise was consistent with the average Radiohead fan's fervor. At a time when *Rolling Stone* reserved its five-star reviews for washed boomer icons, Pitchfork didn't wait to anoint Radiohead as peerless geniuses in the moment. For fanboys like me, this was vindicating—confirmation that our generation was bearing witness to legendary talents of our own, and that *obviously* this stuff was better than the new Mick Jagger albums that were getting gassed up by *Rolling Stone*. Schreiber, a Radiohead fanatic himself, reached out to the many Radiohead fan sites to tip them off about the 10/10 review. "The web traffic was literally off the charts," he told *Billboard*.

Even before the *Kid A* review streaked across the internet like the shooting star from its opening line, Pitchfork was finding a consistent audience. "It was maybe something like 2,000 readers a month or something," Schreiber told Media Bistro in 2013. "But at that point it had sort of become, in this very, very small, niche way, the main, online resource for independent music." He began selling ads, mostly to record stores and labels. Soon Schreiber was able to quit his day job.

His growing roster of writers, though, were still making little to no money for their work. These were passionate hobbyists doing it for the love of the game. Their enthusiasm came through in hot takes, outrageous scores, and formal/conceptual experiments—like a 2001 pan of Tool's *Lateralus* conceived as a teenage prog rock fan's class report on his summer vacation (score: 1.9), or a 2002 rave about a deluxe reissue of Pavement's *Slanted and Enchanted* hand-scrawled on pages from a legal pad (score: 10).

This was the era when Pitchfork became a fixture of my internet routine. By the time I arrived at college in fall 2002, every day I was loading up the homepage, clicking on all five new reviews (at least long enough to see the scores), and perusing the news section to see when the best bands in indie rock would be touring within driving distance. Not only was the site introducing me to a whole new class of artists, it was also expanding my concept of what a music review could be. The writers' distinctive approach, heartfelt conviction, and stellar track record of recommendations inspired intense loyalty in me, spurring countless album purchases and concert road trips.

I wasn't alone. By 2003, Pitchfork's newly introduced Best New Music designation—a stamp of approval affixed to the top of the site's most reverent, ecstatic reviews—was enough to launch an artist's career. It happened to Sufjan Stevens, an ambitious singer-songwriter from the weirdo corners of the Christian rock scene. Pitchfork's lukewarm review of Stevens's album *Michigan* had slipped past many readers unnoticed, but a few weeks later the site replaced it with a breathless 8.5 endorsement by Brandon Stosuy, instantly turning "Sufjan" into an indie household name.

When Schreiber plucked *You Forgot It in People*, the sophomore release from the Toronto indie rock collective Broken Social Scene, from a pile of promo CDs months after its release, his 9.2 Best New Music exultation turned the band (and affiliated acts like Feist and Metric) into underground stars overnight. "The next tour we went on, we suddenly found ourselves selling out venues," Broken Social Scene's Kevin Drew told *Wired* in 2006. "Everyone was coming up to us, saying, 'We heard about you from Pitchfork.' It basically opened the door for us. It gave us an audience." It's the kind of story many Pitchfork darlings were circulating back then.

That power and influence worked both ways. A negative Pitchfork review could destroy an artist—including ones who'd previously been among the site's absolute favorites. The most infamous instance was *Travistan*, the 2004 solo debut from the Dismemberment Plan's Travis Morrison, produced by Death Cab for Cutie's Chris Walla and released through Death Cab's former label Barsuk. Pitchfork's hearty endorsements, including naming *Emergency & I* the No. 1 album of 1999, had been key to the Plan's success. But critic Chris Dahlen was so disgusted with *Travistan* that he rated it 0.0, calling it "one of the most colossal trainwrecks in indie rock history."

The fallout was instant; *Travistan* might as well have been erased from Earth. College radio stations pulled their support. Ticket sales waned. "One indie record store even said that they wouldn't carry it because of the Pitchfork review," Barsuk's Josh Rosenfeld told *Wired*. "Not because they heard it—because of the review." In a series of tweets years later, Walla was still stung by the impact. "It was judge, jury, executioner all at once," he recalled. "The pre-p4k [Pitchfork] review response really was positive. A little confused! But genuinely enthusiastic, and the degree to which that enthusiasm disappeared cannot be overstated. Like, most of the pressing got shipped to retail . . . and most of it got shipped back."

Shamefully, even an obsessive Plan fan like myself barely gave *Travistan* a chance. "Up until the day of the review, I'd play a solo show, and people would be like, 'That's our boy, our eccentric boy.' Literally, the view changed overnight," Morrison told *The Washington Post* in 2006. "I could tell people were trying to figure out if they were supposed to be there or not. It was pretty severe, how the mood changed." His verdict: "The review isn't the story. The reaction to it is. The seriousness with which everyone takes Pitchfork is kind of mind-boggling."

Pitchfork didn't evolve into a real business until after it had already become a kingmaker. In 2004, Schreiber hired the site's first employee, Chris Kaskie, to handle ad sales, payroll, and other business operations. By 2005, Pitchfork had a basement office space in Chicago, Scott Plagenhoef was on board as managing editor, and the site was pulling 120,000 daily readers. That total ballooned to 240,000 in 2007, by which point Pitchfork employed twelve full-time staffers and had finally moved out of a basement into a loft in Chicago's trendy Logan Square neighborhood. In 2005, Pitchfork also launched its own music festival, then called Intonation, drawing 30,000 to Chicago's Union Park (myself included) for a lineup headlined by Tortoise and the Decemberists. In subsequent years, the festival continued evolving its scale and sensibility in parallel with the site.

The fest showed Pitchfork's burgeoning real-life impact—as did a flurry of mid-2000s news articles about Pitchfork's undeniable influence—but nothing revealed the site's clout like the rise of Arcade Fire. If the *Travistan* treatise left a smoking crater where Morrison's career used to be, David Moore's awestruck tribute to *Funeral* ("Their search for salvation in the midst of real chaos is ours; their eventual catharsis is part of our continual enlightenment") blasted Arcade Fire into the stratosphere, rocketing them toward mainstream rock stardom and proving that Pitchfork could move the needle beyond the indie rock bubble.

At the time, Ed Roche was label manager for Touch and Go Records, the longstanding Chicago company that distributed Merge Records releases. "We sent out one hundred advance copies [of *Funeral*] to the mom and pop stores prior to that review, and across the board nobody really cared," Roche said in the Merge oral history *Our Noise*. "It was viewed as an okay record, but nobody really got excited. And then, literally, that review hit within a few days of the release date, and within hours, everybody who had thought the record was okay now thought it was the greatest record of all time."

Funeral was soon touted by more established media institutions like *Rolling Stone* and *The New York Times*. Commercial radio behemoths like KROQ put Arcade Fire in heavy rotation. Hipster icons like David Byrne and Lou Reed cozied up to the band. U2 used "Wake Up" as their entrance music on tour, while David Bowie invited Arcade Fire to perform the song with him at Radio City Music Hall for a CBS primetime special called *Fashion Rocks*. *Funeral* surpassed Merge's top sales mark of 150,000 within a few months of release and went on to sell 500,000 copies in the US alone. It was nominated for a Grammy and a Juno, the Canadian equivalent. And when Pitchfork launched its festival in 2005, Arcade Fire turned down an invite to headline, instead performing across town at Lollapalooza a few weeks later for a crowd more than double the size. Their days of playing 250-cap clubs were over.

* * *

The night of Arcade Fire's jam-packed CMJ showcase at Mercury Lounge, my future boss was also present. "They're Canadian, they love moths, and this show proved the Merge showcase headliners deserve all the hype," Scott Lapatine wrote on *Stereogum* the day after the show. "Helmets, silkscreened blazers, an accordian [*sic*], blood (Win had a guitar mishap early in the set) . . . these guys know how to put on a show."

Lapatine had founded *Stereogum* less than three years earlier, on New Year's Day, 2002. The Long Island native was living in Manhattan and working in digital media for VH1 when he launched his own side hustle on LiveJournal, one of the many early blogging platforms that proliferated online post-Y2K. He named it after a lyric from "Radio Number 1," a then-current song from the loungy, atmospheric French band Air.

Along with peers like NYC's *Fluxblog* and Montréal-based *Said the Gramophone* (which was posting music by local favorites Arcade Fire long before their Pitchfork breakthrough), *Stereogum* was one of the first MP3 blogs, sites where readers could download a selection of new songs handpicked by the proprietor. Not all of this music was legally available; bloggers eagerly posted leaks, unofficial remixes, and whatever else in their inbox piqued their interest. Often, these download links were accompanied by no more than a sentence or two of commentary. Although MP3 bloggers' quest to unearth new music mirrored a reporter's hunt for scoops in some ways, it was less an act of journalism than one of curation—like a DJ turning listeners on to new artists and debuting new songs by old favorites.

Blogs like *Stereogum* were part of an ecosystem of indie-rock websites that emerged in the early aughts, all orbiting Pitchfork, taking cues from it or reacting against it. Message boards like Hipinion and I Love Music essentially functioned as Pitchfork's comments section. A flurry of indie-focused webzines sprung up, like Tiny Mix Tapes, Drowned in Sound, and Stylus Magazine, where several future Pitchfork fixtures honed their craft. PopMatters and *The Onion*'s non-satirical offshoot, The A.V. Club, covered the full spectrum of pop culture, but indie music coverage was a huge aspect of their appeal. In contrast to these operations, most MP3 blogs did not attempt to pull off robust, magazine-style journalism. The posts at destinations like *Brooklyn Vegan*, *Gorilla vs. Bear*, and *Largehearted Boy* were quick and to the point: just links to MP3 downloads, MySpace pages, or other blogs. Words by the author were far outnumbered by words in the comments section.

At first, bloggers fiercely protected their independence. As sites developed influence, they were inundated with pitches from industry sources, but none of the bloggers wanted to look like they were letting publicists and managers influence what they posted. In a much-publicized 2004 incident, Warner Bros. became the first major label to submit their music for coverage at MP3 blogs. "We are very interested in blogs and I was wondering if you could post this mp3," Warner's Ian Cripps wrote to bloggers.

The Secret Machines were not, in today's parlance, "industry plants," a term referring to artists plucked from obscurity by powerful forces and thrust into prominence without organically building their careers. They had been touring with Pitchfork-approved acts like . . . And You Will Know Us By the Trail of Dead for years and were respected among their peers. David Bowie even sang their praises on his website's official forum, naming their album *Now Here Is Nowhere* as the only CD to rival Arcade Fire's *Funeral* that year. But with a few exceptions, most blogs opted not to post Secret Machines MP3s when Warner reached out, lest they appear to be shilling for a major label. Still, if bloggers were wary of looking like sellouts, some of them weren't averse to all interest from the corporate world. One company called Buzz Media bought blogs including *Stereogum*, *Gorilla vs. Bear*, *Idolator*, and even *The Hype Machine*, all of which had grown from passion projects into lucrative businesses.

To return to the DJ parallels, part of the sport of MP3 blogging was the race to feature new artists before anyone else knew about them. This impulse to dig up a new Arcade Fire every day led to blogs—and Pitchfork—rushing to anoint new bands, sometimes before the bands were ready to shoulder those kinds of expectations. Before the internet, indie bands could spend years touring and releasing albums before developing a large following. Now, they could become a sensation with one MP3—and be cast aside just as quickly in favor of tomorrow's new discovery.

One of the bands to benefit (and then suffer) from this accelerated timeline was Clap Your Hands Say Yeah. The Brooklyn band channeled hip influences like Talking Heads and Neutral Milk Hotel into danceable tunes topped off with Alec Ounsworth's exaggerated nasal bray—a voice that dared you to hate it, singing melodies too catchy to ignore. Clap Your Hands Say Yeah self-released their self-titled debut album without a manager or publicist. The album attracted lots of blog buzz in the months and weeks leading up to release; in a sort of holy trinity moment for O.G. MP3 blogs, a *Stereogum* guest post by *Fluxblog*'s Matthew Perpetua directed readers to two Clap Your Hands Say Yeah tracks at *Said the Gramophone* on June 9, 2005.

That hype funneled upward into a 9.0 Best New Music review from Pitchfork, and suddenly CYHSY had gone supernova. The praise took on a meta quality as people celebrated not just the band's music but the way they rose to fame—i.e., without industry support. It suggested that there was a path forward for artists too arty or obscure to attract the attention of legacy print magazines. "While a lot of bands view the promotional apparatus as a necessary evil, Clap Your Hands Say Yeah prove that it's still possible for a band to get heard, given enough talent and perseverance, without a PR agency or a label," Brian Howe's Pitchfork review concluded. "Indie rock has received a much-needed kick in the pants, and we have the rare chance to decide what a band sounds like of our own accord before any agency cooks up and disseminates an opinion for us. Damn, maybe this is how it's supposed to work!"

By the time Pitchfork interviewed Clap Your Hands Say Yeah that fall, they'd self-distributed over 40,000 copies of the album and were selling out their tour dates opening for hungry young NYC band the National, with many concertgoers clearing out before the headliners performed. (Big mistake!) Print media institutions caught on too, eager to report on both CYHSY and their decidedly online pipeline to stardom. In a *New York Times* profile, the band revealed that they'd turned down an appearance on *The O.C.* "I don't like the idea of being overexposed," Ounsworth told *The Times*.

Too late, brother. A second *NYT* profile followed at the end of 2005, again focused on how CYHSY were spurning the machinery of indie-rock fame. But you can't control what other people say about you, and over the next couple years, the blaring hype around Clap Your Hands Say Yeah morphed into backlash. Curious onlookers started to clock that the band was, per *The Times*, "not exactly a crack touring outfit," and, come to think of it, Ounsworth's vocals *were* kind of obnoxious. When the more abrasive follow-up *Some Loud Thunder* dropped in 2007, the moment had passed. "Online opinion is like a magnifying glass in sunlight: Whatever it admires too closely for too long is enlarged, then incinerated," Howe wrote in his 7.2 Pitchfork review. "There was truth in the emerging narrative, but it reflected longing more than reality; the band's story became the stuff of myth, and myths beg to be debunked."

Clap Your Hands Say Yeah became the definitive example of a phenomenon known as "blog rock." "The term, of course, referred to music that had gained popularity through MP3 blogs—specifically those giving coverage to the more left-field, less image-obsessed artists largely ignored by the mainstream music press," wrote *The Guardian*'s Tim Jonze in 2011. In the same article, he called blog rock "unquestionably one of the decade's biggest indie trends, especially to those for whom 'indie' didn't just mean 'guitars' but rather a vaguely outsider/underground music made predominantly by skinny white men."

All that was on point, but Jonze fell victim to a common error: imprecisely wielding blog rock as a synonym for all of 2000s indie rock. He cited Animal Collective, TV On The Radio, Grizzly Bear, and Fleet Foxes as prime examples of the form, but those bands were too popular, too talented, and too long-lasting to be saddled with this somewhat derogatory term. Blog rock connoted something more specific: a cloying sort of indie band with fleeting success manufactured online, apart from real-world communities and institutions. Does the name Architecture in Helsinki mean anything to you? What about I'm From Barcelona? If you weren't rocking with Someone Still Loves You Boris Yeltsin, were you even in these blog-rock streets?

Clap Your Hands Say Yeah exemplified blog rock in their arty and precious sound, their unwieldy band name, their rapid rise and fall, and success rooted almost totally in online hype. "They did not emerge from any kind of scene," Ian Cohen explained at Pitchfork ten years later. "They had not developed a passionate fanbase based on their live performances . . . There was no single that started to circulate until it broke through into the mainstream. They did not represent some kind of innovative new sound."

The influence of acts like Sufjan Stevens, Arcade Fire, and the Decemberists hung heavy over blog rock in the form of instruments like glockenspiels, a movement toward large collectives, and a tendency toward the plucky, quirky, earnest, and twee. (Blog rock, by definition, does not *rock*.) But straightforward guitar-based indie bands like Tapes 'n Tapes and Cold War Kids could be blog rock too, as long as they were propped up by the online critical apparatus long before they were ready for the spotlight.

New York's savvy and eclectic Vampire Weekend fared far better than some of their blog-era peers—creatively, critically, commercially—but they also went through a full circuit of praise and backlash before their 2008 debut album dropped. Pitchfork's 8.8 Best New Music review called it "already one of the most talked-about and divisive records of the year," a divide illustrated by *The Village Voice* publishing concurrent positive and negative reviews of the album. Old-guard media was becoming quicker to take cues from the internet, too. *Rolling Stone*, *The New York Times*, and *The New Yorker* all weighed in during 2007, a year that ended with Vampire Weekend becoming the first band to be photographed for a *Spin* cover story before they'd released an album. By March of 2008 they'd played *Saturday Night Live*.

Notably, *Spin*'s Vampire Weekend cover story remarked on the state of music blogs, which were crucial to the band's rise. "It's hard to credit the rise of MP3 blogs with a revolution when they are in the midst of dramatic change themselves," journalist Andy Greenwald wrote. "While smaller blogs fight for exclusives, the heavyweights have begun sounding more and more like the old guard they seek to usurp. Listen to Stereogum's Amrit Singh on Vampire Weekend's long-term prognosis: 'With the ball rolling and growing support overseas, there's an opportunity to make some money on the distribution and larger-scale touring.'"

Greenwald's piece also touched on the tricky cultural waters the band was navigating: "[Ezra] Koenig claims the right to cherry-pick across lines of culture, race, genre, and class because, as the descendent of Eastern European Jewish immigrants, he is himself an outsider of sorts. And having wrestled with issues of authenticity and cultural appropriation as a deracinated fourth-generation Ivy Leaguer, he's concluded that he's allowed to do whatever the hell he wants. It's charming, but it's also indicative of the sort of confidence that only exists in the very young, the very successful, or both."

The discourse surrounding Vampire Weekend was tangled up

in questions about race and class: Did this group of well-off recent Columbia grads, three white guys and a Persian-American, have the right to play around with African music? Was it disrespectful or inspired to describe their musical style as "Upper West Side Soweto" and to make their songs character studies about the privileged elite? Was devilishly clever singer-guitarist Ezra Koenig honoring his influences or exploiting them? These questions stemmed from an interrogation into indie rock's demographic makeup that took hold, among journalists and artists alike, just as the music was ascending into the mainstream—part of broader changes in critical thought that contributed to the genre's utter transformation.

* * *

Let's circle back to that 2004 Arcade Fire show at Mercury Lounge one last time. Also in attendance that night was *New York Times* journalist Kelefa Sanneh, who was profiling Arcade Fire during their busy CMJ week, chronicling life in the suddenly bright indie music spotlight. Sanneh is one of the finest music writers of his generation, and two weeks after his Arcade Fire feature, on Halloween 2004, he articulated ideas that were percolating "among the small but extraordinarily pesky group of people who obsess over this stuff" in a *Times* article titled "The Rap Against Rockism."

In the essay, Sanneh outlined a conversation that had been building up for decades:

> A rockist isn't just someone who loves rock 'n' roll, who goes on and on about Bruce Springsteen, who champions ragged-voiced singer-songwriters no one has ever heard of. A rockist

is someone who reduces rock 'n' roll to a caricature, then uses that caricature as a weapon. Rockism means idolizing the authentic old legend (or underground hero) while mocking the latest pop star; lionizing punk while barely tolerating disco; loving the live show and hating the music video; extolling the growling performer while hating the lip-syncher.

Many critics and music fans had inherited a set of biases about what makes music honorable and valuable, leading to distinctions between, for instance, who gets to make "classic" albums and who is relegated to the realm of "guilty pleasure" singles. In the same way that political zealots frame events through the lens of their established grievances, rockists applied their faulty received wisdom to each new release, reflexively dismissing certain kinds of music outright or qualifying their praise with hedges like "pretty good *for a pop song*." Rockism was a way to dismiss entire genres—and entire listener demographics—and elevate your preferences about art into a form of moral superiority. Never mind that, as Sanneh explained, its logic wasn't internally consistent: "It could mean loving the Strokes (a scruffy guitar band!) or hating them (image-conscious poseurs!) or ignoring them entirely (since everyone knows that music isn't as good as it used to be)."

Sanneh went on to explain that rockism was worth discussing because it was rooted in other prejudices like sexism, racism, and homophobia. In his view, the anti-disco backlash of the late 1970s—culminating with 1979's notorious Disco Demolition Night at a Chicago White Sox game, where thousands of disco records were burned—was not only a revolt against a pervasive form of dance music. It was a white male revolt against sounds popularized by women, minorities, and gays.

This rejoinder wasn't coming from a rock hater. Sanneh came from a punk background, and his Arcade Fire profile noted that the band's "unhinged" live show "managed to exceed all expectations." He was merely expressing viewpoints that were becoming commonplace among music critics, including the tastemakers at indie-rock stronghold Pitchfork.

As these ideas came to the forefront of the critical conversation, an alternative to rockism emerged. In short, "poptimism" is supposed to mean that all music deserves a fair shake regardless of artist, genre, or how the sausage was made. Under poptimism, there's no such thing as a guilty pleasure, no need to qualify your enjoyment of a song by appealing to assumed biases about what constitutes real, respectable music. It is poptimism that moves critics to treat blockbuster pop albums as serious works of art worthy of the same deep thought and critical rigor as a new Radiohead LP. Theoretically, the philosophy is not about equating popularity with quality, but just refusing to write off any music based on your presuppositions.

Projecting an image of sophisticated music fandom has always required an eclectic, wide-ranging taste. Look no further than James Murphy's litany of references in LCD Soundsystem's 2002 classic "Losing My Edge," in which he knowingly plays the part of a hipster trying to prove his cred. In his lyrics, Murphy cites lots of painfully hip rock bands but also house music (Larry Levan), jazz (Pharoah Sanders), salsa (Fania All-Stars), retro soul (the Bar-Kays), old-school hip-hop (Eric B. & Rakim), and spoken-word legend Gil Scott-Heron. Murphy's narrator was flexing his far-reaching musical expertise, but he touted nothing too popular, nothing too manufactured.

By comparison, under poptimism, a music fan could show off their worldliness by expressing their heartfelt appreciation for hit-makers like Ciara, 50 Cent, or even Ashlee Simpson, whose *SNL* lip-synch debacle had inspired Sanneh's anti-rockism manifesto. It was not so different from hipsters embracing trucker hats and PBR, except this time the mashing up of so-called "high" and "low" culture was increasingly without irony. Partially, this change was spurred on by a predominantly white, educated indie establishment recognizing how insular it could be and sheepishly trying to engage with a world beyond underground rock. Partially, it was a function of hipsters fleeing from indie rock's *O.C.*-era breakthrough stars, who were no longer their little secret, and seeking some other genres to define themselves by. The rise of music piracy and iTunes opened people's ears, too. But also, who wouldn't want to buy into a worldview that knocks down arbitrary barriers and encourages people to like what they like?

This evolution was reflected in Pitchfork's changing attitude toward pop music over the course of the aughts. In the early part of the decade, when the site was beginning to wield serious subcultural power, its year-end album lists always included a range of sounds beyond indie rock—mostly left-field hip-hop and electronic music, with occasional nods to critically respected mainstream rap stars like Eminem, Missy Elliott, and OutKast. But even though the site's writers were conversant with debates about rockism, they weren't all immediately convinced that those old biases needed to go.

One of the most notorious takedowns in Pitchfork history was a 0.0 directed at Liz Phair in 2003. Phair had become a sensation with her fearlessly raw, gleefully provocative debut album *Exile in Guyville*, winner of *The Village Voice*'s Pazz & Jop critics poll in 1993. Two more '90s albums for Matador Records, both co-released by major labels, fortified Phair's reputation as an indie icon. But for her 2003 self-titled LP, she shifted to Capitol Records exclusively, teamed with songwriters and producers best known for their work with Avril Lavigne, and swapped her scrappy indie sound for sparkling pop-rock tunes that could easily slot into radio playlists alongside Lavigne and Michelle Branch.

Many Phair fans saw this as a betrayal, and the response was intense—especially among the critics who'd previously worshiped her. Not only was Phair's fan base mad that she had musically "sold out," but in an ageist, sexist twist, many also scolded her for continuing to write salacious, frankly sexual lyrics now that she was a thirtysomething mom (see: "H.W.C.," with its chorus, "Give me your hot, white cum"). What once was alluring now was dismissed as "desperate." *The Washington Post* reported that *Liz Phair* "inspired some of the most vitriolic music press in ages, with bad (and surprisingly personal) reviews outgunning the occasional good ones by a huge margin."

In that *Post* feature, Phair remarked, "I can't remember getting incensed over something that wasn't extremely, graphically violent or child pornography. The fact that people can get so angry about this record makes me realize these are people that I don't know. I get the bad reviews—'Yeah, it's not my thing,' or, 'I like *Guyville* and now she's in this pop thing and I'm not into that.' But I don't understand the vehemence with which people are going after it."

A few critics applauded Phair's boldness. In *The Village Voice*, self-proclaimed "Dean of American Rock Critics" Robert Christgau, the founder of the Pazz & Jop poll, praised the album for "successfully fusing the personal and the universal, challenging lowest-common-denominator values even as it fellates them." At *Blender*, the great Ann Powers wrote that "the best songs on *Liz Phair* cut through the bullshit to portray a hot young mom reflecting on lust and guilt. Let's hope people can hear the smarts behind the sheen."

Many people didn't. There were pans in *The New York Times*, *The Guardian*, and most famously that 0.0 from Pitchfork. "Ten years on from *Exile*, Liz has finally managed to achieve what seems to have been her goal ever since the possibility of commercial success first presented itself to her: to release an album that could have just as easily been made by anybody else," a nineteen-year-old Matt LeMay lamented. The tone was so scathing that, sixteen years later, LeMay felt compelled to apologize for it in a lengthy thread on Twitter (now X).

Though Pitchfork had risen to prominence as an alternative to traditional media, its *Liz Phair* review was perfectly in step with old-school rockist rhetoric. Soon afterward, the site began to grapple with those biases. Citing the power of file-sharing to broaden listeners' horizons, the intro to Pitchfork's list of the Best Singles of 2003 enthused that "commercial pop seems to be at its most creative height since the 1960s." The author somewhat bashfully explained that although rock music lends itself to albums and pop to singles, "in 2003, there were more than enough brilliant tracks from both sides, and friends, coming from a reformed tightass, there's just no reason to deny it." The list itself was dominated by hip-hop and R&B, with lots of pop and electronic dance music also sprinkled among the indie hits.

These attitudes continued to permeate Pitchfork over the next few years. Not only did the site incorporate hits by mainstream fixtures, it also celebrated a class of obscure artisanal pop stars like Annie, rap acts like M.I.A., and electronic producers like M.I.A.'s close collaborator Diplo—hipsters' own proprietary iteration of popular music. Soon poptimism was coming to bear on the album reviews, too. Contributors like Nick Sylvester and my future *Stereogum* colleague Tom Breihan showered praise on the likes of Cam'ron and Lil Wayne, hit-making street rappers whose music did not cater to rockists. In 2006, Justin Timberlake's "My Love" topped the year-end singles list. Pitchfork, a publication that partially defined itself by all the popular music it ignored, was well on its way to becoming an entity that applied critical scrutiny to music's biggest stars.

These changes did not take hold without a fight. In a 2005 Pitchfork column, Chris Dahlen pushed back against the anti-rockist tide. "In case you don't follow the debates on 'rockism' and 'authenticity' and Ashlee Simpson's 'career,' here's an update: It is currently deeply uncool to judge music by how it's made or who really made it—or to expect that the performer nominally attached to the song wrote it, or played on it, or even sang a single note that wasn't fixed by a computer," Dahlen's piece began, thick with sarcasm. "If you think that a performer with a career and proven talents, like say Bruce Springsteen, isn't playing the same game as, say, Ashlee Simpson—who's still shorthand for 'phony'—then you're stunted by prejudices that impair your ability to love music."

Dahlen's column became an apology for the "adult alternative" indie rock that was becoming deeply uncool among hipsters as it was embraced by their more basic friends and relatives. This was Starbucks music, NPR music, *Paste* magazine music: indie stars like Death Cab, Arcade Fire, and Feist as well as more singer-songwriter-y acts like Gillian Welch, Rufus Wainwright, and Aimee Mann. The adult alternative cohort was anything but cutting-edge, and it was losing hipster cred fast in the poptimist era. The more your music appealed to *Grey's Anatomy* viewers, the less chic it seemed.

Part of the reason critics were so delighted by Vampire Weekend at first was how intuitively they had internalized the logic of poptimism. The group adhered to strict rules designed to avoid coming off like a schlubby indie rock band: no distortion, no T-shirts onstage, etc. Koenig rhymed "Benetton" with "reggaeton" and cited Dharamsala in the same song that quoted Lil Jon's "Get Low" at length. It was a masterclass in mashing up disparate cultures. But if the band found success by distinguishing itself from the indie-rock pack, it still caught a lot of flak within the music-critic culture wars.

The prevailing tone in coverage of Vampire Weekend had grown much more hostile by the time Vampire Weekend released their second album, *Contra*, in 2010. Jessica Hopper's *Chicago Reader* essay "Appropriation, Vacation" crystallized the critiques. "Indie rockers are supposed to be grubby proles, not graduates of Columbia University, and front man Ezra Koenig obviously knows it," Hopper wrote. "Yet he made an album about rich girls and vacations—so when he struggles to downplay the band's background, it's sort of like if Jay-Z tried to claim that growing up in the projects didn't have shit to do with *Reasonable Doubt*."

Nitsuh Abebe, a Pitchfork critic and *New York Times* editor born to African immigrants, had authored Pitchfork's rave review of Vampire Weekend's debut. In a widely circulated Tumblr post, he dismissed Hopper's critique as a form of white liberal posturing he called The Game:

> The Game is largely played by people who are white and/or middle-class, and much of it involves trying to outmaneuver one another about precisely that fact. At the heart of The Game is fear and loathing and boredom concerning the possibility of being *bourgeois*. Being bourgeois is The Game's great sin, and

it is often referred to using the code word "white." If you can't avoid this sin by virtue of being working-class or Ghanaian or something, your best bet is to deftly corner the market on wary "whiteness"-based critiques of anything that smacks of being bourgeois. The critique will try to present itself as an incisive dismantling of class/race/privilege, but at its heart it will just be "oh noes *bourgeois*." The great paradox here, of course, is that The Game is itself an incredibly bourgeois pastime.

Koenig repeatedly claimed his band's detractors were responding to a version of Vampire Weekend that didn't exist, but as interviewers kept bringing up sticky questions about race, class, and colonialism, the band's defensiveness became the album's dominant media narrative. Even Mike Powell's 8.6 Best New Music review acknowledged that "haters will still find plenty to hate about *Contra*, and they'll hate it with vigor." But if Vampire Weekend could not emerge from the poptimism wars unscathed, the conflict was not about to sink them. Within a few years, they'd be on the front lines of an indie-world movement against the concept of the rock band itself.

Chapter 5 Soundtrack

Jet, "Are You Gonna Be My Girl" (2003)

U2, "Vertigo" (2004)

Caesars, "Jerk It Out" (2002)

Gorillaz & De La Soul, "Feel Good Inc." (2005)

M.I.A., "Galang" (2004)

Arctic Monkeys, "I Bet You Look Good on the Dancefloor" (2005)

Lily Allen, "Smile" (2006)

CSS, "Music Is My Hot Hot Sex" (2006)

Feist, "1234" (2007)

Los Campesinos!, "You! Me! Dancing!" (2007)

Kate Nash, "Foundations" (2007)

Calvin Harris, "Acceptable in the 80's" (2007)

The Ting Tings, "Shut Up and Let Me Go" (2008)

Coldplay, "Viva La Vida" (2008)

Santigold, "L.E.S. Artistes" (2008)

The Submarines, "You, Me and the Bourgeoisie" (2008)

Chairlift, "Bruises" (2008)

The Pains of Being Pure at Heart, "Young Adult Friction" (2009)

Cymbals Eat Guitars, "... And the Hazy Sea" (2009)

Fine Dining, "Here Comes the Warm Jets" (2005)

5

Music Is My Boyfriend

iTunes, MySpace, & indie's digital revolution

My sophomore year of high school, I watched a friend download tracks from Rage Against The Machine's *The Battle Of Los Angeles* directly to his family's desktop computer using a program called Napster. I couldn't believe this was real. Sure, there were some mislabeled files out there, and thanks to dial-up internet speed, each song took more than ten minutes to download. But what were a few minutes of patience and some occasional disappointment in exchange for completely free music? As soon as I got home, I put Napster on my own family's computer and started building my MP3 library.

Napster really was too good to be true. After a flurry of lawsuits from the likes of Metallica, Dr. Dre, and the Recording Industry Association of America, the peer-to-peer network shut down in the summer of 2001. The dream of file sharing would persist via other peer-to-peer networks like Audiogalaxy, Lime-

Wire, and Kazaa, but because its brief lifespan overlapped with my high school years, Napster was entangled with my musical coming of age. My journey from Limp Bizkit listener to budding indie rocker played out on Napster's gray interface, interrupted only when someone in my house picked up the phone.

It's hard to overstate the impact of file sharing on my listening habits. Previously, barring a glimpse of something great on MTV or the radio, the only way to preview an album before spending about $15 on a CD was checking it out from the library, borrowing it from a friend, or putting on headphones at a record store's listening station. Now, at my leisure, I could sample a little bit of this, a little bit of that. I never would have bought a novelty hit like King Missile's "Detachable Penis" on CD, but I happily shoveled it onto my hard drive along with Radiohead B-sides and West Coast rap classics.

Mix CDs were revolutionized, too. The purchase of our first CD burner had already been a game-changer: You mean I can put Sublime *and* Red Hot Chili Peppers songs on *the same CD?* But with file sharing, instead of ripping songs from my available discs, I could now assemble an eighty-minute tracklist out of anything I wanted. Once cable and DSL connections entered the picture, I could crank out new volumes of ChrisMix™ even faster. And when I got my first iPod in 2004, liberating me from the portable CD player that skipped every time I hauled it across my college campus, the mix-and-match listening experience went into overdrive.

It would be impossible to recall how many artists I came to love because I illegally downloaded their music. Before pirating music helped me familiarize myself with every release that got Best New Music on Pitchfork, it opened my mind to a vast landscape of sounds that might have otherwise remained out of reach. There were obvious downsides to millions of people internalizing the idea that music should not cost anything, but in the moment, free-flowing MP3s broadened the horizons of a whole generation. That included indie snobs who'd been previously closed off to mainstream music, who collectively underwent a major philosophical change when presented with the chance to slot Kelis's "Milkshake" into WinAmp alongside M83 and Black Dice. In the twentieth century, many music fans had closely defined themselves by their favorite genre—punk rockers, hip-hop heads, and so forth—but in the MP3 era, eclecticism was the wave.

"The great thing about music right now is that listeners don't have to be 'staunch' anymore," explained the intro to Pitchfork's 2003 year-end singles list. "In an age when all music is free, dedicating yourself to just one specific genre or type only denies you the hedonistic musical bliss that is rightfully yours. Sure, we all still buy albums for their increased sound quality, tangibility, artwork and artist support, but let's be straight about one thing: singles are for downloading."

MP3s didn't only help indie rock fans acclimate to the rap and pop hits enjoyed by their mainstream peers. The technology also provided outsiders a convenient gateway into indie rock. It helped that the company most closely linked with the MP3 revolution went out of its way to link itself with user-friendly, indie-presenting sounds—and that alt-leaning music became the cornerstone of the first great social media network.

*   *   *

You remember the silhouettes.

Apple is great at developing sleek, intuitive consumer technology, but the company has always been just as good at marketing those products. To promote its digital music player and Discman-killer, the iPod, faceless human shadows wearing the company's unmistakable white earbuds thrashed their bodies against solid color backdrops, set to music that struck a balance between hip and accessible. The idea of a pocket-sized device containing dozens of albums was already revolutionary, but Apple made sure that it was also *cool*.

Though the first iPods were released in 2001, the dancing silhouette ads began in 2003 with the launch of the iTunes Music Store, Apple's industry-supported attempt to provide a legal alternative to piracy. "Consumers don't want to be treated like criminals and artists don't want their valuable work stolen," Steve Jobs said in the introductory press release. "The iTunes Music Store offers a groundbreaking solution for both."

There were other digital music stores in the 2000s, like the indie-focused eMusic and, eventually, shops from Apple's fellow tech mammoths like Amazon and Google. But iTunes arrived early, and—thanks to savvy marketing, stylish design, and affordable pricing—became the dominant force in the industry. By 2010, Apple owned two-thirds of the online music market and was the number one music retailer on Earth.

Prior digital music stores had failed because they tried to charge $3.50 for an MP3 and limited how the files could be used once you paid for them. At iTunes, individual songs cost 99 cents, and most albums sold for $10. Once it became evident people were willing to pay for MP3s at those rates, iTunes proved to be extremely popular with record labels, who could now sell music without having to manufacture products. And major labels weren't the only ones to benefit from the arrangement.

Syd Butler of Les Savy Fav and Frenchkiss Records said as much in a 2013 *Billboard* feature. "Back in 2003 . . . people were still buying CDs. But to get paid on CDs was difficult," Butler said. "For a small label like Frenchkiss, we needed that money to come in every quarter. When the physical distributor would say, 'Hey, sorry, these all broke,' or, 'The stores lost the CDs,' or whatever excuses came up, it would stall our money. As digital started to grow, it allowed [labels] to get paid more promptly."

The overhead was also basically nonexistent. "That thing that people were paying $12 for in the store cost $5 to make, but then the distributor's taking 14 percent," Laura Ballance of Merge Records explained in a 2019 talk at Drexel University. "And there's all the cost of promoting it. So really, you made a dollar off that record. And then you're splitting it with the band. So you each made 50 cents. Then Apple started selling downloads, 99 cents a song. The label gets paid 66 cents, and you're splitting it with the band. You didn't have to do anything except record and master that record. So it felt almost like free money."

This was thrilling for Merge, a label that had spent a lot on elaborate packaging for albums like Magnetic Fields' three-disc *69 Love Songs*. By the time iTunes arrived, Merge was also benefiting from indie rock's mainstream breakthrough. Spoon, who'd retreated to Merge after being dropped by a major label, were enjoying exposure through MTV2 and *The O.C.* in the early 2000s. Thanks to iTunes, people could buy "The Way We Get By" quickly and easily. And per Ballance's calculations, both band and label would make the same amount from that download as they would have from selling a full copy of *Kill the Moonlight* on CD.

Even for artists who weren't getting on TV, the level playing field of the iTunes store and the "a little bit of everything" mentality inherent to the iPod created an environment where independent music had a better chance to break through via word of mouth. A song no longer needed radio support to blow up, therefore it no longer needed to fit into a radio format—which was handy because the Telecommunications Act of 1996 had so narrowed the scope of terrestrial radio, allowing companies like iHeartMedia (then Clear Channel) to buy up and standardize hundreds of stations. Once *Billboard* started factoring digital downloads into the Hot 100 in early 2005, iTunes gave bands like the Strokes and Death Cab for Cutie a better chance to chart. And through promotions like the Single of the Week, which offered a featured song as a free download, blog-world mainstays like Bright Eyes, M.I.A., and Tegan and Sara were exposed to a vast cross-section of listeners.

Apple did not just create a legal pathway to virality for indie artists. They also latched onto hip music as a reflection of the company's own self-image. Apple spelled out its approach in 2006's "Get a Mac" campaign, in which Justin Long's whip-smart millennial in a hoodie declared, "I'm a Mac," and John Hodgman's doofy businessman announced, "And I'm a PC." Years before that, I instinctively understood that Apple was the fashionable computer company. Their deployment of music was a factor in that branding, even if the exact tunes they chose weren't always aligned with the boilerplate hipster perspective.

In 2004, those selections included "Vertigo," the surprisingly rocking lead single from U2's *How To Dismantle An Atomic Bomb*. U2's iTunes commercial, essentially a short-form music video in which the legendary arena rockers appeared alongside Apple's dancing silhouettes, was the first time the band had allowed their music to be used in advertising. It kicked off a long relationship with Apple that would also include the release of a black-and-red U2-branded iPod in 2006 and the disastrous 2014 stunt in which the band's new album *Songs of Innocence* was automatically loaded into every iTunes user's library. Turns out not everyone wanted a new U2 album on their iPhone, and it was exceptionally hard to delete.

I like U2, but even when they were the biggest band in the world, they tried way too hard and cared way too much to be *cool*. If they were ever hip, no one thought so anymore in 2004, except perhaps corporate executives who liked to blast "Elevation" in their luxury sedans on their commutes from the exurbs. Still, U2's status as credible, serious artists was taken for granted in the mainstream, and Steve Jobs surely saw some of himself in Bono's messianic gestures. The link-up between the two institutions made sense on an intrinsic level. Whatever that union said about U2's stature, it said even more about the power of association with iTunes. Everyone with a TV could soon recite Bono's goofy "Uno, dos, tres, *catorce!*" introduction.

People were just as likely to recognize "Are You Gonna Be My Girl," a rowdy party-starter from Australian rockers Jet that sounded like Iggy Pop's "Lust for Life" blaring at a frat house. Soon enough the public would also have their brains imprinted with "Jerk It Out," a stupendously catchy '60s throwback from the Swedish band Caesars. Shazam (owned by Apple since 2018!) wasn't around yet to help people easily identify the infectious garage-rock throwbacks, but both still ended up on the Hot 100 after they soundtracked those silhouettes busting a move. They charted way higher than any Strokes song, too, despite finding their way into the zeitgeist as outgrowths of *Is This It*'s big bang.

By 2005, there was no shortage of professionalized garage bands riding that wave, and tastemakers were growing suspicious of them all. Pitchfork had panned major-label signees Jet and Caesars before Apple made them ubiquitous, and they panned them again after their iPod-ad boosts—including the infamous peeing monkey review. The site's readership internalized the loathing for this class of bands. My college bandmate David, the same friend who got me into Radiohead in high school, even wrote a Strokes-esque song called "Here Comes the Warm Jet" lamenting all the wack garage bands on the rise. (You can find it on your streaming service of choice, and yes, the title is a Brian Eno reference.)

But people who weren't snobby webzine readers probably detected minimal difference between Jet ripping off Iggy Pop and the Strokes lifting from the Velvet Underground—if they recognized the source material at all. At Apple's scale, it didn't matter if America's hipster brain trust considered these bands anathema. They *sounded* trendy. The danceable old-school rock 'n' roll movement fomented at New York's Shout! party and in Detroit dive bars had reached its cultural zenith, and Apple was there to capitalize. It wasn't so different from *Grey's Anatomy* bringing a coffeehouse-friendly version of indie rock to the masses.

Speaking of coffeehouse-friendly indie: In 2007, Apple turned its spotlight on an artist the cool kids actually liked, leading to one of the biggest "indie" hits ever—never mind that Leslie Feist, like Jet, was signed to a major. Feist had built up a sterling reputation within the indie-rock world, both with her 2004 solo album *Let It Die* and as a part-time member of Broken Social Scene, when Apple built a 2007 iPod Nano campaign around "1234" from her new album, *The Reminder*. The lyrics were as simple and infectious as a nursery rhyme but shot through with the wistfulness of adulthood. Feist's vocals were quaint and conversational but also robust and expressive. The musical backing bloomed from acoustic guitar chords to an ornate swirl of banjo, brass, and backing vocals. And then there was the elaborate one-take music video in which a flash mob's worth of color-coordinated dancers crowd-surfed Feist around an empty room.

Feist was already on the path to stardom before Apple got involved. Thanks to a chorus of raves from the likes of *Entertainment Weekly* and *The Village Voice*, Pitchfork—who graced *The Reminder* with an 8.8 Best New Music review—was hardly her only cheerleader in the press. A *New York Times* feature set at the "1234" video shoot called *The Reminder* "the album that should transform her from the darling of the indie-rock circuit to a full-fledged star, and do it without compromises." Even before Feist's iPod Nano ad, *The Reminder* had sold 200,000 copies.

Feist was working in the increasingly profitable but perilously unhip adult alternative genre, but many tastemakers found her music too compelling to dismiss—or else her association with Broken Social Scene gave them cover to admit liking an artist whose music sounded not so different from Norah Jones. Ryan Dombal's Pitchfork review hinted at the tension between appreciating Feist's artistry and balking at the commercialized bourgeois: "You might hear her over cappuccino-machine hisses in Starbucks, but her direct-line moans easily cut through the biscotti muzak."

When Apple intervened, Feist was exposed to a far broader audience who knew nothing about that kind of scene politics—normal people, who liked what they liked. In the ad, a series of iPod Nanos in various colors played the "1234" video, giving both the song and its visuals a U2-grade showcase while connecting Feist to Apple's nifty boutique device. This inevitably led to sales on iTunes. Within a month of the ad's premiere, weekly downloads of "1234" had risen from 2,000 to more than 70,000, and the song had climbed all the way to No. 8 on the *Billboard* Hot 100.

That kind of success occasioned a 2008 *New York Times* article headlined "Is Apple the Oprah for Indie Bands?" Besides Feist, the report cited CSS, a Brazilian electronic rock band whose "Music Is My Hot, Hot Sex" soared to No. 63 on the Hot 100 after soundtracking a 2007 ad for the iPod Touch. The song is a funky, infectious "new rave" track with a digital drumbeat that resembles Nine Inch Nails' "Closer" and a squelching, distorted bassline seemingly inspired by electronic producers like Daft Punk. It centers on singer Lovefoxxx's playful, ecstatic proclamations like "Music is my boyfriend/ Music is my girlfriend/ Music is my dead end/ Music is my imaginary friend." In another example of Apple's power compared with their competitors, "Music Is My Hot, Hot Sex" had been used in an ad for Microsoft's doomed iPod competitor, the Zune, a year before Apple turned it into a hit.

CSS, whose full band name, Cansei de Ser Sexy, translates to Tired of Being Sexy, represented one flavor of artist that was consistently elevated by Apple: those that blurred the line between alternative and pop. CSS was an indie rock band of sorts—they signed to Sub Pop, they were willfully quirky, and they had plenty in common with dance-punk bands like LCD Soundsystem—but they did not disguise their crowd-pleasing inclinations. You didn't need any context to appreciate what they were doing. Their music sounded cool, but even more than that, it sounded *fun*.

That ethos put CSS in step with Gorillaz, the multimedia project led by former Blur frontman Damon Albarn. Gorillaz's propulsive cartoon rap-rock track "Feel Good Inc." climbed all the way to No. 14 in the US, partially thanks to a silhouetted iTunes ad in 2005. Albarn was a tabloid-level celebrity in England, where the song nearly hit No. 1, and Gorillaz had cracked the US chart before with 2001's "Clint Eastwood," but "Feel Good Inc." became by far their biggest hit. It was also the chart peak for legendary rap trio De La Soul, whose feature on the track provided loud, cartoonish energy to match Gorillaz's animated element.

Those kinds of genre-mashing hits felt like an iPod shuffle come to life. They became a crucial component of the indie music landscape in the mid-aughts, as artists and listeners alike liberated themselves from genre boundaries. But Apple wasn't the only tech company defining itself by alternative music and helping to foster an eclectic style. Friends, we need to talk about MySpace.

* * *

And if we're going to talk about MySpace, we should probably talk about emo.

During the same 2000s era when indie rock was rising to mainstream prominence, emo was blowing up even bigger. In terms of public profile, artists from the Warped Tour scene towered over the biggest Pitchfork sacred cows. This was the era of Fall Out Boy and My Chemical Romance, of Paramore and Panic! at the Disco, of sideswept bangs and belts strewn with bottle caps and seat belt buckles. At the peak of their popularity, emo's biggest stars were scoring Top 10 singles, enjoying extensive MTV airplay, and commingling with the world of big-budget rap and pop—pressing much farther into the mainstream than the likes of Modest Mouse or the Shins ever ventured.

Emo's explosion was not an outgrowth of indie rock's crossover moment but rather a separate glow-up happening in parallel. At times indie and emo have shared a lot in common. In some sense they sprang from the same well, and they both fit loosely into 2000s alternative radio playlists. Some people's iPods undoubtedly included bands from both worlds. But those bands would have never been booked onto the same package tours, guested on each other's albums, or otherwise associated publicly in any way. In the George W. Bush era, indie rock and emo were entirely distinct music industry ecosystems. They might as well have been separated by the Berlin Wall.

As is often the case where indie rock is concerned, that separation had a lot to do with concepts of cool. Indie is not an entirely emotionless endeavor, but it says a lot that the genre was defined by the chilly demeanor of bands like Pavement, Sonic Youth, and Dinosaur Jr. Even when more vulnerable performers like the tragic balladeers Elliott Smith and Cat Power came to prominence, they were treated as untouchable geniuses whose songs were practically incantations. Ditto Neutral Milk Hotel's Jeff Mangum, who developed a reputation as a mystic philosopher operating on a different plane. Mangum's wide-eyed intensity and fearless nasal blare was an indie-rock outlier. There was usually a guarded quality within the scene—"guarded" referring to performers' self-protective irony or cutesy twee affectations, but also to gatekeeping among the fan base. Even Mangum, who threw himself into every lyric, left a lot of room for interpretation within his vivid, inscrutable songs about two-headed boys, semen-stained mountaintops, and the ghost of Anne Frank.

It's not a coincidence that indie rock found a larger audience as it grew more danceable (via garage rockers, disco-punks, and the encroaching influence of electronic music) and made room for big feelings, clearly expressed (via sensitive poets like Death Cab for Cutie and bellowing anthem slingers like Arcade Fire). But even when indie rockers let go of their inhibitions and a wider circle of listeners got in on the action, there was still an element of snobbery within the scene—a fixation on discovering the obscure and cutting-edge once too many people catch on to your old favorites, a tendency to define yourself by what you're *not* as much as by what you are. A handful of charismatic trendsetters might manage to be hip by virtue of their own magnetism, in the sense that anything they like will become cool by default. For the rest of us, projecting a hip image involves some posturing.

To embrace emo was to give up all pretense of ever becoming hip. It's right there in the title of Saves the Day's revered 1999 album *Through Being Cool*. Musically, emo shared a lot of DNA with indie rock, including roots in hardcore and a widespread appreciation for the Smiths and Weezer. But the human side of it, the way emo bands carried themselves compared with indie bands, was entirely different. Lyrically, indie music erred on the oblique side, while emo songs tended to present painfully honest portraits of a singer's grudges, crushes, and neuroses, a trend that often took the form of young men spewing bile at the women who'd allegedly wronged them. Those indictments were often delivered in whiny melodies and wailing roars, vocals that necessitated letting it all hang out. Two of the genre's foundational albums are rightfully titled *Diary* and *Nothing Feels Good*.

"Emo" has historically been almost as slippery a term as "indie." What is and isn't emo is open to debate, and many bands that are obviously emo have rejected the designation, claiming that they were actually punk or indie—a trend that dates back to the very first "emocore" bands in 1980s Washington, DC, and continued into emo's second wave in the 1990s, which centered on the Midwest but sprawled coast to coast.

Most '90s emo was closer to indie rock than to the pop-punk and ska that thrived on the Warped Tour, and some of the more sensitive indie bands at the time, like Bright Eyes and Death Cab for Cutie, were slapped with the "emo" tag more than once. The music of Kansas City's plucky emo heroes the Get Up Kids was sometimes indistinguishable from indie legends Superchunk. There's a reason why, when the second-wave emo nostalgia festival Best Friends Forever launched in 2024, the lineup included a bunch of bands—Built to Spill, the Dismemberment Plan, Unwound, even abrasive noise-rockers the Jesus Lizard—that most people would file in the indie section. The overlap between emo and indie in the '90s was significant.

Nonetheless, Pitchfork *hated* emo. Seminal bands like the Promise Ring were punchlines. Arizona's Jimmy Eat World scored a 3.5 for 1999's *Clarity*, widely hailed as their masterpiece—and when the score was revised to 8.6 years later in one of the site's retrospective Sunday Reviews, drummer Zach Lind made it known on Twitter that he had not forgiven the original insult. Sunny Day Real Estate's *How It Feels to Be Something On* (a truly incredible album, please listen to it) earned a rave review by essentially leaving emo behind to channel Smashing Pumpkins, Led Zeppelin, and U2 instead. The consistent implication was that emo was wussy, whiny music for uncool people with no taste. Pitchfork dismissed Dashboard Confessional, aka Florida emo singer-songwriter Chris Carrabba, as the province of "sensitive, gender-role-enlightened, bedwetting emo boys."

Why did the indie world so vehemently despise emo? In that revised Jimmy Eat World review from 2021, critic Ivy Nelson offered one potential explanation:

> I hated emo in high school—Saves the Day, Dashboard Confessional, all the sad boys with guitars getting airtime on MTV2. Any band that wielded emotions I felt acutely every day made me feel like a vampire exposed to daylight. Resentment, alienation, unrequited love—these already made up the

emotional landscape of one's teenage years, high school hallways without end. There was something mortifying about listening to music that echoed that experience so directly back at me. I preferred indie rock bands whose lyrics were opaque enough to disintegrate in your grasp. This, it seemed to me, was fundamentally more adult and dignified, as if abstracting your angst instead of contending with it was obviously the more mature thing to do.

Disdain from the internet's most influential hipsters did nothing to stop emo from barreling into the mainstream. By 2002, widely cited as The Year Emo Broke, the genre blasted into the public consciousness as both a musical and visual sensibility. Dashboard Confessional was all over MTV and radio with the power ballad "Screaming Infidelities" and popularized the "fauxhawk" haircut in the process. Thursday and Saves the Day were in MTV2 rotation. Jimmy Eat World soared to the Top 10 with their pop radio hit and future karaoke crowd-pleaser "The Middle." The subculture was suddenly popular enough to merit a *Seventeen* magazine spread instructing readers how to dress like an emo kid.

Before spilling over into traditional media, the emo phenomenon had developed online. In his 2023 MySpace oral history *Top Eight*, Michael Tedder surveyed the ways the scene was cultivated by file-sharing networks like Napster, blogging platforms like LiveJournal, and chat services like AOL Instant Messenger, where plentiful emo lyrics were repurposed as away messages and some bands even made themselves available to communicate directly with fans. There was also Makeoutclub, a message board and dating service that was deeply embedded in emo culture. As Say Anything's Max Bemis told Tedder, though Makeoutclub eventually commercialized and "went the way of Hot Topic," early on, "It was more like a basement show of social media."

If 2002 was a tipping point for emo, 2003 was the same for social media. In February, investor and engineer Jonathan Abrams launched Friendster, the first prominent social media network. On Friendster, you could create a profile, connect with friends, and explore a web of social connections. To those of us who'd spent our youths traversing the web, the concept was intuitive, and Friendster took off quickly, with widespread media coverage and an appearance on *Jimmy Kimmel Live!* for Abrams. But by 2004, the site was losing momentum. Friendster did not scale up its engineering to handle increasing public demand, so some pages took half a minute to load. Users found that, because you could only view the profiles of friends and friends of friends, there wasn't much to do after checking up on your social network. And, crucially, a more dynamic competitor had arisen.

In August 2003, just six months after Friendster launched, MySpace went live. It was the creation of Chris DeWolfe, the former sales and marketing head for a data-storage company called Xdrive, and Tom Anderson, who DeWolfe had hired as an Xdrive product tester and copywriter. Anderson—a UCLA film student who'd spent the '80s as a teenage hacker and the '90s as frontman of an alt-rock band called Swank—impressed DeWolfe with his honesty about how bad Xdrive sucked. They hit it off quickly and co-founded a direct marketing company called ResponseBase, which was sold to the marketing company eUniverse in 2002.

While working for eUniverse, Anderson noticed how many page views Friendster was getting. He saw an opportunity to create ad impressions for eUniverse's slate of products, from Razor scooters to diet pills. Anderson also recognized that Friendster's growth was hindered by an overly sanitized interface. There was no way to search for people based on mutual interests. Most importantly, you could create profiles only for people, not entities—like your pet or, say, your band that aspired to one day headline a Makeoutclub party.

MySpace solved all those problems. Profiles were customizable to a radical extent; the opportunity for open-source HTML coding resulted in some extremely gaudy webpages. In a step beyond AIM's away messages, users could program their profile to play a favorite song. You could send direct messages and post "bulletins" to all of your connections on the site. Each profile could showcase its "top eight" friends, a collection of bands and people curated to demonstrate your social connections and good taste. You could also upload hundreds of embarrassing photos from your digital camera.

This was an era when the hottest new technologies encouraged a close personal relationship with music. If iTunes and the iPod had allowed people to keep a mixed-and-matched library of songs as their constant companion, MySpace helped them broadcast that love affair with music to the world. The site essentially taught a whole generation how to present and promote themselves online—including bands, who were able to establish their own MySpace profiles and stay close in touch with all the music fans swarming the platform.

Emo bands flocked to MySpace early on, and the site quickly became associated with this music's continued rise. As the genre became a lucrative commercial proposition in the early 2000s, a third wave of emo bands took hold—bands whose aesthetics matched the bombastic, attention-grabbing style of a pimped-out MySpace page, even as their fan bases largely identified as a subculture of geeks and outsiders. With theatrical pomp and arena-scale ambition to go along with weapons-grade pop appeal, groups like Fall Out Boy and My Chemical Romance steered emo into its "hair metal" era (flatirons instead of perms, this time), complete with *TRL* celebrity status.

Mirroring what had happened a half decade earlier on the pre–social media internet, emo's biggest stars found their way to MTV after first building their coalitions on MySpace. The site had essentially combined Napster, LiveJournal, AIM, and Makeoutclub into one streamlined hub for distribution, promotion, and community-building. Kindred spirits could find each other and geek out over their favorite music. Bands could market directly to their own fans—or to fans of other bands in the same genre. They could share new music instantly, with no corporate interference, and that music could spread rapidly. This was an incredible tool for assembling a grassroots fan army, and the emo scene harnessed it in extremely profitable ways.

Crucial to that buildup was an infusion of women into a scene dominated by men. "From a T-shirt perspective, all of a sudden you're printing youth medium T-shirts. That was a classic early 2000s girl size," Tommy Corrigan of Merch Direct said in Chris Payne's 2023 emo oral history *Where Are Your Boys Tonight?* "Back in the '90s everything was extra large, double extra large. All of a sudden there's hundreds of youth mediums being added to every order. That was a signifier of who was actually going to the shows."

In emo, female-fronted bands remained scarce all throughout the MySpace era, with rare exceptions like Paramore. But as the genre ascended into the mainstream, many bands saw their fan bases split evenly between women and men. Some, like Dashboard Confessional and the Starting Line, attracted *more* women than men. "Part of the reason for that is the same reason with everything, because the dude is cute," journalist Jessica Hopper said in Andy Greenwald's 2003 emo trend report *Nothing Feels Good*. "It's also expressive—in its way—which automatically appeals to teenage girls. There's also a fetishization of the emotional aspect of desire."

In that breakout moment, emo's relationship with women was fraught at best, which led Hopper to write about her deep concern for "the teenage girls I see crowding front and center at emo shows" in her famous 2003 *Punk Planet* essay "Emo: Where the Girls Aren't." She had good reason to be concerned—not just due to the psychological impact of participating in a scene where women existed as muses to be yearned for and raged against, but also due to rampant sexual misconduct epitomized by the grooming allegations against Brand New's Jesse Lacey. The Brand New situation inspired Pitchfork's Jenn Pelly to write a similar essay in 2017. "Third-wave emo—bubblegum emo—needed its female fans, as evidenced by the swaths of girls who screamed this music back, who took photos, who muscled against stages to get as close as possible without being crushed," Pelly wrote. "But the scene did not really want us."

These problems were apparent when Greenwald published his book in 2003, but so was the internet's role in ushering women into the scene. "In the meantime, the place where the real male/female dialogue is occurring and the rules are being rewritten is not on record, but online, where the huge number of women fans have their say and assert themselves in varied and surprising ways," Greenwald wrote. This sentiment became even truer as the online emo world migrated to MySpace.

It's not like MySpace was some kind of paradise, free of the creepers you might encounter at a concert. But it opened up pathways for people of any gender to obsessively study their favorite bands, and it fomented the kind of moodboard-oriented self-expression and community-building later mastered by teenage girls on Tumblr. In 2008, a philosophy PhD candidate at Bowling Green State University even wrote her doctoral thesis on young women's use of MySpace to construct their identities, perform their genders, and build community, framing MySpace as a continuation of physical media traditions like scrapbooking.

Like so much modern music fandom, the MySpace experience was holistic. The site did not only turn people on to new bands. Along with the mall-punk fashion boutique Hot Topic, it also showed young emo fans how to style themselves according to the "scene aesthetic"—even kids who had no connection to any tangible scene. "It was the flatiron, big hair, the cranberry eyeshadow, the pouty lips, the selfies," Leslie Simon of emo bible *Alternative Press* said in Tedder's *Top Eight*. "Before Instagram, selfies were invented for MySpace. It was people holding their Sidekick as far away from their face as possible and trying to look sad but sexy. And that's still true to this day."

Emo was hardly the only kind of music that thrived on MySpace. As the platform grew, reaching past 1 million unique monthly users in 2004, its potential was readily apparent to all kinds of upstart musicians. That year, when I formed my own scrappy indie band (the one with the song making fun of Jet), I rushed to create a MySpace page for us, then kept close tabs on it throughout our two-year run. I scrutinized which songs to include on our profile's audio player, which bands to include in our top eight, and which image to use as our profile photo. I clicked around in search of artists from around the region who might want to play a show with us and posted on the walls of groups I considered peers. For my band, connections forged on MySpace maybe led to a couple gigs with more established acts.

But there were artists for whom the site became a golden ticket to fame and fortune.

Among the most oft-cited cases were a group of teenagers from Sheffield, UK, called Arctic Monkeys. The Arctics' rowdy and incisive rock 'n' roll was clearly inspired by the Strokes' spindly guitar attack, but they'd also internalized the manic energy of dance-punk, a sentiment telegraphed through song titles like "Dancing Shoes" and "I Bet You Look Good on the Dancefloor." They were kids who'd come of age with the early aughts garage rock boom, and they connected instantly with other kids like them. It helped that their friends were smart enough to create them a profile on MySpace, where their fans took over, street-team style, to spread the word.

The ensuing virality led to a bidding war and a deal with Domino, the same indie label that had launched Franz Ferdinand a year prior. In November 2005, the Arctics' official debut single "I Bet You Look Good on the Dancefloor" hit No. 1 in the UK. Two months later, their album *Whatever People Say I Am, That's What I'm Not* became the fastest selling debut in UK history. The notoriously hyperbolic *NME* declared *Whatever People Say I Am* the fifth-best British album of all time in a list published when it had only been out *for three days*. In the US, the album peaked at a healthy No. 24 but did not spawn a Hot 100 hit. Inevitably, in Britain the post-Monkeys acts kept coming, few of them as potent as the Arctics. By 2008, critic Andrew Harrison had coined the phrase "landfill indie" to describe the glut of interchangeable British guitar bands.

In a *Guardian* feature looking back on the Arctic Monkeys frenzy a decade later, music business journalist Eamonn Forde noted that there had previously been "a disconnect between the internet as a sales-and-distribution channel and the internet as a social space. Arctic Monkeys were one of those acts, certainly at the mainstream level, that brought those two things together." In the same feature, *Later . . . with Jools Holland* booking agent Alison Howe posited that Monkeymania probably wouldn't have happened if the band hadn't arrived at the dawn of social media. "If they'd come out 10 years earlier or 10 years later . . . none of that magic would have happened," Howe said. "It felt like a moment that a generation would remember for the rest of their lives."

The Arctic Monkeys were oblivious to how much social media had factored into their rise. In 2005, drummer Matt Helders claimed to the webzine Prefixmag that the Arctics hadn't even heard of MySpace: "We were on the news and radio about how MySpace has helped us. But that's just the perfect example of someone who doesn't know what the fuck they're talking about. We actually had no idea what [MySpace] was." Unfortunately for Helders, the historic association between the band and the social network became so strong that in 2019, the *NME* called Arctic Monkeys "undoubtedly MySpace's biggest success story."

Another UK artist who soared even higher than the Arctics for a time was Lily Allen, a former raver with a foul mouth and a sense of style to match her influence-mashing sound. In 2005, at age twenty, the playfully cheeky singer signed to the Parlophone imprint Regal Records. The label had never heard of MySpace, but Allen learned about it from her friend, the British rapper Lady Sovereign. She began posting her rap- and ska-inflected pop demos there in November 2005, only to watch the songs go supernova in 2006: first "LDN," a chipper satire about what goes on behind London's polished facade, then the even bigger "Smile," on which she savored telling a cheating ex, "When I see you cry/ Yeah, it makes me smile." The attention led to

"Smile" hitting No. 1 in the UK and Allen's label fast-tracking her promo plan. She went on to become one of her country's biggest pop stars for the next few years and even enjoyed some US chart success, joining T-Pain and Wiz Khalifa on the Top 10 single "5 O'Clock."

People weren't just coming to Allen's MySpace page for the music. In the beginning, she was running her own profile, with all the sassy blogging, selfie uploads, and even fan-mail responses that entails. Like all those American emo bands, Allen was directly accessible to her fans in a way no pop star had ever been. The persona she projected on MySpace, where she'd accumulated 57,000 followers as of her August 5, 2006 *New York Times* profile, was at least as important as her music. Image cultivation has always been a central tenet of pop stardom, but here was someone doing it herself through social media. Of course, that transparency stopped once the press started paying attention. "It definitely became annoying when I would write something and it would end up in the tabloids the next day, completely twisted around," Allen told Pitchfork in 2006.

Allen represented an archetype that became increasingly common in the MySpace era: the pop star with a genre-jumbling sound, embraced by the indie world even as they climbed the ladder into the mainstream. Bloggers loved Allen for her saucy pull quotes and sometimes-messy public behavior, which made for good tabloid-style coverage of her every move. But they also appreciated the way her charismatic tunes hybridized disparate musical worlds. Such an approach had been rendered extremely hipster-friendly around the 2004 explosion of M.I.A., a British-Sri Lankan emcee who rapped over wildly eclectic production from Diplo and Switch. It continued through Lily Allen and the late-aughts blog star Santigold, a Black punk rocker whose debut album melded new wave, reggae, dub, electro, and more. They all helped develop a new class of pop stardom annexed into indie rock's jurisdiction by tastemakers, even when it was neither indie nor rock.

The mix-and-match approach to genre had been encouraged by MP3 blogs, where one person's personal taste held more sway than any radio format, and iTunes, where songs that didn't fit into the existing industry infrastructure could still do numbers. As both fans and musicians gathered en masse at MySpace, the site became a petri dish for new omnivorous music scenes. "We knew that it was the music that lived in between or outside of genres that would ignite global communities of niche kids who depended on MySpace to find others like them," the site's Nate Auerbach told *Forbes* in 2019.

MySpace wasn't populated by *only* hip pop stars and cultishly beloved rock bands, and it didn't appeal only to kids with niche interests. In the era when Lily Allen and Arctic Monkeys were popping off and thousands of rappers, DJs, and Warped Tour bands were growing their empires, the biggest artist on the platform by far was Tila Tequila. The model and reality TV star used MySpace more like a modern-day Instagram influencer, posting thirst traps and riding the page views to the top of the site's daily unsigned artists chart. There were songs on her profile, but in her case, the music was incidental to the brand.

Tila Tequila types aside, music became so essential to the fabric of MySpace that in 2005, the platform founded its own record label, though it never amounted to much. Far more successful were the free, intimate concerts known as MySpace Secret Shows. Launched in 2006, the gigs featured MySpace-friendly acts like Panic! at the Disco, Lily Allen, Yeah Yeah Yeahs, and Gnarls Barkley, but also featured older artists who predated the platform, like the Cure, Ice Cube, and even Neil Diamond. "We have such a large social network we can pull from that we literally can go into any city and announce a show 48 hours in advance and fill an entire venue," MySpace's Isac Walter told Reuters in 2008, as the site held its 150th secret show.

The popularity of those concerts reflected MySpace's centrality within the late 2000s music world. As the decade rolled on, it became normal for bands to distribute their new music by streaming it on their MySpace profiles rather than supplying bloggers with free MP3s. Blogs (and Pitchfork's blog-like Forkcast section, where stars could be born with a single blurb) often linked out directly to MySpace pages, both from newly discovered talents and established names. The first thing I'd do when I discovered a new band was look them up on MySpace. Even artists who didn't use the site as their home base felt a need to have some kind of presence there, and some artists had no web presence *except* for a MySpace page. For a while, it was all you needed.

And then, near the end of the 2000s, it all fell apart. MySpace had never been an entirely virtuous project—you'll recall that DeWolfe and Anderson envisioned it as a way to create ad impressions for eUniverse's catalog of junk. So it shouldn't have been surprising that they sold MySpace to Rupert Murdoch's News Corp for $580 million in 2005, just as the site's power was becoming undeniable. Still, it was painfully ironic that the Fox News people were controlling the platform where hip young subcultures flourished—a joke that became less and less funny as News Corp ran MySpace into the ground.

When Murdoch bought MySpace, the site boasted twenty-two million users, but another social media network was coming up behind it like the Undertaker in that meme. Facebook improved upon Friendster's design flaws but kept its streamlined, standardized look. Though it was originally intended for college students, among adults who felt too old for MySpace—where the often tricked-out interface was beginning to feel as clunky as an Angelfire page—Facebook became a powerful Rolodex filled with friends new and old.

MySpace's competition didn't stop with Facebook. 2005 also marked the debut of the user-generated video hub YouTube, which would one day evolve into the internet's foremost music library among its many other functions. In 2006, a short-form messaging app called Twitter got started, offering celebrities and would-be celebs an even more direct pipeline to the public. So did Spotify, a streaming service that would placate users with a passive version of the active music discovery practiced at MySpace's peak. 2007 saw the launch of Tumblr, another microblogging site that built upon MySpace's social networking and personal design aspects. New user-driven music streaming hubs SoundCloud and Bandcamp debuted that year, too. And in 2010, a new photo-sharing app called Instagram hit the scene.

In the midst of all that innovation, as new competitors attacked MySpace on every front and the site's influence began to fade, News Corp launched MySpace Music. An early attempt at a Spotify-style subscription-based music streaming service, it would double as a marketplace for products like ringtones, concert tickets, and merch. News Corp valued the venture, a partnership between MySpace and the three biggest major labels, at $2 billion. Maybe in some other timeline it was that valuable, but in this one it was a disaster—in no small part because MySpace was widely accused of blocking independent labels from getting their music onto the service, undermining one of the main reasons the company had blown up in the first place.

The MySpace Music fiasco unfolded as MySpace hemorrhaged a million users per month and Facebook surpassed its user base. DeWolfe and Anderson departed the company in 2009. By the time News Corp gave up and sold MySpace to the ad company Specific Media in 2011, the sale price was rumored to be $35 million: about 6 percent of what Murdoch paid for it in the first place. It wasn't the first time corporate interests bungled their involvement in a grassroots music phenomenon, and it wouldn't be the last.

Chapter 6 Soundtrack

Daft Punk, "Aerodynamic" (2001)

Junior Senior, "Move Your Feet" (2002)

Ratatat, "Seventeen Years" (2004)

The Go! Team, "Huddle Formation" (2004)

The Knife, "Heartbeats" (2002)

of Montreal, "Wraith Pinned to the Mist and Other Games" (2005)

LCD Soundsystem, "Daft Punk Is Playing at My House" (2005)

Justice, "Waters of Nazareth" (2005)

Hot Chip, "Boy From School" (2006)

Junior Boys, "In the Morning" (2006)

Simian & Justice, "We Are Your Friends (Justice Vs. Simian)" (2006)

Girl Talk, "Hold Up" (2006)

Simian Mobile Disco, "Hustler" (2006)

Cut Copy, "Hearts on Fire" (2007)

Does It Offend You, Yeah?, "We Are Rockstars" (2008)

Crystal Castles vs. Health, "Crimewave" (2007)

MSTRKRFT, "1,000 Cigarettes" (2009)

The Bloody Beetroots & Steve Aoki, "Warp 1.9" (2009)

Yeah Yeah Yeahs, "Heads Will Roll (A-Trak Remix)" (2009)

Caribou, "Odessa" (2010)

6

D.A.N.C.E.

The ballad of bloghouse and indie sleaze

Picture a young woman on a dance floor at some warehouse party in a major metropolitan area. Her hair is a long, unkempt poof cut into bangs across her forehead. She is wearing a shiny silver leotard, and the can of Sparks in her hand spills with each gyration. Flashes of golden eyeshadow encircle both of her eyes, though you may not be able to see them clearly because someone just handed her a pair of bright red "shutter shades" as worn by Kanye West circa *Graduation*. Dancing next to her is a guy with scraggly shoulder-length hair and the faintest sliver of a mustache. He's rocking skinny jeans and a white baseball tee, its blue three-quarter-length sleeves obscured by a green zip-up hoodie with white drawstrings.

Also spotted in the vicinity: plaid skirts, ripped tights, Converse sneakers, crop tops, ballet flats, jorts, deep V-neck T-shirts, Doc Martens, ironic graphic tees, and sweepy fringe haircuts under headbands. Oh, and plenty of digital cameras ready to shovel party pics onto the internet the next day, stoking FOMO and fashion inspiration for an audience around the world.

What kind of tunes are blaring in this scene? More than likely, you're hearing a kind of trend-conscious, internet-native electronic dance music, perhaps promoted as "electro" or "fidget house" or "nu rave" or simply "indie dance." It's as loud and colorful as the fashion—crisp and accessible but also hard-hitting and chaotic. Fizzy disco grooves give way to piercing, serrated synths. It's the soundtrack for a trashy, sloppy, probably unhealthy night they might not even remember the next morning, music plucked from MySpace pages, MediaFire links, and MP3 blogs. Almost every song is a remix.

This is the peak of indie nightlife in the mid-to-late 2000s. The hipster wardrobe has been commodified, sold to the masses not only by Urban Outfitters and American Apparel, but big-box stores like Target. A trend that has already been fully subsumed by capitalism (the runoff from *Vice*-era cool-kid fashion) is colliding with another underground phenomenon that is *about* to succumb to the same forces (the dance party scene that preceded the EDM boom). Not that this nylon bacchanal you've stumbled into is somehow pure and liberated from corporate interest—just look at all those Scion and Red Bull logos everywhere.

Nowadays, it would be easy enough to sum up this scenario by describing these people's fashion sense as "indie sleaze" and their favorite DJ's playlist as "bloghouse." In the moment, those terms were not yet in circulation—especially "indie sleaze," a phrase that didn't pop up until a TikTokker coined it more than a decade later. But like "yacht rock," another phrase invented many years later that has come to define an entire era, just because people weren't saying it back then doesn't render it invalid now. Sometimes language or a single word comes along and retrospectively sums up a moment's whole vibe.

* * *

Bloghouse was an eclectic scene with many tributaries, but for many indie rockers like me, the dance-punk bands paved the way. It helped that one of the best of them was explicitly connecting the dots between their music and Daft Punk, the group that did more than anyone to lay the groundwork for the movement.

"Daft Punk Is Playing at My House," the opening track from LCD Soundsystem's 2005 self-titled debut album, was a spiritual sequel to "Losing My Edge," the 2002 single that put Murphy's project on the map. On "Losing My Edge," James Murphy played a not-so-loosely autobiographical character: an aging hipster, anxious about being eclipsed by the kids coming up behind him, flexing his impeccable record collection and impossible concert history in an attempt to cling to relevance. "I was the first guy playing Daft Punk to the rock kids," he asserts in the song. "I played it at CBGB's/ Everybody thought I was crazy."

With "Daft Punk Is Playing at My House," Murphy ventured out of satire into the realm of outright fantasy, imagining a guy who spends years saving up enough money to hire the French production duo to perform in his basement, robot costumes and all. "I'll show you the ropes, kid," the narrator boasts, sounding smug and self-satisfied but also ecstatic as he contemplates what is about to go down in his own home.

It's telling that in both songs, Murphy, one of his era's premier arbiters of all things hip, framed Daft Punk as absolute titans of clout. With their 1997 debut album, *Homework*, the duo of Thomas Bangalter and Guy-Manuel de Homem-Christo had taken the funky disco-house style known as "French touch" all the way to MTV, pairing their singles "Around the World" and "Da Funk" with memorable videos by acclaimed directors Michel Gondry and Spike Jonze. By the time Daft Punk dropped their bigger, bolder, more bodacious sophomore album *Discovery* and disappeared behind robot masks in 2001, they were already your favorite indie rocker's favorite DJs. *Discovery* was so obviously cool that not even a mediocre Pitchfork review could stop it from becoming a widely beloved, massively influential totem, shoehorned into the indie-rock canon despite an approach to guitars that had more to do with Van Halen than Camper Van Beethoven.

It wasn't long before you could hear echoes of Daft Punk all over the indie music landscape. Danish duo Junior Senior scored a Pitchfork hit with 2002's jubilant "Move Your Feet," a song so user-friendly that, like *Discovery* opener "One More Time," it ended up in a *Trolls* movie years later. Like Daft Punk, the sample-happy English electronic rock band the Go! Team turned to childhood for inspiration, channeling retro TV show themes and playground chants on their euphoric 2004 album *Thunder, Lightning, Strike*. Steering things in a less cartoonish but still playful direction, the Brooklyn duo Ratatat built temples of sound out of electric guitars, synthesizers, and electronic beats on their own 2004 debut.

As the audience for garage rock and dance-punk became more accustomed to programmed drums and a club environment, more and more electronic bands entered into the modern hipster pantheon. Dancy synth-pop groups like the UK's Hot Chip and Australia's Cut Copy became fixtures of the indie ecosystem, and both left audiences in a rapturous state at large-scale events like Pitchfork Music Festival. The quirky psychedelic pop band of Montreal rose to unanticipated heights by adding electronic beats, cranking up the idiosyncrasies, and landing a song in an Outback Steakhouse ad. As the aughts rolled on, British "nu rave" acts like Klaxons and Does It Offend You, Yeah? put a more aggressive spin on dance-rock. But those were all bands; this was also a time when the indie world was opening up more and more to DJ-producer types.

Perhaps no one did more to introduce indie-rock audiences to electronic dance music than Diplo. Starting in 2002, the man born Thomas Wesley Pentz built his legend deejaying Philadelphia's Hollertronix parties alongside DJ Lowbudget, blurring Atlanta crunk, Miami bass, Baltimore club, Italo disco, electro, bhangra, and more into boundary-obliterating dance mixes. At the time, combining so many disparate genres was a radical approach, and it clicked with the revelers who flocked to a musty Ukrainian social club on Philly's far north side. Buzz for the parties built up rapidly, and they soon spread to other cities. By the end of 2003, the Hollertronix crew's *Never Scared* mixtape had cracked the *New York Times*' list of the year's best albums, with critic Kelefa Sanneh praising their decision to lay a Missy Elliott rap verse over the Clash's "Rock the Casbah." The following year, the ultra-hip glossy magazine *The Fader* chronicled Diplo's trip to Brazil, where he channeled the country's baile funk scene into another acclaimed mixtape called *Favela on Blast*.

In 2004 Diplo also connected with Maya Arulpragasam, a British-Sri Lankan rapper known as M.I.A., after hearing her cracking, pounding electro-dancehall banger "Galang." With M.I.A.'s debut album, *Arular*, caught up in music industry purgatory, she and Diplo nudged her career along by spending ten days in his Philly apartment crafting yet another mixtape called *Piracy Funds Terrorism, Vol. 1*. This one was essentially an official leak, matching her vocal tracks for the album with a very Hollertronix range of pre-existing tunes, from rap to reggaeton to new wave. *Piracy Funds Terrorism* was another critical smash, including at Pitchfork, where an utterly cringe Best New Music review tabbed M.I.A. as "a chicken-legged Sri Lankan with so much sex in her self-spun neons you might as well get wasted off penicillin with Willie Nelson at a secret Rex the Dog show."

Yeesh. Anyway . . .

Diplo was exactly the kind of young, omnivorous trendsetter James Murphy had been so intimidated by. His eclectic approach to dance music was the perfect match for an era when technology was collapsing the borderlines between genres—and for a class of listeners who prized exotic, forward-thinking sounds. Lots of hip-hop mixtapes at the time found rappers rhyming over the music from existing radio hits, but Diplo appealed to the hipster lizard brain by pulling his beats from across the timeline and all over the map. If you were reading about indie music via Pitchfork or *Vice* at the time, you were likely greeted with hype about this DJ who was curating sounds from around the globe into party mixes that felt much more cutting-edge than Rogue Wave or whatever. That 2004 *Fader* feature about Diplo's Brazil trip praised Hollertronix for mixing "the Dirty South abject rap of Cash Money Millionaires' 'Project Bitch' with the ineffable feyness of Soft Cell's 'Tainted Love' at parties from London to LA."

Mashups of that ilk were all the rage in the aughts. DJs had been combining audio from multiple songs for decades, and in the '80s, producers like Prince Paul, the Dust Brothers, and the KLF collaged elements from dozens of songs into "sampledelic" fantasias. But as legal threats against uncleared samples mounted, it became all but impossible to distribute mashups, with a few exceptions on the fringe of the industry like Columbus, Ohio's own Evolution Control Committee. The internet allowed unofficial recordings to proliferate without records being pressed or money changing hands, so tracks like Freelance Hellraiser's 2001 hit "A Stroke of Genie-us"—which laid the vocals from Christina Aguilera's "Genie in a Bottle" over music from the Strokes' "Hard to Explain"—were able to catch fire on file sharing servers.

A few more noteworthy mashups emerged in the ensuing years, including 2004's *The Grey Album*, on which the producer Danger Mouse combined vocals from Jay-Z's *The Black Album* with music from the Beatles double-LP known as the White Album. That same year, Jay-Z's music became the basis for *Collision Course*, an officially released mashup album with the nu-metal band Linkin Park. With those projects in mind, it might be tempting to dub Sean Carter the patron saint of the mashup. But nobody did more for the form than Girl Talk.

Gregg Gillis was a biomedical engineer in Pittsburgh with a background in experimental noise music. At first, his electronic solo project Girl Talk channeled the abstract, abrasive sounds of artists like Merzbow. But when he released *Night Ripper* in 2006, his music had veered all the way to the other extreme, cramming together dozens of fragments from the most popular rap, rock, and pop songs in the world into epic album-length mashups—including beloved indie rock songs from the likes of Pixies and Neutral Milk Hotel, which surely greased the wheels for Pitchfork's Best New Music review. Gillis blazed through samples at a frenzied clip that made his music extremely stimulating. By the time your brain processed the fact that the Ying Yang Twins were whispering about their penises over the Verve's "Bitter Sweet Symphony," he was on to the next wild juxtaposition.

The label Illegal Art released *Night Ripper* on CD, which Gillis saw as a legitimizing factor for music many might write off as pure novelty. But piracy felt like a natural way to engage with an album like that. Even better was to witness Girl Talk's live show, which featured Gillis wilding out behind his laptop, gradually stripping off layers of clothing, his audience swarming around him onstage.

"The shows have been great recently because I'll play a plush dance club and then I'll play someone's living room for 40 people on a Saturday night and then I'll play an art gallery," he told Pitchfork in 2006. "I'm blurring the lines as far as where this music is appropriate." The following year, when Girl Talk performed at the Mexican restaurant in my former college town, I of course made my return to campus and spent time contorting onstage, possibly shirtless—an experience all those Dismemberment Plan concerts had primed me for.

Night Ripper was an extreme manifestation of the mixture that was happening every day online at *The Hype Machine*. After devoting unmanageable amounts of time trawling blogs for new music, the Brooklyn-based Russian Anthony Volodkin launched the blog aggregator in 2005 as a way to track which songs were being posted the most. *Hypem*, as it was sometimes known, essentially functioned as the pop charts for music blogs, presented without prejudice or manipulation. Like *Billboard* for the underground, it became a well-traveled crossroads of many variegated online communities—yet another way for fans of one genre to be turned on to everything else.

The Hype Machine was not strictly for electronic music, but *so many* electronic artists flowed onto those charts and into DJ sets around the world. An ecosystem for indie dance music was growing—one where fresh tracks and remixes, often unauthorized and transmitted via low-quality 128kbps MP3s, would circulate through MySpace accounts and websites of fuzzy legality, sometimes onto the hard drives of big-name DJs whose events were peppered with tabloid celebs like Lindsay Lohan and Paris Hilton.

The artists soundtracking this scene came from all over, including from indie rock bands. Jesse Keeler from the belligerent Toronto dance-punk duo Death From Above 1979 started the funky and hard-hitting MSTRKRFT. James Ford and Jas Shaw, two members of the Manchester psych-pop band Simian, became in-demand DJs and producers through Simian Mobile Disco, a side project that eventually eclipsed their original gig. The Belgian band Soulwax had been making snappy pop rock for a decade before pivoting to rave music (key lyric: "It's not you, it's the E talking") and emerging as kings of the bloghouse remix.

The connection to the indie world made projects like these a natural fit for indie-focused blogs, as did bloghouse artists' tendency to remix indie rock artists for the dance floor. The German producer Boys Noize even turned Feist, the queen of the coffee shop, into a bloghouse staple with his remix of "My Moon My Man." Inevitably, new hybrid bands emerged from that genre-colliding context, like Crystal Castles, whose self-titled debut veered from hypnotic minimal electro to searing noise-punk and back. When it dropped in 2008, I didn't even realize those two sounds could coexist on the same record, but I was entranced by what I was hearing.

Most of this would not have happened without Daft Punk, who themselves had first been in a '90s indie band called Darlin', fatefully described by *Melody Maker* as "a daft punky thrash." The duo's iconic Coachella set in 2006, in which they rocked a packed Sahara Tent from within a giant pyramid, loomed large over the entire sprawling bloghouse movement. But their manager, Pedro Winter, aka Busy P, had a hand in stimulating the scene beyond his work with the robots. During the downtime between Daft Punk albums in the early aughts, Winter founded the label Ed Banger Records and began signing other French house artists following in Daft Punk's wake. There were DJs like Cassius, Breakbot, and SebastiAn. There was Uffie, a rapping white fashionista with a quasi-ironic song called "Pop the Glock" that accidentally predicted hyperpop. Most importantly, there was Justice.

Gaspard Augé and Xavier de Rosnay began making remixes for a contest intended to parody Europe's famously cheesy Eurovision competition. One of the first was a raucous, trashy spin on Simian's "We Are Your Friends," which made its way to Busy P and became the second release on Ed Banger. Thanks to Simon Lord's electro-shocked vocals and an undercurrent of aggro synth bass, "We Are Your Friends (Justice vs Simian)" had a lot in common with dancy rock bands from earlier in the decade like the Rapture and the Faint, or even quirky, danceable indie tunes like Modest Mouse's "Tiny Cities Made of Ashes." But while those bands were injecting rock music with dance elements, Justice made their name on dance music infused with rock.

If Daft Punk turned French house music into arena rock, Justice took that impulse to aggressive new extremes. *Cross*, the duo's 2007 full-length debut, is gloriously blown-out in a way that caters to the same pleasure centers as the Darkness's cheeky throwback "I Believe in a Thing Called Love" or Andrew WK's earnest, ballistic "Party Hard." Justice's biggest single "D.A.N.C.E." tones down that dance floor–sledgehammer vibe, opting instead for filter disco and chipper schoolyard chants that feel like an extension of what Junior Senior or the Go! Team were doing a few years before. But mostly *Cross* makes its synthesizers resemble electric guitars on fire and its programmed drums pound like Keith Moon on a bender. It's no wonder that *this* was the dance music that clicked with the indie cognoscenti.

Justice-style bloghouse wasn't the only dance music being hailed by the Pitchfork crowd at the time. A hiccupping subgenre called "dubstep" presented a darker, headier, more mysterious strain of cutting-edge electronic beats. Dubstep had emerged from UK pirate radio culture. It was an offshoot of the skittering subgenre known as "UK garage" (Americans, it rhymes with "carriage") and the associated British hip-hop style known as "grime." Burial, a dubstep producer who kept his identity closely guarded, was the standard-bearer of the scene, serving up shadowy syncopated beats that played like art music *and* dance music, as if grabbing the torch from the IDM artists that made electronic music feel like serious business. Burial's 2007 opus *Untrue* was a masterpiece, but it wasn't exactly built for parties.

Cross, by comparison, was so gleefully ostentatious that, per Pitchfork reviewer Jess Harvell, the album scandalized self-serious electronic music fans who didn't appreciate all this rock 'n' roll sleaze creeping into their realm. "Justice takes this history of the French rave era and blows it out by embracing 21st-century stadium-rock production," Harvell wrote. "They squeeze everything into a mid-range frequency band so loud that the riffs on tracks like 'Let There Be Light' and 'Stress' practically cock-slap you in the face." (Again, Pitchfork, yeesh!)

This kind of aggro playfulness was the purest embodiment of bloghouse, so much so that Justice is the first artist most people would list when trying to explain what bloghouse is. The fact that their sole web presence was a MySpace page only underlined their association with the genre and its wild-frontier ethos. So it's surprising that the blog post that coined the phrase bloghouse, a 2008 *Hipster Runoff* entry called "WTF Is Blog House?" by the culture-chronicling satirist and provocateur known as Carles, excludes Justice from the genre for being too "bangery."

At that point, there was plenty of other music to be included under the bloghouse umbrella, and it was coming from all over the world. Europe gets credit for making bloghouse pop off, but a lot of groundwork was laid in America, too. By the time Justice released *Cross*, Diplo was well into his ascent and had founded his own record label, Mad Decent. The label doubled as the promoter for the genre-blurring Mad Decent Block Party, which started as an actual block party in Philadelphia in 2008 and expanded into a touring festival. Operating in parallel was Fool's Gold, a label founded by the DJ A-Trak that connected the dots between rap and dance music through tracks like the duo Crookers' smash hit remix of Kid Cudi's "Day 'n' Nite."

Out in California, former hardcore kid Steve Aoki spent the 2000s transforming his label Dim Mak Records into a power player in electronic music. Aoki got his start booking bands like At The Drive-In in his Santa Barbara living room during college. Upon moving to LA, he linked with Franki Chan, a Seattle punk who'd been inspired to host his own after-hours romps after seeing K Records founder Calvin Johnson DJ an oldies dance party in Olympia. In 2003, Aoki and Chan began throwing a party called Fucking Awesome that mixed rap, indie rock, and '80s pop with performances by some of indie rock's rising stars. "I think all those deep electronic parties hated us—we were throwing these impromptu parties and we were barely DJs," Aoki told Lina Abascal in her bloghouse history *We Are Your Friends*. "We sucked at deejaying!"

Some of the rock bands who came through Fucking Awesome

rejected the party as too cheesy, but with persistence and exuberance, Aoki and Chan kept up their pursuit of the wildest nights possible. When Dim Mak signed Bloc Party for the 2005 release of *Silent Alarm*, the label had its first major hit record, and Aoki got a foothold in the recording industry to go along with his growing stature in the LA party scene. By the next year, he had split with Chan and founded Dim Mak Tuesdays, the party that would attract many of Hollywood's young nightlife mavens. (There's a great photo of Aoki with a pre-fame Katy Perry, both of them rocking what appear to be American Apparel hoodies.)

It's easy to see why some bands were confused by Aoki's events. With their flash, hedonism, and penchant for attracting celebrities, bloghouse parties had basically nothing to do with the indie rock I fell in love with a few years earlier. It's hard to picture Yo La Tengo pounding Four Lokos while a Bloody Beetroots remix blasts in the background. But from my perspective, as someone who'd come of age with indie rock, this scene somehow felt like an extension of the same alternative music culture. It wasn't just that indie-rock bloggers were circulating some of the same music as alternative dance blogs like *Gotta Dance Dirty* or *Missing Toof*, or that the music coursed with an edgy, lo-fi energy that ran parallel to certain kinds of underground rock. It was also that the generation who'd learned to cut loose from dance-punk and garage-rock bands, who'd had their ears opened to new worlds by Diplo and James Murphy, was now building a nightlife culture out of electronic music that felt specially catered to a rock audience.

The nightlife part was extremely important. This wasn't just geeks trading files on their computers. The nexus of bloghouse culture was online, but it manifested in real life dance nights at destinations like Studio B in Brooklyn and Cinespace in Hollywood, events that were somehow scuzzy and glamorous at the same time, in that distinctively gaudy 2000s way. Although digital cameras, disposable cameras, and camera phones were flourishing at the time, this was the last gasp of a moment before everyone was constantly photographing everything with their smartphones, dancing with devices in hand, or burying their faces in screens. Instead, roving photographers would capture stills of fashionable revelers and funnel those images back onto their websites to be ogled, mocked, or imitated—a trend popularized by New York's Misshapes party, websites like Last Night's Party, and photographers like LA's Mark Hunter, better known as the Cobrasnake.

Another way this scene felt connected to indie rock was the fashion. The styles people were wearing in these party photos were as eclectic and unkempt as the music, in a way that dovetailed perfectly with the Cobrasnake's no-Photoshop approach. "The overarching theme was rock n' roll energy," Hunter told *Vogue* in 2022. "Coming to a party half put together was more exciting than a fully snatched look." Bloghouse attire was a neon, hyper-stylized evolution of the thrift-shop wardrobe long associated with underground rock. And a lot of it came from American Apparel and Urban Outfitters, brands that did for indie fashion what *The O.C.* mixes and iPod ads did for indie music.

In the '90s, thrift-store clothes were an essential component of the hipster lifestyle, be it out of financial necessity, as a rejection of mainstream consumerism, or as a way to express your quirky individuality. It was the sartorial equivalent of recording on a four-track instead of in a fancy studio. As the 2000s-vintage hipster became a well-known trope, newcomers to the indie world adopted not only the music but the clothes. But as only the most dedicated music fans are willing to dig through crates to find rare vinyl at a record store, not everyone wants to actually buy used clothing or spend hours perusing thrift stores. Wouldn't it be so much easier to grab those looks straight off the rack from stylish retail storefronts?

"Urban Outfitters and American Apparel identified their target audiences, moving into neighborhoods with a high density of 18 to 25 year olds who were beginning to experiment with their personal style and values," Elizabeth Segran wrote at Racked in 2015. "In college towns, students looking to express their newfound interest in indie rock or '80s nostalgia could put together an entire look in a matter of minutes at one of these stores; they didn't need to dig through bins of old T-shirts at Goodwill anymore."

Urban Outfitters got an earlier start. Dick Hayne and some college classmates launched the first store, originally known as Free People, in Philadelphia in 1970. It expanded around the world slowly and steadily, developing a balance of modern bohemian style and retro nostalgia. By 1996, *The New York Times* was describing Urban as "the apparel company that caters to the young and multiple-pierced," noting how profitable it had become.

As the company continued to grow in the 2000s, it became a destination for those seeking to replicate the styles seen in Williamsburg, Silver Lake, and on all those Flickr accounts full of dance night photo dumps. It did so by presenting an easily digestible version of hipster fashion, but also by lining its stores with records and knickknacks and selling wares designed to transgress and provoke, like a racist Monopoly parody called Ghettopoly or a Kent State sweatshirt that seemed to be splattered in blood. Hayne also faced backlash for his support of Republican senator Rick Santorum.

Those kinds of scandals were tame compared with the ones that haunted American Apparel, a company that hinged its reputation on progressive bona fides. Dov Charney got his start in the clothing business by taking the train into New York and smuggling out basic Hanes white tees into Montréal, where he sold them to friends and businesses. He was quite literally hawking American apparel to his Canadian countrymen. In 1989, Charney founded American Apparel as a wholesaler and eventually started manufacturing his own tees in South Carolina. In 1997, he opened a factory in Los Angeles, touting his products as American-made and his company as a beacon of progressive causes. In 2003, the brand opened its first retail store in LA's hip Echo Park neighborhood, with dozens more to follow around the world. By 2006, Charney sold American Apparel to an investment group for nearly $400 million. He remained the company's face and driving force until he was removed as CEO in 2014 after years of financial struggles and sexual harassment allegations.

In the 2000s, American Apparel staples like monochrome zip-up hoodies, raglan three-quarter-sleeve baseball shirts, V-neck T-shirts, skinny jeans, and cotton spandex bodysuits became essential components of the hip millennial wardrobe. They weren't exactly thrift-store clothes, but they were simple, affordable, and ethically made. With their solid colors and distinct lack of branding, they cut against the conspicuous consumption that flourished in the early aughts mainstream, though they surely became their own kind of status symbol. And after scaling up to an extent that drew constant comparisons to Gap, what started as the province of young creatives in urban centers eventually became ubiquitous even among social circles who couldn't name a single MP3 blog. "They made a hard-to-define bohemian lifestyle accessible to an entire generation of young people growing up in the cookie-cutter suburbs," Segran wrote in Racked, referring to both Urban Outfitters and American Apparel.

Charney liked to talk about ethics—about immigrants' rights, about fashion photography without Photoshop—but American Apparel's rise had more to do with marketing. Most profiles of Charney noted that he styled himself like a 1970s pornographer, with thick-framed glasses and wide-open collared shirts. The company's ads, which tended to feature scantily clad women staring directly into the camera, were also uniformly described as amateur softcore porn. Charney shot some of those images himself. Others were by Terry Richardson, a photographer with similar statement eyeglasses (the statement being "I am a huge creeper") who got famous by bringing that lo-fi porn sensibility to the world of high fashion photography. The "sleaze" in indie sleaze refers in part to debauched partying, but it also connotes that skeezy vibe advanced by Charney and Richardson, both of whom skated through years of sexual misconduct allegations before finally watching their empires crumble.

All this made American Apparel a perfect match for *Vice*, the media company that did so much to define brash, button-pushing 2000s hipster culture. It was not uncommon for Richardson to shoot editorial photos for the magazine *and* American Apparel ads that appeared throughout its pages. Beyond an aesthetic, these companies shared a shameless drive for world-conquering success that *Brooklyn Magazine*'s Chris Chafin identified as typical of early 2000s youth culture. "Those companies are us: antiauthoritarian capitalists obsessed with being cool and monetizing that coolness," Chafin wrote in 2017. He went on to dismiss *Vice* magazine as *Maxim* for hipsters who sneered at *Maxim* and to call American Apparel's online store "as much a porn site as an online commerce portal for buying clothing." Where's the lie?

Garage rock, dance-punk, club rap, and indie dance music

spent the first half of the 2000s colliding and commingling, then spilled over onto the bloghouse dance floor in the latter half of the decade. Along with the music came the look and feel of brands like Urban Outfitters and American Apparel, as well as actual thrift stores, colliding styles just as boldly. For a moment there, bloghouse seemed to be some kind of trashy utopia where disparate elements could come together to rage. "It was a point in time where a lot of people and influences converged," A-Trak told *Vice* in 2015. "There was an openness to what the sound really was."

But like so many thriving underground cultures, it would eventually be supplanted by something more plastic, with little to no connection to its Wild West origins. By the end of the decade, MySpace success story Calvin Harris would make the leap from bloghouse parties and unauthorized remixes to bottle-service clubs and chart-topping Rihanna collabs. DJs like Aoki and Diplo would pull off similar transitions, headlining massive festivals and producing songs for pop royalty. Sonny Moore, a Warped Tour emo frontman whose gamer tag was Skrillex, would help popularize a high-octane version of dubstep that would have frat bros losing their minds with every dial-up-modem-connecting, Optimus-Prime-transforming bass drop.

Bloghouse was about to wither away, to be replaced by something even gaudier. It wasn't the only indie subculture that was about to go boom. All while the bloghouse party raged on, an entirely different, earthier wave of indie music was blossoming into its own kind of corporatized sensation.

Chapter 7 Soundtrack

The Mountain Goats, "The Best Ever Death Metal Band in Denton" (2002)

Wilco, "Jesus, Etc." (2002)

The Decemberists, "Here I Dreamt I Was an Architect" (2002)

Neko Case, "I Wish I Was the Moon" (2002)

Damien Rice, "The Blower's Daughter" (2002)

José González, "Heartbeats" (2003)

My Morning Jacket, "Golden" (2003)

Sufjan Stevens, "For the Widows in Paradise, for the Fatherless in Ypsilanti" (2003)

Animal Collective, "Who Could Win a Rabbit" (2004)

Joanna Newsom, "Bridges and Balloons" (2004)

Devendra Banhart, "Little Yellow Spider" (2004)

Iron & Wine, "Naked as We Came" (2004)

Espers, "Caroline" (2004)

Bright Eyes, "First Day of My Life" (2005)

Beirut, "Postcards from Italy" (2006)

Jenny Lewis & The Watson Twins, "Rise Up With Fists!!" (2007)

Glen Hansard & Markéta Irglová, "Falling Slowly" (2007)

Fleet Foxes, "White Winter Hymnal" (2008)

Bon Iver, "Skinny Love" (2007)

Edward Sharpe & The Magnetic Zeroes, "Home" (2009)

7

Upward over the Mountain

The evolution of indie folk

It's a sacred ritual and a clown show. Right now, somewhere around the world, some troubadour is lugging their instrument onstage at a bar or coffee shop—or into the corner of the room where they set up the microphone. Perhaps they're hardened veterans of this routine, or maybe they're anxiously shuffling toward the mic for the first time. Probably, they're clutching an acoustic guitar. Possibly, they're wearing a knit cap. There's no telling what could happen when this person opens their mouth. You could be moved to tears, or to get up and race out of the room. You might involuntarily laugh out loud.

For a couple years in the early aughts, open mic night was my native environment. Within days of arriving at college in rural southeastern Ohio in 2002, I made my way to the one at the ethically sourced, locally owned coffee shop uptown. On that first visit, I merely observed the proceedings, but as someone whose AIM screen names included Guitar247 and MadGuitarSkillz, the chance to demonstrate my musical acumen without actually having to book a show was too enticing to resist. In my dorm room, I hashed out a handful of half-baked originals and covers, and by the fall of my sophomore year, I was a regular on the campus open mic circuit. My sets usually included a performance of OutKast's "Hey Ya!"—a painfully cliché white-guy-with-guitar maneuver that I believed to be fun and quirky at the time.

During winter break back home in Columbus, I took this act to yet another open mic with David—the friend who got me into indie rock in high school, accompanied me to many concerts around the Midwest, and would eventually write that anti-Jet rock song for our band. Like me, David had prepared a mix of his own material and other people's songs, designed to show off not only his talent but also his impeccable taste, which meant he played Neutral Milk Hotel's "Two-Headed Boy."

In hindsight, this seems . . . unwise. "Two-Headed Boy" is an incendiary ballad of Jeff Mangum's fervent strums and even-more-fervent vocals, eerie and electrifying, alluring and disturbing. Mangum's piercing, borderline-grating vocals slice across the mix even on songs like "Holland, 1945," where he has to compete with a rumbling rhythm section that constantly threatens to go off the rails and unkempt distorted guitars that leave dust clouds in their wake. So when he's only accompanied by an acoustic, every sustained syllable feels like staring a madman in the eye: You're afraid of what horrors you might glimpse, but also how much you might relate to what you see. "In the dark, we will take off our clothes!" Mangum howls, leaving much to the imagination. "And they'll be placing fingers through the notches in your spine!" Performing a song like that at open mic night is not corny like covering "Hey Ya!," but unless you're Jeff Mangum, it's a losing proposition.

In 2003, David was hardly the only indie rocker taking inspiration from Neutral Milk Hotel. The supernaturally powerful Athens, Georgia, band became a word-of-mouth sensation with their 1998 sophomore album *In the Aeroplane over the Sea*, then disbanded before they could be subsumed into the music industry and risk contaminating the pure, friendship-driven dynamic that helped make them so great in the first place. In their absence, imitators proliferated.

Half a decade later, NMH's shadow loomed large over the landscape in upstart groups like Arcade Fire and Okkervil River—most obviously in the Decemberists, a bookish Portland combo known for donning old-timey garb and singing about soldiers, sailors, cathedrals, etc. Colin Meloy, the band's bespectacled auteur, took inspiration from '60s British folkies like Fairport Convention and '80s college rockers like R.E.M. But when your arrangements are tinged with accordions, your voice seems to originate from right behind your nose, and the first song on your debut album is about the ghost of a stillborn girl who wanders parapets and clings to petticoats, you're going to draw comparisons to Jeff Mangum.

The Decemberists broke through by releasing two great albums in the same year. Kill Rock Stars, the Pacific Northwest label that made stars of Elliott Smith and Sleater-Kinney, reissued their 2002 debut *Castaways and Cutouts* in early 2003. The album made waves at Pitchfork, where reviewer Eric Carr knocked Meloy as a *Twilight Zone* version of Mangum but concluded he had the goods. Six months later they were back with the less pastoral, more theatrical *Her Majesty the Decemberists*, again dubbed Best New Music.

The Decemberists were great counterprogramming for the New Rock Revolution, and for a few years there, I connected with their music deeply. As a dork, no matter how much I loved some of those ultra-louche New York bands, I never entirely felt like I belonged in their world. Could I picture myself getting shitfaced with Julian Casablancas at Shout! or snorting lines with Carlos D at Misshapes? Absolutely not. Meloy's soft, pretty librarian music, on the other hand, was so dweeby that it made me feel cool by comparison—but not too cool to keep immersing myself in his records. "To be honest, so much of that stuff—writing about Dickensian characters, pulling people out of Dylan Thomas stories and putting them into songs—it was because it was funny initially, and it felt kind of at odds with the expectations of what writing indie pop was at the time," Meloy told *Newsweek* in 2015.

Beyond providing a nerdy, fantastical alternative to the grit and grime of the *Meet Me in the Bathroom* bands, the Decemberists were helping to lay the groundwork for indie music's next big trend. Just as the mainstream always has singer-songwriter figures like John Mayer or Noah Kahan to balance out popstar types like Justin Timberlake or Dua Lipa, there's usually some kind of folksy music percolating within the underground. Every few years, a new permutation of that sound bursts into the zeitgeist. So it went in the early months of 2004, when—within months of anointing the Rapture's howling dance-punk freakout *Echoes* as the best album of 2003—Pitchfork went all in on a style of music that would come to be known as "freak folk."

* * *

Freak folk began to dominate the underground—as a loosely defined aesthetic, and certainly as a buzzword—at a time when the dance-punk wave was going mainstream through the likes of Franz Ferdinand and the Killers, user-friendly indie favorites like Death Cab for Cutie and the Shins were blowing up, and the Brooklyn hipster was becoming a well-known trope. For people whose identities hinged on being ahead of the curve, on being different, the widespread embrace of these entities meant a change of aesthetic was needed. In a *New York* magazine piece from 2010 titled "What Was the Hipster?," Mark Greif identified a shift from the ironic "white" hipster—with his "wifebeater" tank tops, PBR tallboys, and subversive performance of dive-bar machismo—to a "green" hipster fixated on nature, nostalgia, and the recovery of lost innocence.

"Certainly the points of reference shifted from midwestern suburbs to animals, wilderness, plus the occasional Native American," Greif wrote. In this movement toward primitivism and the great outdoors, we also see the seeds of Coachella-era music festival style, of flower crowns and sundresses and the whole neo-hippie ordeal—a shift that inevitably involved women taking a more prominent role in the public conception of what it meant to be a hipster. "Where the White Hipster was relentlessly male, crowding out women from public view (except as Polaroid muses or SuicideGirls), the Hipster Primitive feminized hipster markers," Grief wrote. "One spoke now of headdresses and Sally Jessy Raphael glasses, not just male facial hair."

Ugh, yes, the headdresses. Remember that 2004 was also the time when indie rock tastemakers were beginning to reckon with their overwhelming whiteness. One way they sought to push back against insularity was to fill their iPods with rap music; another was the clumsy appropriation of indigenous culture in an attempt to tap into some kind of borrowed authenticity. Indie music's sometimes problematic quest to get back to some pre-corrupted point of origin was a significant subplot in the 2000s, and it kicked into overdrive with the rise of freak folk. In 2004, the trend was inescapable.

If freak folk had a messiah, it was Devendra Banhart, who certainly looked the part. In that case, I guess freak folk's John the Baptist would be Sam Beam, a mild-mannered Florida man whose scratchy four-track demos paved the way for a hype cycle centered on earthy eccentricity.

Beam would have killed at open mic night. It's possible he *did* kill at open mic night, but he might not have ever bothered getting up there. Music was not Beam's passion. The robustly bearded South Carolina native went to film school, worked video production jobs across the South, and was teaching cinematography in Miami when his home recording project Iron & Wine took off.

Beam started writing songs and recording them at his house because it was a more cost-effective outlet for creativity than making movies, and he famously adopted his hushed vocal approach partially so he could record without waking up his young children. If the lo-fi sound was an economic choice, it was also a wondrous aesthetic for his music, like a grainy, sepia-tone Instagram filter over his acoustic ballads. Beam's music was a relentlessly Southern blend of tender lullabies and bluesy folk, with song titles like "Bird Stealing Bread," "Muddy Hymnal," and "Upward over the Mountain." The rougher, gnarlier material helped earn him some cred with those who worship old Delta blues legends, but it was the exquisitely pretty stuff that lifted him to prominence.

Sub Pop released Beam's home demos as Iron & Wine's 2002 debut *The Creek Drank the Cradle*. Despite his plans to flesh out the songs into a more polished product, the label wisely left the music as it was, recognizing an unrepeatable magic in the intimate recordings. *The Creek Drank the Cradle* was an outlier in an indie scene that was trending toward immediacy and accessibility—solemn, bucolic, full of gentle harmonies and contented sighs—but by the time he released his second album, Beam's music was suddenly au courant.

That record, 2004's *Our Endless Numbered Days*, professionalized the Iron & Wine sound without undermining its appeal, and—with hearty approval from both Pitchfork and Zach Braff—it made Beam one of the biggest artists in indie music. I preferred when his tracks sounded like lost artifacts rather than majestically rendered studio creations, but Beam and producer Brian Deck managed not to taint the soul of the project. The glittering fan favorite "Naked as We Came" definitely should have been in *Garden State* instead of Beam's hokey Postal Service cover.

The *Garden State* soundtrack wasn't the only noteworthy compilation album to feature Iron & Wine in 2004. Not long after *Our Endless Numbered Days* arrived, Iron & Wine's hushed stunner "Fever Dream" was included on a disc called *The Golden Apples of the Sun*. The comp was curated by Banhart, an art-school dropout who'd grown up in Texas and Venezuela before landing in California. With his long hair, Jesus beard, and tendency toward shirtlessness, Banhart looked like a bohemian shaman, and he knew how to sell that image. His own spring 2004 album *Rejoicing in the Hands* set his quivering warble against not much more than acoustic guitar, save for the occasional tasteful string arrangement. But despite his skills as a singer-songwriter, Banhart may have been even more talented as a curator.

The Golden Apples of the Sun was essentially Banhart's mixtape showcasing his peers to the world. Banhart recognized a rising wave of earthy, psychedelic nouveau folkies taking inspiration from '60s and '70s psych-folk acts like the Holy Modal Rounders, the Incredible String Band, Vashti Bunyan, and Bert Jansch. He funneled twenty of those acts onto a CD for the upstart art and music magazine *Arthur*—which had profiled Banhart in 2003, labeling him a "freaked folknik" on their cover—and the rest was history. *The Golden Apples of the Sun* quickly became a definitive text for a scene that spanned far beyond Banhart and his friends, and association with it helped bands like Espers, Vetiver, and CocoRosie to establish a foothold in the music industry. But if there was one breakout star on the compilation, it was another young San Franciscan named Joanna Newsom.

Newsom would have stood out among nearly any group of performers. Her main instrument was a giant harp, and her voice was even more striking than Mangum's, a cooing, squawking force of nature that elicited strong reactions from listeners on impact. In the decades since Newsom's breakthrough, many journalists have taken their 2004 counterparts to task for the ways they wrote about her vocals, and in some cases, critics absolutely went overboard. The idea that it's misogynistic to call Newsom's voice "squeaky" or "childlike" feels like an overcorrection—were people supposed to ignore this incredibly distinctive and polarizing aspect of her music?—but you can see why Newsom's supporters would be on guard against anything that scanned as a backhanded compliment because there were definitely cases when descriptions of her voice descended into cheap mockery. Especially vile was the review at Stylus, which included the phrase, "RIYL: Shrill, esoteric female singer/songwriters that play harp and sound like they're ten years old with a possible, though not certain, mental problem."

It was also unfortunate whenever Newsom's highly affected

vocal style became an excuse to dismiss her formidable artistic vision. "Bridges and Balloons," which appears on *Golden Apples* and opens *The Milk-Eyed Mender*, is more than an introduction to a peculiar aesthetic. It's a gateway into a fantastical world, one full of gorgeous sonic flourishes, narrated with wonder, melancholy, and jolts of humor. By the time she returned with 2006's *Ys*, a mammoth achievement she produced with baroque-pop hero Van Dyke Parks, Newsom had cemented herself as one of her generation's most brilliant composers and arrangers. At the time, it already felt like a privilege to see such a prestigious artist perform in a small Columbus nightclub and not some ornate theater in one of North America's six largest media markets. She developed such a serious-artiste reputation that it was delightful when she later married *Saturday Night Live*/The Lonely Island comedian Andy Samberg, who spent Newsom's *Ys* era making digital shorts like "Dick in a Box."

Banhart, Newsom, and their cohort were not the only artists pushing folk traditions into new experimental realms. In 2003, *The Wire*, a UK magazine focused on outré music, coined the saying "New Weird America" in a cover story on the "free folk" movement of the Northeast, where bands like MV & EE and Sunburned Hand of the Man were combining ancient folk and blues traditions with avant-garde psych and drone. In Louisville, early Newsom supporter Will Oldham had spent years making haunting folk records under guises such as Bonnie "Prince" Billy, and My Morning Jacket were developing a strain of spectral Southern rock that could glimmer and glow but also blow you down. In Chicago there were Califone, a group whose junkyard folk rock felt both futuristic and old as dirt, and Wilco, a major-label band who had been hailed as "the American Radiohead" (and earned a perfect 10 from Pitchfork) by deconstructing their alt-country sound on 2002's *Yankee Hotel Foxtrot*. And then there was Brooklyn, from whence seemingly all the most popular indie acts emerged in the 2000s.

Their number included Animal Collective, childhood friends from Baltimore who moved to New York and made a name for themselves donning masks and playing primitive experimental folk music. (Their early album *Ark* was originally called *Here Comes the Indian* because of course it was.) In 2004 AnCo became Pitchfork celebrities with an 8.9 Best New Music review for *Sung Tongs*, a warped, hallucinogenic travelogue through the backwoods of their minds. Recorded by core members Avey Tare (Dave Portner) and Panda Bear (Noah Lennox) under a red lightbulb in Colorado, *Sung Tongs* was full of druggy campfire music, sometimes wildly catchy, other times hallucinatory and expansive. Though far from poppy, it was the most approachable thing Animal Collective had ever released, and it began their transition from outsider artists to underground stars with crossover appeal.

Subsequent releases brought more force and structure to their music (2005's *Feels*) and began to lace their left-field psych folk with electronic elements (2007's *Strawberry Jam*) while maintaining its weirdo edge. Long after the freak folk hype died down, Animal Collective remained one of the most beloved bands in indie, popular enough to headline a night at Pitchfork Music Festival in 2008. Lennox contributed to the band's popularity with a string of stunning solo albums as Panda Bear, most famously 2007's loop-based psych-pop odyssey *Person Pitch*. But no matter how far out of the forest they ventured, I'm not sure anyone predicted the quasi-mainstream breakthrough Animal Collective would achieve by the end of the decade—another story for another chapter.

As with any buzzy subgenre that captures the imaginations

of music critics and then marketing agents, the term "freak folk" was widely rejected by the artists who were aligned with it. At the time, Banhart told *The New York Times*, "All of us have known each other for a long time. It's not music made for magazines or labels, it's made for each other. If you were to ask me how I feel about any of the term freak-folk, it's cool—you have to call it something—but we didn't name it. We've been thinking about what to call it, and we just call it the Family."

Nine years later, after getting a haircut and putting some clothes on, Banhart told the same paper that he didn't think freak folk was "an apt descriptive label." Similarly, Newsom dismissed freak folk as a "media construction" in a 2015 *Fader* interview: "It wasn't offensive, it was just so not accurate." That same year, in a Quietus feature, Animal Collective's Josh Dibb, aka Deakin, told Vashti Bunyan, "We were very indignant to being lumped in with that Brooklyn, freak folk thing"—though recording 2005's *Prospect Hummer* EP with Bunyan, the godmother of freak folk, didn't do much to dissociate Animal Collective from that movement. I get it; artists are unique flowers who *hate* being labeled. But even if "freak folk" was invented by journalists as a lazy shorthand for a vast spectrum of sounds, it was a helpful descriptor, a term that identified real currents sweeping through the underground.

One artist sometimes categorized as freak folk who was perhaps less deserving of the designation was Sufjan Stevens. Stevens was a softspoken Christian from Michigan who'd moved to New York and fallen in with the Danielson Famile, a rock-band-as-left-field-religious-art-project in which members wore something like Boy Scout uniforms and frontman Daniel Smith sometimes dressed up as a giant tree. 2003's *Michigan*—or, if you prefer, *Greetings from Michigan, the Great Lakes State*—had lifted

Stevens to indie-celeb status thanks to a rave Pitchfork review. On that album, Stevens borrowed some of Danielson's community theater vibes for his own auteurist approach. He deployed banjo, an indie-pop choir, and jazz and orchestral instruments from the post-rock playbook in service of profoundly moving songs about his home state. Some tracks, like "Oh Detroit, Lift Up Your Weary Head! (Rebuild! Restore! Reconsider!)," were big productions full of homespun pageantry. Some, like "For the Widows in Paradise, for the Fatherless in Ypsilanti," were aching hymns, stripped-down and vulnerable.

2004's *Seven Swans* doubled down on the softer, sparser side of that sound, and it arrived just as the freak-folk hype was gaining steam. Recorded in fits and starts with Smith at his family's New Jersey home, the album presented some of Stevens's most overtly Christian material, playing out like a collection of modern psalms. Some song titles referenced scripture, and closing track "The Transfiguration" straight up retold a Bible story. The music was often bare bones, only Stevens's quivering tenor and a guitar or banjo, but bursts of sonic color sometimes entered into the frame like divine apparitions. On the title track, his supporting cast exploded to life, conjuring an apocalyptic vision that blurred together terror and euphoria. "He will take you," Stevens sang. "If you run, He will chase you/ 'Cause *He is the Lord*."

As someone from an evangelical background who had abandoned religious music but still felt a connection to the faith of my youth, I loved the idea of a "cool" Christian singer-songwriter. But Stevens wouldn't have broken through to the extent he did simply by appealing to former youth group kids. Secular listeners connected with even Stevens's most openly devotional music, in part because he was approaching spirituality from a different angle than the cookie-cutter worship music that proliferates in many white American churches. Albums like *Seven Swans* felt like something real and personal, not just an empty ritual dressed up in the trappings of arena rock. Just as Christian rock tends to manufacture the religious equivalent of certain popular artists, here was hipster culture's alternative to Christian music, artfully rendered and obscure enough to share with your less tapped-in friends as a flex.

"My faith informs what I'm doing. It's really the core of what I'm doing in a lot of ways," Stevens told the *Los Angeles Times* in 2005, in a feature touting the "soft revolution" of indie folk music. "But the language of faith is a problem for me, and I try to avoid it at all costs. You could say that I have a mind for eternal things, for supernatural things, and things of mystery. I'm more comfortable with using those terms because they can be used without controlling or stigmatizing anyone."

Stevens's difference in perspective from your average Christian balladeer became even clearer years later as he gradually revealed his queer identity to the world, but before that dimension of his life was evident, he stood out as a complex persona with a staggering creative outpouring. It helped that he wasn't *only* singing about God. 2005's *Illinois* was a tour de force tackling Mary Todd Lincoln, John Wayne Gacy, zombies, UFOs, predatory wasps, the unjust fate of the indigenous population, a cancer patient's teenage romance, and much more, with an expansive musical palette to match. Centered on "Chicago," a Jesus-streaked coming-of-age epic that sounded like a busy metropolis breaking out into joyous choreography, it was an album so theatrical that someone literally adapted it into a Broadway production. When I saw Stevens's 2005 tour supporting *Illinois*, despite costumes and some minor pageantry, the production still felt small-scale and DIY. Yet on the album itself, you could hear his music growing less amateur in real time, and in the surrounding scene, his influence was palpable.

It wasn't long before the scraggly hippie vibes of freak folk gave way to something more sanitized, scalable, and twee. When I say "twee" here, I mean it in the broader Merriam-Webster sense of "affectedly or excessively dainty, delicate, cute, or quaint," not the more specific musical subgenre known for its proudly amateurish qualities. Because there was nothing amateurish about the indie folk that began to arise in the second half of the aughts and on into the early 2010s. As so often happens, a vibrant subculture was transforming into something more like a product—not always a *sterile* product, but certainly a product more accessible to a normie audience. If freak folk was like a local vegan co-op, the stuff that followed was Whole Foods.

Stevens, with his meek narration and co-ed chorales and ostentatious orchestrations, had something to do with that change. So did the Decemberists, who signed to a major label and kept indulging their most precious theater-geek tendencies, even acting out a maritime battle with a whale onstage at Pitchfork Music Festival. The edgeless indie balladry propagated by Hollywood and Starbucks played a role, as did a swarm of quirky blog-rock bands with a dozen members and a brass section. And acts like Beirut (sort of a Neutral Milk Youth Hostel) and Andrew Bird (a whistler and violist formerly from Squirrel Nut Zippers) injected a fancy baroque pop element into the scene.

Not every new act in this sphere was smoothing out its music. Bands like New York's Gang Gang Dance were still delving into druggy, tribal sounds at the outskirts of polite society. The artist now known as Anohni was applying her peerless voice to cabaret-ready balladry with assists from artists like Devendra Banhart and Lou Reed. Two years after *Golden Apples*, newer freak-folk artists like New England's Feathers and NorCal's Brightblack Morning Light were still emanating trippy vibes. But the iconoclasts' reach was far exceeded by the likes of José González, a Swedish singer-songwriter whose crystalline acoustic cover of the Knife's indie synth jam "Heartbeats" became a coffeehouse sensation.

There were a lot of catalysts and reference points for this more streamlined indie-folk sound, not all of them strictly musical. The rise of the fussy, meticulous, unflinchingly precious filmmaker Wes Anderson was a helpful parallel—and not just because Team Zissou's hats looked like something you might see on the guy at the house party with an acoustic guitar, desperately seeking people's attention while strumming Damien Rice songs. After *The O.C.* and *Garden State* and *Grey's Anatomy* came *Once*, a 2007 indie movie musical in which musicians Glen Hansard and Markéta Irglová play buskers who briefly find creative inspiration and romance. *Once* became a sleeper hit, and Hansard and Irglová—who fell in love in real life for a while, too—toured the world performing songs from the film under the name the Swell Season.

Also illuminating was the spread of publications like *The Believer*, Dave Eggers's literary magazine for and by would-be Wes Anderson characters, devoted to "the concept of the inherent Good." But perhaps nothing captured the spirit of this movement better than *Paste*, an Atlanta-based music mag focused on adult alternative and Americana, which began carving out a softer, friendlier, less esoteric indie canon than the cred-obsessed Pitchfork. There was some great writing in *Paste*, but it's hard to imagine many of the artists it championed being celebrated in a photocopied zine. What's easy to imagine is someone paging through an issue of *Paste* at their local coffee shop, where many of the albums discussed on the page might be circulating in the background.

Coffee shops and soft, pretty indie folk were made for each other. Many such establishments hosted open mic nights, but beyond that, these spaces were set up to become the favored haunts of young city-dwelling music fans. In the '90s, the rapid expansion of Starbucks and the massive popularity of *Friends* made coffee shops an avatar of the urbanite lifestyle—a place where college students could gather to sip lattes and socialize while pretending to do their homework. Many coffee shops were set up for those gatherings, full of couches and large upholstered chairs fit for sinking into for hours at a time. In a 2024 *Dwell* article, aesthetics expert Evan Collins described the vibe as "javacore," typified by "faux-worn furniture, brushed paint on a dresser, French country vibes, lots of flowers . . . found furniture, a thrift shop aesthetic."

If you ever planted yourself in one of these businesses, perhaps your visit was soundtracked by a mix of acoustic singer-songwriters whose music leant itself to the cozy environs. More than a few Iron & Wine converts were made that way. As the 2000s progressed, advancements in technology made these kinds of spaces even more popular, both for Central Perk-style group hangouts and for hours frittered away in isolation. It was not uncommon to happen upon a hipster brooding in a corner, scribbling in a journal or perusing a novel while listening to their iPod. Midway through the decade, laptops began to outsell desktop computers as the advent of public Wi-Fi revolutionized the ability to get work done (or procrastinate) at a boutique café.

This was all happening in the long tail of 9/11, at the height of George W. Bush's Iraq War, and one thing freak folk offered was a sense of escapism. Bunyan speculated as much in 2004, telling *The New York Times*, "It's a particularly difficult time to look at the world, and maybe right now it's just easier to create your own." Although Banhart and his peers were inspired by their elders, their sensibility diverged from more conventional approaches to folk music, which were focused on traditional songs to be passed down. Indie folk was less about connecting with an ancient lineage and more about dealing with heavy emotions by disappearing into highly stylized worlds, full of not just outlandish characters but small-batch wares that connoted high quality and good taste.

But trend-sniffing companies tend to find ways to mass-produce even the most bespoke products, and just as trucker hats had quickly gone mainstream, freak folk's return-to-Eden vibe was quickly converted into something cute you could pick up from Urban Outfitters. The culture described on the back of Marc Spitz's book *Twee* was starting to congeal: "Artisanal chocolate. Mustaches. Locally sourced vegetables. Etsy. Birds. Flea markets. Cult films. Horn rimmed glasses." Music remained a huge part of that lifestyle, but like the fashion and the food, the sound of indie folk was gentrifying into something more clean-cut.

As roots-rock visionaries like Wilco and My Morning Jacket stepped from the avant-garde into jam-band territory and newer, more put-together artists like *Paste* favorites She & Him and the Avett Brothers emerged to grab the baton from the freaks, some previously fringy or chaotic musicians were also finding ways to fit into this quaint new paradigm. Even former teenage prodigy Conor Oberst—whose singer-songwriter-y indie band Bright Eyes had been messy and combustible enough to sometimes qualify as emo, and who preferred confrontational protest songs like "When the President Talks to God" over a retreat into fantasy—cleaned up his sound for 2005's tremendous *I'm Wide Awake, It's Morning*.

In Bright Eyes' case, shaving off some of the rough edges was not a problem. Released the same day as the less fondly remembered electronic experiment *Digital Ash from a Digital Urn*, *I'm Wide Awake* contained some of Oberst's most mature, inspired songwriting, including "First Day of My Life," an instant romantic mixtape staple that coincidentally became the first dance at my wedding *and* my drummer's wedding. More than ever before, the album seasoned Oberst's music with elements of folk and country; he even wrangled some backing vocals from country-rock icon Emmylou Harris. The resulting masterpiece set Oberst on a course toward the lucrative world of NPR-friendly adult alternative—a trajectory matched by his Saddle Creek peer Jenny Lewis of Rilo Kiley on her 2006 solo debut *Rabbit Fur Coat*, a highly enjoyable album of folk rock, soul, and country dismissed by Pitchfork as "indie-yuppie" music.

Iron & Wine broke out the electric guitars on 2007's *The Shepherd's Dog* and shifted their live show toward mirage-like full-band jams. I went to see them on that tour, and I hated how far Sam Beam had drifted from the intimate singer-songwriter fare of *The Creek Drank the Cradle*. If Beam's music was starting to seem less alternative, less unique, less special, so was his audience. Observing an outdoor Iron & Wine show in Brooklyn for her 2008 book *It Still Moves*, the esteemed critic Amanda Petrusich described the trendy neighborhoods around the venue, where "dirty vinyl siding and rusted tin awnings are reminders of a past that's been consumed and commodified by the present." After purchasing an ice cream cone amidst booths for local breweries and eateries, she noticed versions of the same hipster uniform everywhere: "star tattoos, oversized sunglasses, studded belts, canvas bags with woodland animals (squirrels, deer, and finches especially) patched in place, scads of rubber bracelets, American Apparel T-shirts, too much jewelry, choppy haircuts, skinny waists."

The bags emblazoned with forest creatures feel especially relevant to that moment's prevailing sensibility. In the most famous sketch from the hipster-skewering comedy series *Portlandia*, *SNL*'s Fred Armisen and Sleater-Kinney's Carrie Brownstein urge a shopkeeper to put a bird on every item in her inventory but are terrified when an actual bird flies into the store. "I remember going around to little boutiques in Portland, and I felt like it was kind of an insult to my intelligence that just because there was a lampshade with a bird stencil on it, that somehow elevated it to a place of art," Brownstein later told *EW*. "There was a craft explosion, and birds did seem like a shorthand: 'This isn't your average piece of paper—this is stationery now.'"

By the time *Portlandia* premiered in 2011, the public was eminently familiar with this aesthetic. Maybe this lifestyle was not, as *Twee* author Spitz asserted, "the first strong, diverse, and wildly influential youth movement since Punk in the '70s and Hip Hop in the '80s"—your average person knows what punk and hip-hop are and, I assure you, has no idea what twee means. Yet there's no doubt that this precious point of view came to prominence as the 2000s rolled on, morphing the sound of folk rock as it collided with the rustic and rugged.

It didn't get much woodsier than Fleet Foxes, who rocked the requisite facial hair, frequently sang about the great outdoors (trees, mountains, snow, the sun), and slathered their music in vocal harmonies that seemed to echo down through majestic valleys. And, oh yeah, that band name.

Suburban Seattle natives Robin Pecknold and Skyler Skjelset

formed the group in their early twenties based on their shared love of retro touchstones like Bob Dylan, Neil Young, Joni Mitchell, and Brian Wilson. "Fleet Foxes seem to have stepped right out of San Francisco's Summer of Love, circa 1967," *The Seattle Times* declared in an early writeup, in which Pecknold admitted to asking his bandmates if they could sound more like Crosby, Stills & Nash. You can hear that influence loud and clear on songs like expansive slo-mo ballad "Blue Ridge Mountains" and the urgent "Ragged Wood"—driven onward by a rolling drumbeat from Josh Tillman, who'd later go solo as Father John Misty and become one of indie music's main characters.

Those kinds of harmonious acoustic anthems were a bit sweeter and smoother than the median indie-folk acts had been kicking out, but Fleet Foxes struck a chord with seemingly everyone they encountered. Phil Ek—who'd produced classics by Pacific Northwest indie royalty like Built to Spill, Modest Mouse, and the Shins—caught wind of Fleet Foxes and offered to record their demo. They signed to Seattle indie standard-bearer Sub Pop and kept piling up accolades. In a four-star review of their self-titled debut album, *Rolling Stone* hilariously called them "a lower-dosage Animal Collective." *EW* bestowed the album with a perfect 10, while Pitchfork awarded Best New Music to both the LP and Fleet Foxes' introductory *Sun Giant* EP. By the end of the year, the site had named *Fleet Foxes* and *Sun Giant* collectively as the best album of 2008.

Fleet Foxes' big win suggested millennial tastemakers were now comfortable with loving the same new bands as their boomer parents—or in other words, that the taste gap between Pitchfork and *Rolling Stone* was growing smaller. Songs like "White Winter Hymnal," with its crisscrossing vocal melodies and pastoral wordless flourishes, and "He Doesn't Know Why," with its overwhelming blasts of harmony, were too potent to write off as pure nostalgia, even if nostalgia was baked into the band's DNA. Fleet Foxes were triumphant right out of the gate, and they've continued to be a big deal—yet they still aren't even the biggest indie-folk success story of their era.

Bon Iver's origin is the stuff of legend. Justin Vernon had broken up with his band *and* his girlfriend, then spent two months sleeping on his ex's couch, when he got the hell out of Raleigh in November 2006. He drove through the night back home to Wisconsin, stopped at his parents' house, and decided to spend the winter alone in his father's cabin outside Eau Claire. As the story goes, he spent his days chopping wood, hunting for his meals, drinking beer, and watching *Northern Exposure* before opting to do something with the musical equipment sitting in his car.

Sorry to be hokey on Main, but something magical happened that winter. As Vernon began writing and recording, he switched up his approach, pushing his voice from its scruffy midrange up into a trembling falsetto and multitracking it until it sounded otherworldly. The music was largely sparse and hollowed out, with celestial atmospherics manifesting in the empty space—a post-rock deconstruction of singer-songwriter fare, like Sufjan Stevens reimagined by Talk Talk. The songs were strikingly beautiful and alluringly unique; it sounded like Vernon had conjured spirits in that cabin, like everything was recorded in darkness but lit up by a faint supernatural glow. And though there was more than a little freak folk in lyrics like "Only love is all maroon/ Gluey feathers on a flume/ Sky is womb and she's the moon," the end result was remarkably accessible.

Vernon called his new project Bon Iver, a mangled take on the French for "good winter," and titled the album *For Emma,*

Forever Ago. He had wondered if the tracks he made at the cabin should just be demos for some future studio venture, but as with Iron & Wine's debut, the material elicited such a passionate response that it obviously had to come out just as it was. The music was too enticing, its mythic backstory even better. In the summer of 2007, Vernon self-released *For Emma*, and things snowballed from there: word-of-mouth praise from the blogs and beyond, sold-out pressings, and a record deal with the rising Indiana indie label Jagjaguwar before year's end. Obviously, journalists ate up the "heartbroken dude retreats to the wilderness and whips up a masterpiece" narrative.

By March 2008, Bon Iver and Fleet Foxes were big enough deals to be booked for Pitchfork's afternoon showcase at the Austin venue Emo's during South by Southwest (SXSW), the annual festival/conference where buzz bands play many, many sets at venues around town and people like me scramble to see them while snagging as many free drinks as possible. I was at SXSW that year for *Columbus Alive* to cover the rise of my city's ultra-lo-fi indie-pop scrappers Times New Viking, who also played Pitchfork's event, and both Bon Iver and Fleet Foxes stunned me that day. As the year wore on, I noticed many of my friends who weren't nearly as tapped in to the indie music ecosystem raving about *For Emma*. As more and more people discovered Vernon, tastemakers and early adopters did not wash their hands of him. Bon Iver was quickly ascending, seemingly beloved by hipsters and normies alike.

Inevitably, *For Emma* became open mic night manna. Hundreds, maybe thousands of performers around the world attempted to interpret "Skinny Love." From a performance perspective, it's one of the few tracks on the album that relies on nothing but Vernon's vocals and guitar. On a listener level, it's the most basic, least "weird" song on the tracklist. It makes sense that it caught on, but nowadays, more than any other Bon Iver song, "Skinny Love" feels like a harbinger of far more annoying bands that emerged in Vernon's wake. The soulful howls, the impassioned strums, a rhythm that invites both artist and listener to pound on some nearby surface—it was all laying the groundwork for a generation of performatively rustic hit-makers who shot to fame by stomping, clapping, and yelling "Hey!"

Chapter 8 Soundtrack

THE NATIONAL, "Fake Empire" (2007)
FEIST, "I Feel It All" (2007)
ANDREW BIRD, "Heretics" (2007)
LCD SOUNDSYSTEM, "All My Friends" (2007)
YEASAYER, "2080" (2007)
FRIGHTENED RABBIT, "The Modern Leper" (2008)
GRIZZLY BEAR, "Two Weeks" (2009)
DIRTY PROJECTORS, "Cannibal Resource" (2009)
THE ANTLERS, "Two" (2009)
VAMPIRE WEEKEND, "Giving Up the Gun" (2010)
ARCADE FIRE, "Ready to Start" (2010)
ST. VINCENT, "Cruel" (2011)
FLEET FOXES, "Grown Ocean" (2011)
DESTROYER, "Kaputt" (2011)
BON IVER, "Beth/Rest" (2011)
FUN., "We Are Young" (2011)
MUMFORD & SONS, "I Will Wait" (2012)
OF MONSTERS AND MEN, "Little Talks" (2011)
THE LUMINEERS, "Ho Hey" (2012)
PHILLIP PHILLIPS, "Home" (2012)

8

Fake Empire

Prestige indie rock's moment of ubiquity

"What the indie rock movement is doing right now is very inspiring," Jay-Z said in August 2009, talking to MTV about watching Grizzly Bear at the Williamsburg Waterfront. His sister-in-law, Solange Knowles, was tapped into the world of Brooklyn indie rock, and she'd brought Jay and Beyoncé to see one of the scene's most popular bands. The visit made headlines; here were real-deal celebrities gracing the upper reaches of the underground to take in artsy-fartsy guitar music among a legion of Pitchfork readers. On the still-nascent Twitter, footage of Jay and Beyoncé swaying to a slow, woozy track called "Ready, Able" went viral.

In the MTV interview, Jay pushed against the idea that it was surprising for the world's most famous rapper to go see a bunch of white guys playing cerebral chamber-pop. "I don't understand why people are always surprised to see me at shows!" he said.

"I've always said that I believe in good music and bad music, so I'm always at those type of events. I like music."

Jay wasn't about to leave superstardom behind for a niche underground career à la André 3000 and his flutes. Nor did he recruit Nico Muhly—a favorite among Grizzly Bear and their peers—to lace his next album with conservatory-ready string arrangements. But he did see some commonalities between his own rise and that of the bands that had adopted his native borough as their home. Jay even compared indie rock bands to early rappers from back when hip-hop was a burgeoning grassroots movement, not yet recognized by mainstream gatekeepers. "It felt like us in the beginning," he told MTV. "These concerts, they're not on the radio, no one hears about them, and there's 12,000 people in attendance. And the music that they're making and the connection they're making to people is really inspiring."

Grizzly Bear were not the most obvious candidates to entertain the "Crazy in Love" duo—or to attract 12,000 people to an outdoor concert billed as a "pool party." The band had begun as Ed Droste's solo project seven years earlier. His lo-fi 2004 debut *Horn of Plenty* was substantial yet barely there, full of ghostly songs that occasionally got shoehorned, awkwardly, into the freak-folk conversation. By 2006's *Yellow House*—a warm, impressionistic update on the classic pop sounds of the Beatles, the Beach Boys, and Phil Spector—Grizzly Bear had blossomed into a collaborative unit. Co-frontman Daniel Rossen's baroque, proggy tendencies nicely complemented Droste's more straightforward approach, and both men brought a yearning, swooning quality to their vocals that contributed to the sense that this music was high art for old souls.

In 2009, Grizzly Bear were touring behind *Veckatimest*, the album that cemented their status as indie rock royalty. *Veckatimest* has some intense moments; opener "Southern Point" builds to a pulse-pounding finale, and on "Fine for Now," Grizzly Bear sound like an actual grizzly bear awakening from slumber, ready to roar. But most of the time, this was not an especially rocking band. Their music was gorgeous but also could be rather . . . drowsy? Whereas some groups might implore their audience to "make some noise," I once heard Droste praise the crowd at the Wexner Center in Columbus for being so quiet and attentive.

They probably wouldn't have broken through like they did without "Two Weeks," a bouncy pop tune built on plinking piano chords, a hard-slapping backbeat, and a chorus that seemed to encircle you with swirling vocal harmonies. Most Grizzly Bear songs were designed to sneak up on you, but "Two Weeks" grabbed you from the start. It grabbed lots of people, earning ample blog love and a No. 5 finish on Pitchfork's list of the best tracks of 2009 and pushing *Veckatimest* to a Top 10 debut on the *Billboard* 200 albums chart, despite a low-quality leak months in advance.

Jay-Z wasn't the only one from outside the indie rock bubble noticing that Grizzly Bear were pretty cool, and Grizzly Bear were hardly the only indie band reaching people beyond that bubble. In the late aughts and early 2010s, what Jay-Z called "the indie rock movement" reached a peak of cultural saturation. Many trends were coming to a head: Hollywood's embrace of indie music post–*The O.C.*, the star-making pipeline of Pitchfork and blogs, an explosion of indie dance music, the commodification of thrift-store fashion and twee sensibilities, the horizon-broadening impact of MySpace and iTunes, hipsters' embrace of radio hits, indie rock's gradual metamorphosis into pop.

This was an era when marquee indie artists topped the charts (Vampire Weekend), won major Grammys (Bon Iver), or both

(Arcade Fire). Danceable indie-presenting acts like MGMT, Phoenix, and Passion Pit were everywhere, from the radio to TV ads to festival stages. Even the ultra-geeky Decemberists had a No. 1 album; even the ultra-grimy Yeah Yeah Yeahs pivoted to sparkling dance-pop; even staunch weirdos Animal Collective evolved their sound to arena scale. The commercial apparatus built up around "indie" as a lifestyle brand was booming thanks to retailers like Urban Outfitters, and many of the artists who'd ridden that wave were thriving. And though most of the biggest indie rock hits of that epoch barely scraped the bottom of the Hot 100, they were so trendy and ubiquitous that there's no doubt they would have soared up the charts in the era of Spotify and TikTok, when streaming's power began to surpass that of the radio.

In terms of subjective cultural impact, indie rock wasn't quite grunge or nu metal. It was difficult for rock, even increasingly poppy rock, to have that kind of sustained reach at a time when MTV was no longer a tastemaking behemoth, putting the rockers and the pop stars in the same programming blocks. And just as the Hot 100 didn't tell the full story of grunge or nu metal's impact because it did not factor in MTV airplay, the chart could not measure the reach of songs that largely circulated through MP3 blogs, MediaFire links, and BitTorrent.

But this music and its attendant lifestyle would make it to the upper reaches of the Hot 100 one way or another. It loomed large enough that, by 2012, on her first No. 1 hit, ascending world-conqueror Taylor Swift sang scornfully to her ex, "And you would hide away and find your peace of mind/ With some indie record that's much cooler than mine." Another Swift hit from the same album began, "It feels like a perfect night/ To dress up like hipsters/ And make fun of our exes." These references made perfect sense to Swift's young audience. For millennials coming of age, indie was a part of the atmosphere.

Yet for all its potency as a youth movement, indie rock was scoring some of its most noteworthy breakthroughs by skewing more adult—sometimes even adult contemporary. In the process of going pop, some of indie's heavy hitters were also getting fancier, fussier, and more mature. While many indie artists embraced an accessible, youthful sound that thrived at festivals and the mall, others evolved the genre into an eminent institution, making music that connoted grown-up sophistication and played well within the halls of power. This wing of indie rock was designed for cavernous arenas and ornate theaters, for awards shows and political rallies, for Sandy Cohen as much as Seth. It was presented as something weighty and important, fit not for tank tops and sunglasses but the formal attire that many of its core artists rocked onstage.

Because "indie" had become such a fluid term, there was plenty of spillover between the genre's flashy Urban Outfitters side and its stately NPR side. Take St. Vincent, aka Annie Clark. Clark's gifts as a guitarist and composer got her into Boston's illustrious Berklee College of Music, but she dropped out in 2004 after three years, disillusioned with academia's rigid approach to music. She found her way into indie rock via the Polyphonic Spree, a psych-pop choir from her native Dallas. By 2005 she was a member of another plucky twee ensemble, Sufjan Stevens's touring band behind *Illinois*.

Some of those quirky, ambitious Sufjan vibes made it into Clark's first couple St. Vincent albums, but their ambitious arrangements owed at least as much to the British art-pop legend Kate Bush. Clark knew when to keep things prim and proper and when to let 'er rip. Like her fellow chameleon David Bowie and her future collaborator David Byrne, she understood how to make pop music feel like high art and art music connect like pop. In that sense, she was a perfect tour mate for Grizzly Bear in 2009, by which point she was an ascending indie star.

Grizzly Bear also straddled the worlds of poppy, approachable indie rock and serious-business art music, albeit a bit more awkwardly. They dressed casually and played plenty of festivals—in 2013, I saw them perform on the beach at Alabama's Hangout—but one listen through *Veckatimest* was enough to recognize that their native environment was concert halls and art museums. It did not totally compute for them to perform outdoors in Brooklyn on a Sunday afternoon at a venue with a giant Slip 'N Slide. It *did* make sense for a pair of American royals like Beyoncé and Jay-Z to show up at a Grizzly Bear concert, given that some of the band's peers had been hobnobbing with an actual president.

For those who'd been clued in for years, watching powerful people wake up to indie music was fascinating, sometimes even thrilling. But inevitably, the spotlight was fleeting. Before the 2000s indie scene had even begun its victory lap, the music industry was generating big-box versions of it, launching artists who fared far better on the charts than any Pitchfork-approved favorites.

* * *

It's important to acknowledge that indie rock never stopped *rocking*. Amidst all the genre's changes, there remained a baseline of hard-hitting bands that earned rave reviews and built up devoted audiences—from Spoon, the Hold Steady, and Wolf Parade to Deerhunter, Vivian Girls, and Titus Andronicus. Yet some of the biggest success stories were bands who, after making a ruckus in the middle of the decade, embraced a refined accessibility, appealing to the middlebrow prestige of awards shows, political rallies, and self-mythologizing documentaries. Looking back, ground zero for this transformation may have been spring 2007, which saw the release of Arcade Fire's *Neon Bible*, the National's *Boxer*, and LCD Soundsystem's *Sound of Silver*.

I did not see *Sound of Silver* coming. From 2002's "Losing My Edge" onward, LCD Soundsystem had spent half a decade proving themselves as a god-tier singles band. Their 2005 self-titled debut had played more like a singles compilation than a proper album. But with LP2, James Murphy delivered a cohesive masterstroke. The boisterous dance-punk energy and ultra-chic electronic influences remained, but the pop acumen of David Bowie and Talking Heads was turned way up this time. The result was both a dance record and a rock record, a party record and an in-my-feelings record, a procession of anthems for bloghouse listeners who dabbled in indie rock and vice versa. In its 9.2 Best New Music review, Pitchfork declared it "as close to a perfect hybrid of dance and rock music's values as you're likely to ever hear."

There were tracks like "Get Innocuous" and "Us v Them," slow-build dance-floor heaters that grew into all-encompassing grooves. There were cheeky rock songs like "North American Scum" and "Watch the Tapes," fit for fist-pumping and even headbanging even as they kept a trace of that hip-swinging energy. Most importantly, there were *ballads*, though even those could send your body into euphoric contortions. The breakup track "Someone Great" was built around a skittering programmed beat and a symphony of hypnotic synths. "New York, I Love You but You're Bringing Me Down" mostly did away with electronics in favor of throwback piano pop that exploded into a bombastic rock 'n' roll climax— one of those moments when a pivot into traditionalism somehow feels like a left turn. At the center was "All My Friends," one of the most beloved and significant songs in the history of indie music.

Murphy was embarrassed of "All My Friends" at first, fearing that LCD's audience would reject it as too melodic and earnest. The song was inspired by missing his friend group when he went on tour, but it came to stand for much more than that, becoming even more of a generational touchstone for aging hipsters than "Losing My Edge." Musically, "All My Friends" was Murphy's attempt to replicate the rush he experienced from Joy Division's perpetually intensifying "Transmission": "It's the same thing the whole way through, and without any kind of embarrassing rockist gesture," he told *Mojo* in 2007. "It starts off so gentle, and becomes so *fucking* overwhelming. By the time he's going, 'Dance, dance, dance to the radio,' your head's exploding."

To achieve that sensation, Murphy built an eight-minute epic around an incessantly plinking piano chord. It's a sound that conjures possibility and nostalgia all at once, that stands out sharply at first but eventually blurs into a din in the background, that will surely be used in trailers for millennial coming-of-age stories as often as "Fortunate Son" is needle-dropped into Vietnam War movies. Little by little, propulsive bass, drums, and guitar emerge around that central harmonic flicker. Murphy sings about getting older, watching life fly by too fast, wishing he could reconnect with the people he loves. The music keeps intensifying, and so do the emotions, until Murphy finally breaks through the noise and howls, repeatedly, "Where are your friends *tonight?!*" It's an astounding moment of release, shot through with a wistfulness so powerful it could bring you to your knees. Whether in the car, on a run, or at an LCD Soundsystem concert, it never fails to tingle my spine.

When LCD released their third album, 2010's Top 10 hit

This Is Happening, Murphy announced it would likely be the last one. The idea was to send LCD out at the peak of their powers, before they could fall off. The retirement campaign led to a blowout farewell show at Madison Square Garden in April 2011, filmed for a documentary called *Shut Up and Play the Hits* that interspersed footage from the concert with clips of Murphy being interviewed by the journalist Chuck Klosterman and stowing away his musical equipment the next morning. *Shut Up and Play the Hits* worked hard to seal the legend of LCD Soundsystem, and when the band got back together just five years after such a definitive, conspicuous goodbye, the movie started to feel pretty goofy in hindsight. But no cinematic documentation was necessary to validate what LCD Soundsystem had accomplished. The very fact that 2002's paragon of exclusive Brooklyn cool sold out Manhattan's world-famous arena in 2011 was a testament to how far this band had come, how far *indie music* had come.

The National played a big part in that glow-up. The five members of the band all grew up around Cincinnati, but they started their band in New York in 1999, just before the Strokes, Yeah Yeah Yeahs, and Interpol took off. Unlike those bands, the National did not arrive on the scene fully formed. They spent their first few years trying to figure out their sound, which began as a sort of downcast country rock with notes of droll poet-rockers like Leonard Cohen and David Berman. Their early albums were decent, but they lacked a certain intangible magic and were out of step with the rising rock stars of NYC. The band felt that tension acutely, as singer Matt Berninger explained to *Spin* in 2013:

> We practiced next to [Interpol] and I remember hearing them for the first time through the wall and thinking, 'Wow, that band is really, really good and this is great; we're in a

healthy, creative space here. Then, a couple of days later, *Spin* was shooting [Interpol] in the hallway of the practice space and they all just looked so cool in their suits. I had my khaki pants on from work and had to weave through them as they were taking photos, feeling the entire time like, "Fuck, we're definitely not those guys." But we were always aware of the distance between us and those bands. We weren't going to connect with people on that level. From day one, we wished we were cool. But we weren't, not like them. We were going to have to connect with people on an emotional level.

By 2004's *Cherry Tree* EP, they were figuring out how to make their songs come alive, both through the chiming, shimmering, sometimes erupting guitars of twin brothers Bryce and Aaron Dessner and the more forceful, inventive playing of rhythm section Scott and Bryan Devendorf (also brothers). Berninger was similarly growing in confidence, stepping into the loopy free-associative swagger that, along with his unmistakable baritone bellow, would make him one of the most memorable frontmen of his era. "I'm a perfect piece of ass," he sang with an audible shit-eating grin, a few lines before declaring, "And all the wine is all for me."

Cherry Tree was a warmup for 2005's *Alligator*, the National's first masterpiece, which codified their approach while expanding its limits. They even sprinkled in a few distortion-bombed rock songs without compromising their well-honed sad-bastard identity—most famously "Mr. November," which ended with the band going supernova and Berninger screaming, in character as a political candidate, "I won't fuck us over! I'm Mr. November!" As Bryce Dessner told *Spin*, the more aggressive vocals arose organically at live shows for practical reasons: "He was screaming so people would shut up and listen, because they would constantly talk over us."

Some National fans still hold up *Alligator* as the gold standard, treasuring its roughshod and explosive qualities, but the band had even greater albums on deck. 2007's *Boxer* is the one that rightfully rocketed them to the indie A-list (and the Best New Music list). The National were the same band from *Alligator*, but more majestic and bigger than life. Opener "Fake Empire"—with its mesmerizing circle of piano chords, sweeping syncopated backbeat, and ecstatic orchestral finale—was an entryway into a new phase for the National and maybe indie rock as a whole. Their work felt fancy and refined, fit for dinner parties and wine tastings. Yet Berninger narrated each song with a rumpled, neurotic disposition that cut through the pretense, addressing anxiety, depression, and the washed life with candor and bizarre turns of phrase. On the hard-charging "Mistaken for Strangers," he sang of "another un-innocent, elegant fall into the un-magnificent lives of adults"—a perfect summation of the National's vibe.

Boxer elevated the National, and not just within Pitchfork world. Just as R.E.M., the icons and kingmakers of alternative rock, had anointed Radiohead by taking them on tour in the '90s, R.E.M. invited the National to open their 2008 tour with Modest Mouse. And Michael Stipe was not even the most prominent figure aligning himself with the National. That same year, the Bush-critiquing "Fake Empire" became part of the fast-rising Illinois Senator Barack Obama's presidential bid when Hope Hall, who'd directed the "Mistaken for Strangers" video, got a job doing video work for the campaign. "To have a little song you write when you're depressed about the world get used like that, it's hard to describe," Berninger told Ryan Pinkard in the 33⅓ book about *Boxer*.

Meanwhile the Dessner brothers were emerging as leading lights of a new class of indie artists. Back in Cincinnati, Bryce launched the MusicNOW festival, blurring together the indie vanguard with the neo-classical music he composed and performed with the ensemble Clogs. Aaron began to take on production work for artists in the National's sphere, like the powerfully melancholic singer-songwriter Sharon Van Etten and the heart-on-sleeve Scottish rock band Frightened Rabbit. Some of his other production clients like Doveman and Buke and Gase were signed to Brassland, the label the Dessners founded with Alec Hanley Bemis.

The brothers also curated and produced 2009's scene-defining compilation *Dark Was the Night*, a benefit for the AIDS charity Red Hot, documenting a less scrappy, more elegant breed of indie rock acts. The 31-song, 130-minute tracklist brought together a who's who of classy indie types: Bon Iver, Sufjan Stevens, Feist, Arcade Fire, Grizzly Bear, and on and on. The album crystallized a somber, sophisticated sensibility. "On this record, we tried to capture this musical renaissance, which may not have the cultural impact of grunge or punk, but is equally significant from a cultural and creative standpoint," Red Hot founder Andrew Carlin told *Billboard* in 2009. "It's an assertion of Aaron and Bryce's generation. These artists are not fringe or marginal."

By the time the National signed to the venerable 4AD label and released the brooding, searching, cathartically stormy *High Violet* in 2010, they had become one of the defining bands of their era, polished and classy but also a force of nature when they wanted to be. It earned an 8.7 Best New Music review at Pitchfork but also debuted all the way up at No. 3 on the *Bill-*

board 200, indicating that not just chronically online hipsters were buying in. Their appeal was exemplified in a stirring performance of "Afraid of Everyone" on *Letterman*, with Sufjan Stevens on backing vocals. The National were now built for big stages like that. Songs like the fiery "Terrible Love" and the graceful, surreal "Bloodbuzz Ohio" sounded amazing in arenas. Seeing them open for Arcade Fire in Indianapolis in 2011, I marveled at how far they'd risen.

No matter how big those bands grew, Arcade Fire always seemed like the biggest thing going in indie rock—some of the few actual rock stars to come out of the scene. Unfortunately, Win Butler later got up to some rock-star behavior in the derogatory sense, sparking sexual misconduct allegations from multiple people in 2022. The news tainted Arcade Fire's legacy for many listeners, but it hadn't yet impugned the band's reputation in the years after their debut, when they were becoming the indie equivalent of A-list celebrities.

After a debut album that channeled and transcended their personal pain, 2007's *Neon Bible*—somehow darker and more melodramatic than the album called *Funeral*—was the band's grand statement about the world's ills, their turn from an inward to an outward focus. As Stephen Deusner put it in Pitchfork's approving but less rhapsodic review, the album takes aim at "the government, the church, the military, the entertainment industry, and even the basest instincts of the common man," applying a heavy-handed intensity that can feel absurd when you're not on Arcade Fire's wavelength but packs a tremendous wallop when you're in the right headspace.

I liked *Neon Bible* but did not find it as compelling as *Funeral*. I missed the first album's raw, unhinged energy and "where the hell did this come from" mystique, and I thought the second album's attempts to make big statements about The Way We Live Now resulted in songs that threatened to collapse under their own weight. But LP2 did what it needed to, inspiring favorable reviews and debuting at No. 2 in the US, and Arcade Fire continued to ascend. In 2007, they played *Saturday Night Live* for the first time. In 2008, they took the stage at a Bruce Springsteen concert to perform multiple songs with the Boss. In 2009, they even joined Jay-Z as the entertainment at the Obama Campaign Staff Ball, at Obama's personal request, after playing multiple benefit shows for the campaign. Arcade Fire seemed to have ballooned to the largest possible scale for an independent rock band, but their next album cycle would prove there were even more prestigious achievements left to unlock.

As a concept for an album by a Big Serious Rock Band With Important Things To Say, *The Suburbs* is perhaps even more ready-made than *Neon Bible*'s warnings about the dangers of religion, capitalism, and television. A meditation on Win and Will Butler's childhood outside Houston, Arcade Fire's 2010 LP is "neither a love letter to, nor an indictment of, the suburbs—it's a letter *from* the suburbs," Win told *NME*. Suburban life is not exactly a subject that has gone unexamined by artists across disciplines, and for a band splitting the difference between messianic U2 and apocalyptic Radiohead, an opening lyric like "The businessmen drink my blood" is a little on-the-nose. But when you're putting those words in a song as gripping as "Ready to Start," they can be as on-the-nose as you want. Arcade Fire were an arena rock band even when they were playing tiny clubs, and arena rock was made for ostentatious gestures; you just have to come through with electrifying songs to make all the impassioned sloganeering feel profound.

The Suburbs largely delivered on that front. Though a bit meandering at times, the album was adventurous and light on its feet compared with *Neon Bible*. Its more refined but still emphatic sound felt like a natural maturation for the band, and it was dotted with some of their finest songs. The one that most validated the concept was "Sprawl II (Mountains Beyond Mountains)," the album's penultimate track. Sort of an epic update on Blondie's new wave classic "Heart of Glass," the song takes Win Butler off lead vocals and lets Régine Chassagne cook, turning midtempo synth pop into something theatrical and awe-inspiring. Her lyrics depict dead shopping malls as endless mountain ranges and the distant city lights as beacons for those who don't fit into the suburban mold: "Sometimes, I wonder if the world's so small/ That we can never get away from the sprawl."

The Suburbs was another critical and commercial success, debuting at No. 1 and elevating Arcade Fire's tours to the hockey and basketball sheds where they always belonged. Still, I don't think anyone foresaw the events of February 13, 2011. When *The Suburbs* was nominated for Album of the Year at the Grammys, their inclusion was surprising but not inconceivable. Arcade Fire had been in the world of power players and stodgy institutions for a while by then. But no one believed they would actually *win*. When the nominations came out, my future boss Scott Lapatine blogged at *Stereogum*:

Good job to Arcade Fire, who will lose Album Of The Year to one of these LPs:

Eminem—Recovery
Lady Antebellum—Need You Now
Lady Gaga—The Fame Monster
Katy Perry—Teenage Dream

Yet somehow, when Barbra Streisand stepped to the podium and opened the envelope, the name she read was not Eminem, Katy Perry, nor Ladies Gaga or Antebellum. After announcing, "And the Grammy goes to," all a flustered Babs could do was stutter, "The . . . Suburbs? . . . Arcade Fire!" The band was just as mystified, walking onstage with expressions of giddy disbelief. Win Butler's first words: "What the hell?" The band had just performed "Month of May" and was scheduled to return to the stage for "Ready to Start" to close out the ceremony; with that run of show, surely they must have had some inkling of what was in store. Then again, maybe not, because it really did not seem within the realm of possible outcomes. Arcade Fire? Won Album of the Year? For a release on Merge Records? All these years later I *still* kind of can't believe it.

The Suburbs wasn't the first Album of the Year on an independent label. Vaughn Meader's *The First Family*, a comedy LP(!) released on Cadence Records, took the award in 1963. Many subsequent winners were technically released on indies but distributed by majors, like the two prior victors, Taylor Swift's *Fearless* and Robert Plant and Alison Krauss's *Raising Sand*. As those superstar names imply, Arcade Fire were the only winners from anywhere near the world of indie rock, the only ones who could conceivably be considered underground artists—if you can say that about a band with a No. 1 album and heavy KROQ airplay that tours arenas and pals around with POTUS. For Pitchfork readers everywhere, it was a wild night.

The band that once joked about being the flavor of the month was now etched in history—or maybe they were now the flavor of the month on a much larger scale. Despite all the commercial and cultural breakthroughs Arcade Fire and their indie peers had achieved up to that point, the win perversely showed how far they remained from household-name status. In the aftermath, a Tumblr account called Who Is Arcade Fire??!!? compiled angry and befuddled social media posts from people who had no clue who this band was. "The grammy people have lost their mind... who are the Suburbs and how in the heck did they win album of the year... smh," wrote one Twitter user. Another posted, "Wow... really???!!!?! Arcade fire won album of the year?!!??!!???!! Never even heard of these fuggs!!!" Even Rosie O'Donnell chimed in, "album of the year ? umm never heard of them ever."

This was a perfect summary of where indie music stood at the dawn of the 2010s: embraced by gatekeepers, thriving at the box office, yet bereft of high-charting hits and overshadowed by weapons-grade rap, pop, and EDM. The process repeated at the 2012 Grammys, when Bon Iver took home Best New Artist over the Band Perry, J. Cole, Nicki Minaj, and Skrillex. For anyone even slightly familiar with Bon Iver, the win felt late. By that point Justin Vernon was two albums deep for the venerable Jagjaguwar label and had bounded into the mainstream as a guest on multiple Kanye West albums. The week after the Grammys, Justin Timberlake even parodied Bon Iver on *SNL*. Yet a new slew of confused and agitated social media posts manifested, with a special emphasis on the pronunciation of Bon Iver, necessitating the Twitter account @WhoIsBonnieBear to circulate messages like "J Cole shoulda won that shit! fuck that gummy bear group" and "who tf is bonnie bare or however you say that shit and he ugly."

Such tweets underlined the still-significant gap between your average music fan and the internet kingdom of blogs and Pitchfork, where Bon Iver's sophomore LP *Bon Iver, Bon Iver* had been named the best album of 2011 two months earlier. The record reinvented Justin Vernon's music as a remarkable strain of post-rock, making it sound like wide-open landscapes a world away from the woodland cabin of Bon Iver's origin story. Surprisingly, it also incorporated adult contemporary elements like smooth, sensuous saxophone and, on closing track "Beth/Rest," electric piano straight out of an '80s soft-rock ballad. Of course the first indie rocker to win Best New Artist at the Grammys did so by channeling Peter Cetera and Bruce Hornsby.

When Vernon received that trophy, soft rock and adult contemporary were having quite a moment in indie rock. In the mid-2000s, the comedic web series *Yacht Rock*, which lovingly satirized the smooth sounds of the '70s and '80s, had spread virally through blogs like *Stereogum*. Soon, elements of Steely Dan, the Doobie Brothers, Kenny Loggins, and the like started to work their way into indie rock with less and less irony. It might've started with Grizzly Bear, who—days after Jay-Z came to their show—released an alternate version of "While You Wait for the Others" with Michael McDonald on lead vocals. The cheesy AM pop revivalism of Ariel Pink's Haunted Graffiti became an indie sensation in 2010. By 2011, without even a trace of a wink, impassioned saxophone blasts could be heard on indie synth-pop band M83's nostalgic masterpiece "Midnight City," a sleek widescreen paean to the 1980s of our collective imagination.

One of the most acclaimed albums of 2011 was *Kaputt* by Destroyer, the project of the scruffy, professorial poet-crank Dan Bejar (also known as the New Pornographers' secret weapon, whereas Neko Case was their not-so-secret weapon). Bejar, a perennial critics' favorite, has changed up the sound of Destroyer a lot over the years, keeping only his wispy, Dylan-esque rasp and elliptical lyrics as a throughline. With *Kaputt*, he embraced a luxuriant sound that came off like a lite-jazz dream state, wearing it like a costume but not as a joke. "It slides between soft rock, smooth jazz, and new romantic pop," Mark Richardson wrote in Pitchfork's 8.8 Best New Music rave. "The bass is fretless; the synths have the blocky contrast of a Nagel painting; there are heavily reverbed trumpets and saxophones that almost serve as a Greek chorus, trilling away at the end of every line to enforce the beautiful plasticity of these songs."

This was a sound that would have been anathema on Lollapalooza '95 alongside Pavement, Hole, and Sonic Youth, yet in 2011 *Kaputt* became Bejar's most popular album by far among fans and critics alike. Its instant embrace as a canonical classic spoke volumes about how the indie audience's tastes had evolved and how far the word "indie" had been stretched. In 2001, Steely Dan's comeback album *Two Against Nature* beat Radiohead's *Kid A* for Album of the Year at the Grammys. Upon its release, Pitchfork's Brent DiCrescenzo, who wrote the site's infamous over-the-top *Kid A* review, excoriated *Two Against Nature* for its excessive smoothness in a 1.6 takedown. Yet now some of the acts being hailed as the indie vanguard were sounding a lot more like Steely Dan than Radiohead. It was enough to attract some Grammy love for the scene, but not enough to stop the music industry from replacing indie's would-be crossover stars with similar artists who boasted hits, not hipster clout.

* * *

If the public's perplexed reaction to indie music's Grammy breakthroughs was instructive, so was the roster of big winners in 2013, when alt-leaning bands with far less critical acclaim but way more commercial success began to eclipse the longstanding indie favorites. We'll get back to Best New Artist and Song of the Year eventually, but first: Album of the Year.

It went to *Babel* by Mumford & Sons, strummy British blokes who'd blown out indie-folk sounds to blockbuster scale. Mumford & Sons played extremely hearty acoustic music with the unhinged urgency of *Paste* favorites the Avett Brothers, usually without a drum set, while rocking the kinds of old-timey vests once seen on bands like Arcade Fire and the Decemberists. The band's rampant use of banjo felt like a bizarre Sufjan Stevens aftershock, and Marcus Mumford's howling, yowling vocals were like cultural runoff from Frightened Rabbit. At a time when rustic folksiness had become pervasive, Mumford reminded me of an overpriced "artisanal" restaurant that once served me dessert on a repurposed tree stump. Just as Pearl Jam and Nirvana eventually led to Creed and Nickelback, here was the butt-rock Bon Iver.

Mumford & Sons were leaders of a wave of radio-friendly artists that emerged in the early 2010s to make stomp-clap folk rock wildly popular and extremely uncool. The biggest hit of the bunch belonged to Denver's own Lumineers, whose 2012 debut single, "Ho Hey," climbed all the way to No. 3 on the Hot 100. That song plus "Little Talks," a cheerily trumpet-blaring Top 20 single by Iceland's Of Monsters and Men, combined to give this movement the perfectly derisive nickname "hey! folk" among the *Stereogum* staff. In 2012, even former pop-singer factory *American Idol*, in its last meaningful act of starmaking before dipping into irrelevance, launched winner Phillip Phillips with the Mumford soundalike "Home."

A common music industry cycle was underway. It was as if all the increasingly poppy indie-folk bands of the late 2000s had handed the baton to a new wave of artists that could more easily make hits because they were not beholden to hipster concepts of cool. And folk was hardly the only indie subgenre being replicated by more blatantly populist forces, especially when there was an obvious vacuum to swing into. In 2009, under the name Owl City, Minnesota bedroom producer Adam Young scored a No. 1 mega-hit with the saccharine electro-pop song "Fireflies" by shamelessly ripping off the Postal Service.

Similarly, in 2011, right when breakout stars MGMT were retreating from the spotlight, LA commercial jingle writer Mark Foster channeled the duo's festival-ready psych-pop vibe on the airy, whistling No. 3 smash "Pumped Up Kicks." That same year, another LA band called Capital Cities released "Safe and Sound," an EDM-shaded synth-pop track that played like the zombified corpse of MGMT's "Kids." It took years, but in 2013 "Safe and Sound" broke through and soared to No. 8. But of all the many wannabe MGMTs, perhaps no one jacked their swag as brazenly or immediately as Empire Of The Sun, an Australian duo in goofy costumes whose 2008 psych-tinged synth-pop single "Walking on a Dream" was like adult contemporary *Oracular Spectacular*. Empire Of The Sun sounded so much like MGMT that noted indie aficionado Jay-Z called them in to replace MGMT on 2009's *The Blueprint 3*, as MGMT's Andrew VanWyngarden explained in a *Stereogum* interview:

> Our managers connected us with Jay-Z's manager and said that they wanted to collaborate, and they sent us a beat that Kanye West had made. We were like, "This is cool." For over a week, we dropped everything. We're like, "We're gonna fucking make a Jay-Z song! This is insane." We had our whole studio set up, and Ben and I ended up making this vampiric, horror-rap beat with this really strange chord progression. Then we fit

chords over the chorus that was Kanye West's disco beat, and we were just like, "This is sick." It sounded awesome. We sent it and then had a conference call with Jay-Z. He was like, "This is cool, but I want you guys to do your MGMT thing." And we're like, "OK," and at that point, we knew it wasn't really in the cards, but we had this song. I still have it in my email. It's really fun. Anyway, flash forward a few months, and they got Empire Of The Sun to sing the chorus over the chords that we had written.

Foster The People, Capital Cities, Empire Of The Sun: These bands were all flashes in the pan, one-hit wonders hocking the musical equivalent of fast fashion. But not all short-lived success stories are the same. Consider the case of the 2013 Grammy winners for Best New Artist.

Nate Ruess, Andrew Dost, and Jack Antonoff formed Fun in New York City in 2008. All three members had been part of underground bands playing some permutation of emo-leaning indie rock that had little to do with any Pitchfork zeitgeist. Ruess fronted the shimmering pop-rock band the Format. Dost was an instrumentalist in the blog-rocky Anathallo. And Antonoff was doing a twee Springsteen thing as the leader of Steel Train. As Fun, they set loose Ruess's nasal wail on songs that put a shiny modern spin on '70s pop and rock. The band's 2009 debut *Aim and Ignite* channeled theatrical talents like Elton John and Freddie Mercury but still sounded cutesy and sensitive in a very 2009 way: a stack of baroque indie-pop suites piled up with vocal harmonies, violins, and flugelhorns galore, shot through with theater-kid energy and MySpace-emo sass. Fun became a cult favorite, just as the members' prior bands had been, but this time they wanted more.

Like many people back then, the members of Fun had been entranced by the maximalist sound of Kanye West's *My Beautiful Dark Twisted Fantasy*. They wanted their own songs to feel that massive and indestructible, so when they signed to the Atlantic subsidiary Fueled by Ramen for their second album, they worked hard to get the attention of Jeff Bhasker, the producer who'd worked closely with Kanye to craft that aesthetic. Bhasker helped Fun streamline their songs and laced them with powerhouse programmed beats that captured that monolithic *MBDTF* feel. The result was *Some Nights*, an album of sometimes grating but often inspired state-of-the-art pop rock fit for gazing at both your navel and the stars.

Lead single "We Are Young"—the first rock song to top the Hot 100 in a decade, and the 2013 Grammy winner for Song of the Year—expanded from sparse, neurotic verses to a lighters-up chorus about dealing with your problems by getting shitfaced and feeling indestructible. That hook was ideal for shouting in groups at the top of your lungs: "Tonight, we are young/ So let's set the world on fire/ We can burn brighter than the sun!" But no one sang it better than Ruess. "He has a huge voice, all snarl and Broadway panache," Jody Rosen wrote in *Rolling Stone*. "At his full-fathom best, he could send Adam Lambert scrambling for cover."

Title track "Some Nights," a No. 3 hit, worked in part because it stacked that voice into bombastic harmonies and paired it with militaristic rolling snares. All throughout the album, it was as if Fun's old sound was now encased in an Iron Man suit. Ruess could sometimes sound like a twerp when leaning into his starry-eyed underdog routine—an avatar for his generation's struggle with Peter Pan syndrome. But his talent and charisma outweighed his lost-puppy qualities, and the music sounded remarkably fresh, including Ruess's embrace of Auto-Tune (another Kanye-favored technique). Not many rock bands were trying that yet, and the ones who had attempted it were often clowned for their efforts. But as Ruess went full "Runaway" on the album's climactic power ballad "Stars," he sounded like he was forging ahead into the future.

It would be a future without Fun. The band toured *Some Nights* hard and graduated to much larger venues, but when the promotional cycle wrapped up, Ruess opted to turn his next batch of songs into a solo album. That choice left Dost hanging and freed up Antonoff, the band's bespectacled guitarist, to start a new band called Bleachers. The project's 2014 debut *Strange Desire* updated his penchant for '80s nostalgia in stylish new ways. I was impressed.

But Bleachers wouldn't turn out to be Antonoff's most important contribution to the modern music landscape. Not even Fun qualify for that designation. Instead, he'd become best known as a prolific producer and songwriter, a central figure in bridging the gap between the sounds of indie and pop. It didn't happen overnight, but the process started almost as soon as Fun went on indefinite hiatus, around the time he landed some credits on an album called *1989*.

Chapter 9 Soundtrack

Passion Pit, "Sleepyhead" (2007)

MGMT, "Kids" (2007)

Empire Of The Sun, "Walking on a Dream" (2008)

Phoenix, "1901" (2009)

Animal Collective, "My Girls" (2009)

Neon Indian, "Deadbeat Summer" (2009)

Vivian Girls, "Where Do You Run To" (2008)

Washed Out, "Feel It All Around" (2009)

Real Estate, "Beach Comber" (2009)

Toro y Moi, "Blessa" (2009)

Ariel Pink's Haunted Graffiti, "Round and Round" (2010)

Beach Fossils, "Daydream" (2010)

Best Coast, "When I'm With You" (2009)

Wavves, "King of the Beach" (2010)

The Drums, "Let's Go Surfin'" (2009)

Foster The People, "Pumped Up Kicks" (2010)

M83, "Midnight City" (2011)

Beach House, "Myth" (2012)

Tame Impala, "Feels Like We Only Go Backwards" (2012)

Mac DeMarco, "Ode to Viceroy" (2012)

9

Terminally Chill

Vibey psychedelia for fests, fashion, ads & algorithms

I made a lot of mistakes at Bonnaroo 2009. I missed all of Bruce Springsteen & the E Street Band's headlining set while waiting for my friends at our tent. I left early from what turned out to be Beastie Boys' final live show to catch part of David Byrne's performance, not realizing Adam Yauch would be dead from cancer three years later. And I skipped most of what was billed as Nine Inch Nails' farewell concert to go see MGMT.

That last one I can justify to myself, kind of. MGMT were a huge deal at the time. With their 2007 debut album *Oracular Spectacular*, produced by the Flaming Lips' sonic consigliere Dave Fridmann, former Wesleyan classmates Andrew VanWyngarden and Ben Goldwasser had transformed psychedelic rock into commercial-friendly synth pop. *Very* commercial-friendly, it turned out. The album's big three singles—the synth-pop monolith "Time to Pretend," the contagious disco-funk pastiche

"Electric Feel," and the surging keyboard anthem "Kids"—became inescapable fixtures of pop culture. Again and again, those songs appeared in ads and video games, at fashion shows and sporting events, in the background of TV shows and movies. For a few years there, every house party and rock-oriented dance night I attended was guaranteed to feature MGMT on the playlist, and never was I mad about it.

Now I was all set to encounter those same songs at Bonnaroo in the middle of the night. This felt significant, both because of the band and because of the setting. Along with Coachella in the California desert and Lollapalooza in Downtown Chicago, Bonnaroo—held every June on a farm in Manchester, Tennessee—was one of a handful of American music festivals that by the end of the 2000s had developed into tentpole events for youth music culture, like whole chunks of the music-blog ecosystem coming to life one weekend at a time. The 'Roo started out in 2002 with a jam-band focus, but soon enough it was catering to indie fans like me alongside the Phish partisans. And in 2009, I felt *extremely* catered to.

That year, albums by the indie bands Grizzly Bear, Animal Collective, Phoenix, Dirty Projectors, and Yeah Yeah Yeahs were so universally praised by critics that users of the hipster message board ILX coined the term "GAPDY" as a catchall term to mock the overbearing consensus. All five of those bands played Bonnaroo 2009. So did Bon Iver, St. Vincent, TV On The Radio, Yeasayer, Jenny Lewis, of Montreal, the Decemberists, Passion Pit, Santigold, Chairlift, Ted Leo & the Pharmacists, Okkervil River, and the jammy but eternally indie-friendly Wilco. The presence of so many Pitchfork pets on the lineup said something about the evolution of Bonnaroo, but it said even more about the evolution of indie rock. The music of bloggers and MySpace was developing into the music of festivals, a broadly appealing genre jumble that bore less and less resemblance to the insular indie of old. The idea that a field full of indie bands would be a weekend-long dance party now seemed intuitive.

Few bands summed up that transformation better than MGMT. Although they were signed to Columbia and therefore not officially an indie band, the hits from *Oracular Spectacular* were the epitome of indie's shift toward festival-rocking pop. They relied on synths at least as much as guitars, boasted gargantuan hooks and highly danceable rhythms, and stoked nostalgia by calling back to the most accessible elements of '60s psych pop, '70s disco, and '80s new wave. The album cover even telegraphed the festival association: a shirtless VanWyngarden on the beach in board shorts with a colorful scarf around his neck, Goldwasser next to him rocking some kind of tribal getup, both of them looking like they'd either like to sell you some tabs of ecstasy or "borrow" a few of yours. A 2:15 A.M. set by this band—at the height of their fame, at one of the most important music festivals in the world—seemed destined to unfold as a transcendent psychedelic rave. Instead, I was privy to a wigged-out performance from a band way more mercurial than I'd realized.

I had failed to appreciate how much of *Oracular Spectacular* was trippy, exploratory fare that cut against the pleasure-center immediacy of the singles. I had also failed to anticipate that MGMT were more interested in becoming a brilliant weirdo cult band than stadium-filling superstars, and that they were already in the process of recoiling from music industry fame. "We got a glimpse of that and shrunk back," VanWyngarden told *The Guardian* in 2010. "We thought, hmmm, I dunno. Let's write a really weird album."

At Bonnaroo, MGMT seemed ambivalent about their hits.

They appeared to be way more invested in their deep cuts, a cover of 'Til Tuesday's "Voices Carry" with Chairlift's Caroline Polachek, and a crop of anxiously quirky new songs. Many of those would end up on 2010's *Congratulations*, a strange and low-key genius album that played more like an act of self-sabotage at the time. Only when they re-emerged to encore with "Kids" did the crowd properly explode, and even then the guys were only halfway taking it seriously, singing over tracks as if doing a karaoke version of their own song.

There'd been no such messing around the prior evening, when Phoenix took the stage ahead of post-midnight sets from Crystal Castles and Girl Talk. Phoenix were consummate professionals who hailed from the same Parisian music scene that yielded Daft Punk. Their first two albums had dabbled in a kind of chic alternative dance pop, but on 2006's *It's Never Been Like That*, they'd dropped the electronics and leaned into a clean-lined pop-rock format, writing tight little guitar-centric tunes that inspired Pitchfork to dub them the "soft-rock Strokes." Singer Thomas Mars's holographic voice, which had sounded great spitting broken English over synthesizers and programmed beats, was even more winsome crooning neon hooks over breezy, dynamic guitar pop. In 2006, the soft-rock Strokes were making music infinitely more vital than the actual Strokes.

It's Never Been Like That is a masterpiece, but Phoenix's true breakthrough would be 2009's *Wolfgang Amadeus Phoenix*, an also-spectacular album that reapplied some of that old synthetic shine to the band's new guitar-powered sound. It was a record full of smooth, gleaming surfaces, on which every vocal glowed like a smartphone screen and every song glided like a luxury car. Or maybe I'm just drawing that association because Cadillac put the synths-and-guitars joyride "1901," one of *Wolfgang Amadeus*

Phoenix's many boutique-ready bangers, in a commercial for the SRX. The ad helped push "1901" onto the *Billboard* Hot 100 by the end of the year, but by then it had already been inducted into my personal hall of fame. This music felt like pure lifestyle product, far removed from every kind of underground scuzz and socio-political heft. Yet as a pure sonic achievement it was sleek, sophisticated, and deeply satisfying. I couldn't get enough.

MGMT's "Kids" and Phoenix's "1901" were far from the only blog-world favorites received as actual hits at Bonnaroo that year. Massachusetts synth-poppers Passion Pit were there, fresh off the release of their debut album, *Manners*. A year prior they'd nudged indie music in an altogether poppier direction with breakthrough single "Sleepyhead," a synth-pop bomb drop that paired singer Michael Angelakos's helium-voiced falsetto with an even higher vocal sample resembling the "chipmunk soul" production style of early Kanye West. Grizzly Bear were on hand to perform "Two Weeks" two months before Jay-Z got to it. Yeah Yeah Yeahs kicked out "Zero" and "Heads Will Roll" from their synth-pop pivot *It's Blitz!*, sounding just as ferocious in their electronic era as in their garage band days. The often abstract and pretentious Dirty Projectors trotted out "Stillness Is the Move," a surprisingly straightforward alt-R&B gem that will be earning comparisons to Mariah Carey for all eternity.

And then there was Animal Collective, whose rise spoke volumes about the changes in indie music writ large. AnCo had broken through by strumming acoustic guitars and making tripped-out campfire songs, challenging listeners and purposefully operating on the fringes. But for years now they'd been spending their performances hunched over electronic equipment like a DJ crew, steering their music in a direction that might not cause your most basic acquaintances to run away screaming.

The band named 2009's *Merriweather Post Pavilion* after the Maryland amphitheater where they'd grown up seeing large-scale concerts. The album lived up to that billing, blowing out AnCo's Beach-Boys-gone-feral pop experiments into songs fit for EDM laser light shows. *Merriweather* leaked in December 2008, and by the time it officially dropped a few days into the new year, indie critics were hailing the album as an instant classic. Pitchfork dropped a 9.6 on it, and *Stereogum* published a post cheekily headlined, on January 5, "Is *Merriweather Post Pavilion* The Best Album Of 2009?"

Merriweather boasted crowd-pleasers like the frenetic bodymover "Brother Sport" and "In the Flowers," a song that sounded more like a fireworks display than the AnCo song actually titled "Fireworks." But the album's signature track is "My Girls," a jubilant sing-along on which Panda Bear addresses the most commonplace of concerns—providing for his family's fundamental needs—against a backdrop that sounds like aliens landing their spaceship on Earth and teaching humanity how to dance. The middle of Friday afternoon was not an ideal setting for songs that belonged in a nightclub crossed with a planetarium, but the particulars of AnCo's Bonnaroo experience weren't about to alter their trajectory much. By the summer of 2009, Animal Collective were already conquering heroes. Their success raised the question: If even esoteric freaks like these guys could successfully pivot to pop, how high could indie's most accessible talents soar?

* * *

A month after my Bonnaroo expedition, a new trend was cohering within the indie blogosphere. It emerged in the shadow of *Merriweather Post Pavilion*, but whereas Animal Collective's brand of psychedelic synth music was hi-fi, much of this subgenre sounded old and faded, as if dubbed from a cassette tape left out in the sun. The most common read was that young millennials who were graduating into the Great Recession were engaging with their foggy memories of '80s pop as a way of transporting themselves back to childhood to escape their crushing economic situation. Here was the retro technology side of Mark Greif's "green" hipster archetype, obsessed with recapturing lost innocence not by communing with nature in an earthy hippie way but by flashing back to childhood beach vacations and Apple IIe computers.

As is their wont, critics and bloggers tried to tag the emerging style with a snappy genre label. Some called it "glo-fi," which was accurate enough. Others opted for the dreadfully clumsy "hypnagogic pop." For a while there *Gorilla vs. Bear*, a popular MP3 blog that made this kind of dazed, hyper-online pop music central to its ethos, was using the term "dreamwave." The name that ultimately stuck, "chillwave," started off as a joke—kind of? I think? It wasn't always fully clear if Carles was joking.

Carles, later revealed as the alias of Carlos Perez, was the author of *Hipster Runoff*, the smartest, meanest, funniest blog ever to cover indie music and all its cultural scaffolding. Carles could be cruel in his attempts to assess art and see through posturing—both other people's and his own—but he was incredibly savvy about the hipster self-image and how the music industry sausage was made. His posts blurred the line between the hype manufactured by his fellow bloggers and the many corporate attempts to co-opt that hype—always in character, always deploying quotation marks so wantonly that it was never clear how ironic or sincere he was trying to be. A 2015 *Vice* feature headlined "The Last

Relevant Blogger," occasioned by Carles's decision to sell *Hipster Runoff*, succinctly explained his whole deal:

> HRO was part relentless hipster scene chronicle, part relentless satirization of that scene, part shameless clickbait, part self-reflexive critique of the entire online economy ... [Carles's] best trick was repurposing the cumbersome brand jargon that marketers use to describe the experience of the youth they target, and reciting it from his own prismatic stream of conscious. Carles aspires 2 be 'relevant,' bb, and 'authentic' and 2 have a 'meaningful experience' by consuming products 'for all the right reasons,' embracing 'alt' trends like 'chillwave' and rejecting 'lamestream' bros. He bluntly exposes the contrivances that hipsters, tastemakers, and advertisers alike use to create the perception that there exists an experience better and more unique than the one being lived by 'average' Americans—while still asserting them.

On July 27, 2009, Carles published a post titled "Is WASHED OUT the next Neon Indian/Memory Cassette?" It offered up several dozen barely serious labels for this burgeoning scene before landing here: "Feel like I might call it 'chill wave' music in the future. Feels like 'chill wave' is dominated by 'thick/chill synths' while conceptual core is still trying to 'use real instruments/sound like it was recorded in nature.' Feel like chillwave is supposed to sound like something that was playing in the background of 'an old VHS cassette that u found in ur attic from the late '80s/early '90s.'" To his surprise, other people started saying "chillwave" with a straight face, and the term gained purchase far beyond blogger world.

Chillwave's Mount Rushmore comprised four young men

of different ethnic backgrounds from across the East Coast and American South, all of whom simultaneously began accumulating hype in July 2009. The scene's home base was the internet, but if it had a geographical center, it was Columbia, South Carolina, where two of the Big Four resided. One was Toro y Moi, aka Chaz Bundick, whose breakthrough single "Blessa" was a woozy, wobbly, easy listening extension of the Beach-Boys-sound-collage style pioneered by Panda Bear's *Person Pitch*. *Stereogum* called it "some kind of Animal Collective-via-bedroom J Dilla" and "perfect for a breezy summer afternoon."

"Blessa" exuded the quarter-life restlessness and longing for a return to youth that came to typify chillwave. Bundick sang about his desire to reconnect with an ex from his teenage years who'd moved away from their hometown, and about the struggle to make a living through whatever employment he could find after the subprime mortgage collapse: "I found a job/ I do it fine/ Not what I want/ But still I try." He also, of course, sang about summer. Chillwave was about nothing if not the yearning to live in an endless, idealized fantasy summer, and the genre's warped synthesizers sounded better and better as the weather got hotter and hotter. There's a reason this stuff popped off in July.

Bundick's friend, collaborator, and fellow Columbia resident Ernest Greene recorded as Washed Out. Greene's own signature track, "Feel It All Around"—you might know it as the *Portlandia* theme song—slowed down Italian singer Gary Low's sprightly 1983 synth-pop tune "I Want You" until it felt like drifting down a river on an innertube under a scorching, blinding sun. He topped it off with sighing, echo-laden harmonies and lyrics that addressed the possibility of rekindled romance in the language of pure, unadulterated vibes: "You feel it all around yourself/ You know it's yours and no one else." It's hard to think of a more majestic chillwave track, or one that better encapsulates the genre's sonic approach.

Up in Philadelphia, Davye Hawk had been releasing tracks under the aliases Memory Cassette and Weird Tapes for about a year when chillwave surged into the spotlight. Hawk, who switched his band name to Memory Tapes around the time this music became a media sensation, never had a song as iconic as the rest of the main chillwave bros. But he arguably pioneered the style by taking the synth psych practiced by the Flaming Lips, MGMT, and Animal Collective in a blurrier, dancier direction and slapping it with song titles like "Surfin" and "Body in the Water."

And then there was Alan Palomo. The Mexican-born, Texas-raised artist didn't totally fit in with the other chillwave mainstays. His music as Neon Indian was funkier, livelier, more immediate. Most chillwave artists sounded like social outcasts in their childhood bedrooms working through their failure to launch; Palomo sounded suave and charismatic, and he carried himself like a star—perhaps a skill set he learned from his father, Jorge, a former Mexican pop singer. But Palomo made retro synth music, and with track titles like "Deadbeat Summer," "Terminally Chill," and "Should Have Taken Acid with You," Neon Indian's inclusion in the wave of chill was practically preordained.

By the end of 2009's so-called Deadbeat Summer, chillwave had become a huge deal within indie circles. Not everyone liked it, and not every artist was influenced by it, but it grew so big so fast that you had to have an opinion on it. Chillwave took off so quickly not only because of slick branding, but because it fit into a broader cultural convergence of new and retro technologies, of underground and mainstream sensibilities, of art and business. As Ian Cohen put it in a 2019 *Stereogum* retrospective, chillwave was "at the center of a cluster of indie culture trends bubbling up toward the end of the decade—Hipstamatic and the revival of Polaroid, a proliferation of vinyl and cassette labels, Urban Outfitters' incessant need for store-mix fodder, tastemaking music blogs, Tumblr, a curious wave of guitar bands reveling in beach iconography and surf music, and above all, the so-ironic-it-might-actually-be-sincere pose of Carles."

That list of trends shared roots in a prevailing generational mood. In a 2015 *Vice* feature about what he called the Vibe Generation, the insightful critic Larry Fitzmaurice connected the dots between chillwave and other early 2010s indie music that shared its escape-from-reality ethos: "an increased embrace of sampling and electronics, a de-emphasizing of guitars, a sonic approach that favored tactile sensuality rather than the bookish sensibilities that pervaded 2000s alternative music, and an unabashed love of all things retro, from Tangerine Dream to fruit punch Gushers, that has defined this decade's youth as a people that find the present too painful to exist in."

Chillwave artists and their listeners were driven by deep longings to return to some purer, easier, happier time in the hazy corners of their memory. But as with the freak-folk artists who sought a primitive, Edenic state, it was remarkable how quickly the marketplace stripped the bubbling subgenre of its raw pathos and transformed it into pure lifestyle product. The same impulses that gave us chillwave led to a future of "beats to study/relax to" YouTube channels, latecomers like Poolside creating music that seemed to be expressly aimed at Tommy Bahama storefronts, and EDM-adjacent producers like Tycho making the sonic equivalent of a screensaver.

At first, though, this stuff was all pretty amateurish. The main chillwave acts descended upon SXSW in March 2010, at the peak of the festival's buzz-building power, which led to a perfect time capsule of a *Gorilla vs. Bear* post: a Polaroid photo gallery of a Toro y Moi, Warpaint, and Washed Out show at Urban Outfitters. The abundance of chillwave bands in Austin that year also inspired a scathing assessment from *The New York Times* under the headline "Glo-fi—Just Another Blip?" "The songs come across like geek daydreams: half-remembered Top 40 songs and dance hits sung by guys too shy to leave their rooms," wrote Jon Pareles.

The *Times* takedown spawned a *Village Voice* response from Brandon Soderberg titled "In Defense of Chillwave," though even that ostensibly supportive analysis negged the genre as "something solely focused on trying to sound like Christopher Cross on muscle relaxers." The fact that a lot of the singers couldn't really sing could be perceived as punk in the same way that confrontationally soft and amateurish indie-pop bands like Beat Happening were punk. The notion that you don't have to be a conventionally talented singer to sing is certainly in line with punk and indie rock history, but in chillwave's case it existed in tension with production that translated seamlessly to the retail environment.

As chillwave entrenched itself in the indie landscape, its main acts started releasing albums and carving out their own niches apart from the genre's baseline aesthetic. Yet that initial chillwave sound became pervasive as artists working in a similar vein, from Small Black to Wild Nothing, were vacuumed up by indie labels. The phenomenon demanded a genealogy, so visionaries like Animal Collective's Panda Bear and Deerhunter's Bradford Cox, thanks to his dreamy solo project Atlas Sound, were hailed as chillwave progenitors. But the consensus godfather of chillwave was Ariel Pink.

Pink, born Ariel Rosenberg, first rose to niche stardom as a

Los Angeles outsider artist releasing music on Animal Collective's Paw Tracks label. His albums under the name Ariel Pink's Haunted Graffiti, culled from a treasure trove of home recordings he'd squirreled away over the years, presented zonked lo-fi reinterpretations of '70s and '80s retro kitsch, from AM Gold to commercial jingles. Albums like 2004's *The Doldrums* are knotty labyrinths—theoretically pop, but with the hooks buried under layers of impenetrable weirdness. Yet on songs like "Don't Talk to Strangers" and "So Glad," both from 2006's *Loverboy*, Pink pioneered a warped, hazy revival of '80s synth pop at its cheesiest. "It's hard to know how much Ariel's output is responsible for a new crop of musicians running their own tracks through crusty VHS tapes to capture that hazy analog ambiance," Pitchfork's Ryan Schreiber wrote in 2010, "but it's hard to deny that Pink's public access–style demo jams sounded like a lot of what now gets called chillwave as far back as 2002."

Eventually, Ariel Pink's Haunted Graffiti expanded from a concept to an actual band and secured a record deal with 4AD, making them labelmates with indie household names like the National and St. Vincent. Pink became an indie celebrity himself with his first 4AD album, 2010's *Before Today*, recorded in a studio and featuring some of his cleanest, most approachable songs to date. The album's big single was "Round and Round," a melancholy yet majestically funky soft-rock anthem with what Schreiber described as "rollerskate verses" and a "crazy-melodic John Hughes prom chorus."

Pitchfork went all-in on Ariel Pink in 2010, gracing *Before Today* with a 9.0 Best New Music endorsement and ranking "Round and Round" as the best song of the year. "In 2010, Ariel Pink was the strange kid who fucked around all semester and developed a reputation as a hopeless loser who then proceeded to blow everyone's minds at the talent show," Mark Richardson wrote in the site's year-end listicle. "And in the end, 'Round and Round' succeeds brilliantly for the same reason great Burt Bacharach songs work—because every chord change and turnaround and melodic leap is in exactly the right place." A favorable comparison to Burt Bacharach? Best known to my generation as the schmaltzy piano man from *Austin Powers*? This was quite a sentiment coming from the website that introduced me to indie rock a decade earlier, and it spoke to a hipster palate that had been turned completely inside out.

At the peak of all this soft-rock kitsch, at a time when festival-ready synth pop like Passion Pit and prestige arena rock like the National were also proliferating, there were plenty of newly minted underground stars playing lo-fi guitar music, too. But it speaks volumes about the millennial psyche that many of those rockers were just as fixated on the beach and vibey nostalgia as the chillwave bros, and they used similarly hazy recording techniques to get their summer fantasias across. This was the era of Surfer Blood and Sun Airway, of the Drums' "Let's Go Surfin'" and Real Estate's "Let's Rock the Beach," of a dreamy band called Beach Fossils whose guitarist left to start an even dreamier band called DIIV.

The first of the beach bands to come crashing to the shore was literally called Wavves, though to Nathan Williams's credit, his band name predated "chillwave" by a whole year. Williams was a young upstart from San Diego who looked a bit like *Home Alone* star Macaulay Culkin. Pulling inspiration from both skate punk and noise pop, he played deeply distorted Beach-Boys-meet-Nirvana tracks with simplistic arrangements and repetitive titles. Songs on sophomore album *Wavvves* included "Beach Demon," "Beach Goth," "Surf Goth," "Summer Goth," "California Goths," "Sun Opens My Eyes," and "Gun in the Sun."

In late 2008, between the release of his first and second albums, an insane hype storm began to swirl around Williams. In March 2009, LP2 was blessed with Best New Music status and a grade-A review from The A.V. Club among other raves, and by the time Wavves got to SXSW two weeks later, they were both the buzziest and most controversial act in Austin. Some celebrated Williams's preternatural songwriting touch, while others knocked the band's rudimentary approach and messy live show. From *Stereogum*'s festival recap: "Interesting to see how divisive he's been down here—everyone has a strong opinion (e.g. when a friend realized who was about to play, he actually walked out in 'mock' disgust)." The haters included my Columbus neighbors Psychedelic Horseshit—members of a Midwest lo-fi scene that had been building steam for a few years prior, jokingly known as "shitgaze"—who made homemade "WAVVES SUXX" T-shirts despite performing at some of the same showcases with Williams.

The excitement and hostility surrounding Wavves continued to intensify until May, when Williams had a spectacular drug-fueled meltdown onstage at Barcelona's famed Primavera Sound festival, breathlessly detailed in a first-person Pitchfork report by Schreiber himself. "Finally, fed up with Nathan's petulant behavior, [drummer Ryan Ulsh] ran out from behind his drumkit and poured a full cup of beer over Nathan's head," the Pitchfork founder wrote. "The act would be met with their most enthusiastic applause of the evening."

Williams apologized in a note the next day, saying he'd snapped under mounting pressure and an exhausting tour schedule. But Wavves barely slowed down. After a few months laying low, they kept touring, adjusted their lineup, and recorded summer 2010's *King of the Beach*, an album that elevated both their fidelity and their songcraft. Dubbing himself the king of the beach amidst indie music's obsession with sandy shores was an audacious move, but the maniacally catchy, hard-hitting songs backed up the bravado. "You're never gonna stop me!" Williams sang on the title track, and at least until the song ended, it felt true.

By then, a queen of the beach had emerged. Bethany Cosentino was a Los Angeles native who'd been a child actor, a *Fader* intern, and a member of the experimental drone act Pocahaunted. In 2009, she moved back home from New York and founded Best Coast with Bobb Bruno, a local producer who she knew from LA's legendary indie venue the Smell. Early singles like "Sun Was High (So Was I)" were in step with the reverb-drenched Phil Spector revivalism practiced by blogger-adored bands like Dum Dum Girls and Vivian Girls. Cosentino fleshed out the band's moodboard with well-chosen covers by artists like Lesley Gore and the Beach Boys. But the song that crystallized Best Coast's appeal and shot them to indie stardom was "When I'm with You," a surging, jangling echo-chamber love song that could almost be mistaken for a lost girl-group classic from the 1960s.

Best Coast kept releasing tracks and building clamorous buzz until the summer 2010 release of debut album *Crazy for You*, which replicated the "When I'm With You" approach across a dozen more lovesick guitar-pop gems. From the ultra-catchy, reverb-soaked opening track "Boyfriend" onward, it was a clinic in back-to-basics songwriting with an artful touch—like a hip rejoinder to Weezer's sleek and streamlined Green Album, evoking teenage love and heartbreak via sentiments as plainspoken as "I wish he was my boyfriend."

The music was killer, earning Best New Music status and winning widespread praise. But it also attracted more than its share of detractors who took issue with Cosentino's crazy/lazy/baby rhyme schemes, narrow thematic focus, and allegedly formulaic songwriting. At a time when the social web was coming into its own and newly minted celebrities had to navigate that terrain with no guidebook, she faced startling amounts of vitriol in blog comment sections, on social media, and at *Hipster Runoff*, where Carles turned poking and prodding at Best Coast into a sport. Cosentino was subjected to a smaller-scale version of the tabloid treatment that besieged the likes of Britney Spears and Lindsay Lohan—and with Drew Barrymore directing a Best Coast video that featured stars like Donald Glover and Shailene Woodley, for a while there it seemed like Cosentino might ascend to that level of fame.

Amplifying both the public intrigue and the vitriol was Cosentino's status as one half of a buzzy (and perpetually buzzed) power couple with Nathan Williams of Wavves. Williams and Cosentino reveled in their smoked-out, freewheeling existence. They went on tour together. They cracked jokes about giving "joint" interviews and hobnobbed with rappers like Freddie Gibbs. They seemed to be having great fun, but their existence infuriated some people. One *Stereogum* commenter dubbed them "The Heidi Montag and Spencer Pratt of indie rokk," and I can only imagine the misogynistic barbs that once lingered under posts at *Brooklyn Vegan*, where anonymous commenting was eventually shut down because it became too toxic. At *Hipster Runoff*, Carles joked that Pitchfork gave *King of the Beach* and *Crazy for You* the same 8.4 rating to avoid "relationship conflict"; he later posted invasive reports about the couple's personal business, such as one about Williams hotboxing Cosentino's home while house-sitting for her.

Cosentino responded to the attention by tweeting "hipster runoff can eat a dick," which inevitably inspired another Carles blog post. An excerpt:

> Does Best Coast h8 being blogged about on HIPSTER RUNOFF?
>
> Has HIPSTER RUNOFF been "harsh" on Best Coast?
>
> Are buzzbands angry when HIPSTER RUNOFF blogs about them?
>
> Does Best Coast h8 all blogs, or just HIPSTER RUNOFF?
>
> Is Best Coast pissed at HIPSTER RUNOFF for blogging about her everytime she twitpics bags of dank?

Though Cosentino later confessed to taking every bit of criticism personally, in public she seemed unfazed—especially on Twitter, where her knack for personal branding further elevated her indie celebrity stature. Mirroring *Crazy for You*'s lyrical content, Cosentino filled her highly quotable timeline with quips about her love for weed, the sun, California, and her cat, Snacks, who appeared on the album cover and became an important character within the Best Coast extended universe, even getting his own @Snacksthecat account on the same platform. All this tweeting wasn't so different from the way Lily Allen supplemented her tunes on MySpace with cheeky blogging and stylish selfies, and it predicted the way future indie stars like fellow LA native Phoebe Bridgers were able to build a cult of personality with tweets that complemented her music.

A savvy social media presence is not the only way Best Coast helped to map out the future of music celebrity. Just before her debut album dropped, Cosentino became one of many indie musicians to partner with Converse on the release of new music, collaborating with Kid Cudi and Vampire Weekend's Rostam Batmanglij on a song called (naturally) "All Summer." Best Coast and Wavves also teamed up on a track for *The Christmas Gig*, a compilation of original indie Christmas songs, available as a free download at Target's website. Hollywood's indie music fascination was peaking. Brands like Scion and Mountain Dew were throwing concerts and commissioning singles to be distributed as free MP3s. Money from corporate America was funneling into indie music, and lots of artists were doing one-off collabs with apparel brands and giant corporations. But not many had their own fashion lines.

Cosentino's mom was a fashion designer, Bethany herself had dabbled in making her own clothes growing up, and at *Fader* she'd penned a fashion column called "Thrintage" in which she reviewed thrift stores and vintage shops. In 2012 she leveraged that expertise by launching her own line at Urban Outfitters, presaging a world where every pop star's music began to feel like an ad campaign for their personally branded lifestyle products. Cosentino's line was part of UO's vintage-leaning Urban Renewal series, and it directly aligned with the company's standardization of the thrift-store experience. Cosentino said as much in a 2012 Pitchfork interview: "I love thrift shopping, but sometimes I find things that don't fit right, or are just missing something, like a few buttons, or a side zipper. So doing this line was like getting to take my favorite thrift store outfit and turn it into something really cool and modern."

The fashion focus made Best Coast an ideal fit for publications like the rising pop-culture-meets-style women's magazine *Nylon* and the rapidly expanding community of young women and girls on the microblogging platform Tumblr. But the same ventures that appealed so directly to women riled up certain sectors of the male-dominated indie music world, and they tended to become ammunition for Cosentino's critics. "Before people get carried away, realize that there's plenty of precedent for this: Kim Gordon did a line for UO in 2009 and Alexa Chung (though not a musician, obviously) still has a line for Madewell," warned *Stereogum* atop a sarcastic comment section.

Cosentino is not above critique, but it's hard to miss the pattern: When blog commenters took their best shot at mainstream-facing indie stars, there was often an element of misogyny at play. So many of the era's most viciously derided artists were women, especially those who brought an unapologetically girly perspective to their work. The indie world was not accustomed to that perspective—skimming through reviews of Best Coast's 2012 album *The Only Place*, it's impossible not to notice they're all by dudes—and as a more expressly feminine outlook continued to impact the genre throughout the 2010s, the pushback from some quarters would be intense.

Prejudice aside, it did not help Cosentino's cause that *The Only Place*, a clean-lined collection recorded with the great Jon Brion, was a step down from the hazy and inspired *Crazy for You*. Writing in North Carolina's *Indy Week*, the esteemed journalist Grayson Haver Currin dismissed Best Coast LP2 as "symptomatic of a growing tendency for independent bands to serve more as lifestyle soundtracks than actual artistic endeavors." Take it for what it's worth coming from yet another guy, but there's some truth in that assessment, and it nods to a phenomenon far bigger than Best Coast or even indie music: As the decade rolled on, popular music in general would come to feel more disposable, even when the creative output was substantial. In part this was because of the way the emerging technological landscape turned music into "content," less an end unto itself and more a backdrop for scrolling timelines and zoning out.

*   *   *

The fact that music was becoming the functional equivalent of iPhone wallpaper dovetailed with the specific changes that were taking place within indie rock. The genre was getting further than ever from its punk roots—sonically and philosophically, out of opportunity and necessity—which was putting a strange new spin on the age-old tensions about selling out and going pop. People whose tastes and ethics had been molded in the pre-Nirvana underground had been watching alternative rock's mainstream dalliances in horror for years—people like the staunchly opinionated producer and zine writer Steve Albini, who preferred his music as abrasive as possible and took his friends Sonic Youth to task for recruiting bands like Nirvana to major labels.

"[Sonic Youth] chose to join the mainstream culture and become a foot soldier for that culture's encroachment into my neck of the woods by acting as scouts," Albini told *GQ* in 2010. "I thought it was crass and I thought it reflected poorly on them." For Albini, big business was an exploitative force that would only cause harm to a vibrant underground culture, the soft-rock stylings of Steely Dan were self-evidently lame, and reflecting on the good old days was a distraction from the jarring immediacy of a well-recorded snare drum. By the time he gave that interview to *GQ*, those were no longer firmly held positions across the indie landscape. A complex, multifaceted shift was well underway, one that felt like the culmination of several factors.

Thanks to the combination of poptimism's egalitarian approach to listening, the ever-encroaching reach of nostalgia in pop culture, and an open door for careerism thanks to benefactors from Hollywood to Wall Street to Silicon Valley, bands from an indie backdrop had spent a decade writing increasingly accessible songs, reclaiming genres that had previously been rejected as fluff, and reaching listeners like me who hadn't come to indie music via sneering punk rock or a fiercely progressive local scene. A recession that destabilized millennials' financial future sent listeners retreating into faded memories of childhood innocence while also tightening their entertainment budgets. For musicians, whose bottom lines were further compounded by the ongoing persistence of piracy, refusing to license your music for advertisements or get in bed with brands like Mountain Dew or Taco Bell started to feel like a luxury they couldn't afford.

This was the environment that yielded sparkling product like MGMT's "Kids" and Phoenix's "1901" and inspired chic retro offerings like Neon Indian's "Deadbeat Summer" and Best Coast's "When I'm with You." Each of those songs has stood the test of time, but it was easy for indie purists to dismiss so much of the youthful Urban Outfitters music as empty and ephemeral because, frankly, so much of it was. Yet in such a heavily corporatized indie landscape, the line between the sellouts and the serious artists was never that clear-cut. Grizzly Bear, who few would dismiss as a case of style over substance, licensed "Two Weeks" for a Volkswagen ad that premiered during the 2010 Super Bowl, a move that inspired Trent Reznor to make an example of them in a 2017 Vulture interview:

> Something that's struck me as a significant shift, and I don't know when it started, is when the corporate entity became a benefactor as opposed to a thing musicians shunned. When I hear Grizzly Bear in a Volkswagen commercial, it kind of

bums me out. I like Grizzly Bear a lot; I don't want to think of a fucking car when I hear their song. But somewhere along the line it became okay to get in bed with a sponsor. More specifically it became okay for rock bands to talk about. When I started to hear musicians talking about their sponsorship deals as something to be almost proud of, it bothered me.

For Grizzly Bear, the VW ad was less about boosting their egos and more about making ends meet. "The band's had a song on a *Twilight* soundtrack, been repeatedly praised by Jay-Z, appeared on *The Colbert Report*, and opened for Radiohead," wrote journalist Nitsuh Abebe in a 2012 Vulture story. Yet in that feature, Grizzly Bear explained that indie rock success had not bought them a substantially different lifestyle. "People probably have an inflated idea of what we make," co-frontman Ed Droste said. "Bands appear so much bigger than they really are now, because no one's buying records. But they'll go to giant shows." The harder it got for bands to make a living through traditional means like selling records and going on tour, the less of a scandal it became to license your music for commercial purposes.

Some bands became masters of retail-ready vibe-out music while still maintaining a reputation as serious artists, perhaps none more so than Grizzly Bear's friends and collaborators Beach House. Yes, another beach band, but the solemn dream-pop duo from Baltimore predate chillwave and the Wavves/Best Coast moment by several years. After getting together in 2004, Victoria Legrand and Alex Scally released their self-titled debut in 2006, immediately becoming Pitchfork favorites. The band played gothic, narcotized pop centered on drum machines, droning organ chords, Scally's alternately eerie and soothing guitar work, and Legrand's warm, hypnotic vocals. It was a lush and elegant strand of shoegaze that sparked comparisons to totems of cool like Mazzy Star, Nico, and Low—and of course the filmmaker David Lynch, whose *Twin Peaks* became a never-ending source of inspiration and comparison for surreal indie music. ("It is happening again," Legrand sang on 2010's "Silver Soul," drawing a direct line between her music and Lynch's work.)

Beach House made sparse, intimate music at first, but as their profile rose with stellar releases like 2008's *Devotion* and 2010's *Teen Dream*, they gradually beefed up their sound with live drums and more luxuriant production. By 2012's *Bloom*, they were making majestic planetarium music: glittering, grandiose, and shot through with deep personal feeling. The album debuted in the *Billboard* Top 10 and inspired a 9.1 Best New Music exaltation at Pitchfork. "Beach House's decision to call this record *Bloom* is almost too perfect," wrote critic Lindsay Zoladz. "Two people from Baltimore started by making incense-smelling, curtains-drawn bedroom pop. Now, eight years later, they make luminous, sky-sized songs that conjure some alternate universe where Cocteau Twins have headlined every stadium on Atlantis."

People often write that Beach House's albums are like soundtracks for movies that don't exist, so inevitably, they were mined for ads and Hollywood syncs. A 2012 Pitchfork feature explained that, though Beach House approved *Teen Dream*'s windswept "10 Mile Stereo" for a Guinness commercial and the same album's tender "Take Care" for an episode of the "adorkable" Zooey Deschanel TV series *The New Girl*, they'd refused many requests to put their music in a Volkswagen ad as their pals Grizzly Bear had. They simply weren't fans of the concept VW was pitching them.

The carmaker's solution to being rejected by Beach House was to commission a replacement track that even Beach House fans mistook for the real thing. A *New York Times* report at the time indicated that the band's peers including Fleet Foxes, Sigur Rós, LCD Soundsystem, and Grizzly Bear were subject to soundalikes from advertisers who were eager to glom onto indie rock's cool and credibility even (especially?) after being told no. "A feeling and a sentiment and an energy has been copied and is being used to sell something we didn't want to sell," Legrand told *The Times*, lamenting that a legal case against VW would be murky and prohibitively expensive.

Not everyone was tapped into Beach House's feeling and sentiment and energy. "It's beautiful, spectral, dreamy, but never makes your pulse quicken," wrote Maddy Costa about *Bloom* in *The Guardian*, while the *Los Angeles Times*'s Todd Martens declared, "It all makes for a lovely lullaby of an album, but it just doesn't result in many songs." Yet some listeners picked up on the soaring hooks and sweeping dynamics within the moody textures, and for others, the stasis was the point. Beach House kept growing in stature, becoming one of the defining indie acts of their generation. If chillwave and MGMT represented an especially salable form of modern psychedelia, Beach House were the prestige equivalent: the ultimate chillout music for the vape pen and Xanax era, adding an air of sophistication to chic dinner parties, stargazing sessions, or hours wasted browsing Instagram. They made depression sound exquisite.

The other defining psych band of the 2010s presented the flip side of that coin, and they ascended higher than Beach House or almost any other indie band of their era. Kevin Parker, the Perth-based mastermind behind Tame Impala, approached psychedelia from an entirely different direction. His music was acid-fried and distortion-bombed. In a way that directly called back to the '60s and '70s, it rocked. Their 2010 debut, *InnerSpeaker*, combined

Parker's lysergic John Lennon vocals with combustible, kaleidoscopic guitar jams, always laced with hard-knock drums that suggested a lifelong devotion to the Flaming Lips' Steven Drozd. Yet the album's title nods to a tendency for deep introspection and insularity that would direct Parker into vibeyness soon enough.

"You will never come close to how I feel," he sang on lead single "Solitude Is Bliss," but plenty of people were feeling Tame Impala right away. "It's difficult to be so plugged-in to a vintage feel without the music seeming time-capsuled, but the band's vibrance helps these songs sound very much alive," Zach Kelly wrote in Pitchfork's Best New Music review.

Tame Impala toured heavily behind their debut, including dates with MGMT in what amounted to a passing of the big-tent psych-pop torch. They played a ton of festivals, too, ingratiating themselves with a wide range of listeners beyond their wheelhouse and probably picking up some big ideas about how to connect with a diverse field full of listeners. By the time they released their second album, *Lonerism*, in 2012, they'd become a weapons-grade version of a festival-friendly indie band. Whereas *InnerSpeaker* sounded analog at an atomic level, *Lonerism* made psych sound like an LCD screen, glowing and fluid. Its tracks were like video game levels to be explored, and they were so dynamic that they translated brilliantly to the live setting. "Now there are a lot more instruments," Parker told *Interview*. "More synthesizers. The guitars wait in the wings for a lot of the songs, and then suddenly come in right at the end. Each instrument is treated like a weapon."

Tame Impala inevitably ended up in commercials; the hard-stomping "Elephant" was licensed by Audi and BlackBerry. But if "Elephant" was *Lonerism* at its most straightforwardly bluesy, the record's appeal and influence was tied up in the way it moved beyond the old templates that inspired Parker. Its textures reflected the modern festival environment—eclectic, expansive, sleek enough to soothe the average listener's ears but full of fireworks to keep the people entertained. *Lonerism*'s futuristic approach to psychedelia mirrored the bombastic widescreen rap that was being propagated by Kanye West at the time. There were echoes of the then-booming EDM scene, too: "Kevin Parker doesn't sound like an electronic producer, he just thinks like one," Ian Cohen wrote in Pitchfork's 9.0 review.

That latent resemblance would become a lot more explicit on 2015's *Currents* as Tame Impala fully embraced their destiny as the leading rock band on the festival scene and your favorite pop star's favorite band. From Rihanna to Travis Scott, seemingly every A-lister wanted a piece of Tame Impala. Parker was more in-demand than most. Among indie-world stars, his appearances on big-ticket albums were perhaps surpassed by only electronic singer-songwriter James Blake. But in another sense his adventures in the hip-hop world were a sign of the times. In the same years indie rock was reaching its peak of visibility, it was experiencing massive crossover with the realm of pop, rap, and R&B.

Chapter 10 Soundtrack

Cannibal Ox, "Iron Galaxy" (2001)

cLOUDDEAD, "Apt. A (1)" (2001)

The Diplomats, "I Really Mean It" (2003)

Dizzee Rascal, "Fix Up, Look Sharp" (2003)

Lady Sovereign, "Random" (2005)

Clipse, "Momma I'm So Sorry" (2006)

M.I.A., "Paper Planes" (2007)

Kid Cudi, "Day 'n' Nite (Crookers Remix)" (2008)

The Cool Kids, "Black Mags" (2008)

Drake & Peter Bjorn and John, "Let's Call It Off" (2009)

Jay Electronica, "Exhibit C" (2009)

Asher Roth, "I Love College" (2009)

Lil B, "I'm God" (2009)

Kanye West & Bon Iver, "Lost in the World" (2010)

Tyler, The Creator, "Yonkers" (2011)

Kendrick Lamar, "A.D.H.D." (2011)

Mr. Muthafuckin' eXquire, Danny Brown, Despot, El-P, & Das Racist, "The Last Huzzah!" (2011)

Death Grips, "I've Seen Footage" (2012)

Run The Jewels, "Oh My Darling Don't Cry" (2014)

10

Late Registration

The indie rockers warm up to the hip-hop hipsters.

I touched Tyler, The Creator's foot. It was *right there*, so I just . . . reached out and did it. In the frenzy of the moment, squeezed against the stage among hundreds of revelers, I grazed his bright blue skate shoe as if he were the messiah and I was seeking to be healed. Unlike Jesus, Tyler didn't seem to notice. He was too busy wilding out onstage with his friends, yelling stuff like "Kill people! Burn shit! Fuck school!"

I'm not proud of invading Tyler's personal space like that, but in my defense, avoiding physical contact was seemingly not a high priority for a guy who was stage-diving, crowd-surfing, and otherwise careening into the crowd at every opportunity. Everyone else's bodies were colliding, too, in a mass of humanity that was basically one big mosh pit. "This is the gnarliest shit I've ever been to," Tyler announced at one point. "I've got blood on my arm." The blood belonged to a kid named Kyle who had broken his nose in the melee, who Tyler invited onstage to show off his injuries.

This magic moment transpired at the dusty outdoor performance space of Austin's Scoot Inn during South by Southwest 2011. Tyler Okonma and his transgressive hip-hop collective Odd Future Wolf Gang Kill Them All had spent the past year rocketing upward through the media—culminating in a chaotic performance on *Late Night with Jimmy Fallon* and a *Billboard* cover story in the weeks leading up to this show—and now they were marauding through one of the music industry's signature events. Odd Future were already well-known when they arrived at SXSW, and they attracted a storm of attention everywhere they roamed. They were happy to reciprocate with a tempest of their own.

On this Friday afternoon, the crew was sowing anarchy at a party thrown by Converse and the skateboarding magazine *Thrasher*. There were performances from other hipster-friendly rap acts including Das Racist, Danny Brown, and Killer Mike (an astonishing lineup in hindsight) and an indoor stage full of rock bands. But Odd Future was the main event, and they delivered on the hype, bringing *Jackass* levels of adrenaline and personal risk to the stage while performing shout-along horrorcore rap over queasy, discordant beats.

Tyler, rocking a tie-dye T-shirt, cutoff jean shorts, and tube socks up to his knees, jumped into the audience from atop a giant stack of speakers at least ten feet high. Hodgy Beats one-upped him by leaping from the roof that hung atop the stage. There was lots of beer-splashing—mainly from the audience, as Odd Future mostly weren't old enough to buy a drink. I'm glad the show is preserved on YouTube to revisit, but it's not like I'd ever forget a performance like that one. It was hip-hop, it was punk rock, and it felt like the most vital thing going in music at that moment.

Odd Future arrived at a fulcrum point. Their impact extended way beyond indie rock, but they heralded a moment when those artists and an audience of mostly white hipsters embraced the traditionally Black genres of rap and R&B on a much wider scale, while some within those genres leaned harder into the art-damaged trappings long associated with indie music. In the early 2010s, Pitchfork readers obsessed over blockbuster rap releases from the likes of Kanye West, Drake, and Kendrick Lamar, became well-versed in the world of street-rap mixtapes on the download site DatPiff, and listened in awe as hip-hop producers sampled or collaborated with some of their favorite indie bands. Meanwhile, a wave of artful new R&B artists and indie acts started messing around with each other's signature tropes, furthering the line-blurring overlap between genres that had started with blogs and MySpace. Suddenly, to be a hipster meant caring more about rap and R&B than indie rock, and quite a few rappers and R&B singers were rising to stardom by pandering to hipsters. It was a transformative era, and it had been a long time coming.

* * *

Pioneered by Black New Yorkers in the 1970s, hip-hop evolved into first a vibrant subculture and then a universal force, morphing in countless capacities along the way. Naturally, this growth involved the development of myriad subgenres, some more accessible than others. By the time rap was coming into its own as a commercial force, a separate wing of the genre was gaining steam underground.

It wouldn't have been the same without Native Tongues. In the late '80s and early '90s, as rap exploded into the national consciousness, New York groups like A Tribe Called Quest and De La Soul developed an arty, jazzy, playful yet high-minded approach to hip-hop. In general, the Native Tongues movement skewed toward positivity, spirituality, and Afrocentrism, maintaining space for quirky self-expression in hip-hop as novelty hits and various forms of gangster rap took over the charts.

By the mid-'90s, the Native Tongues coalition had splintered, but its disciples were proliferating, and a scene was building. Some called it "conscious rap" because of the tendency to focus on social issues and spiritual enlightenment. Others, sometimes dismissively, dubbed it "backpack rap," a nod to acts like Black Moon who were rarely seen without the bags in their videos. Backpacks were a staple of New York hip-hop, a way to haul around tools of the trade like notebooks, albums, recording equipment, or cans of spray paint on public transportation. For backpack rappers, the bags came to symbolize a dedication to salt-of-the-earth "real hip-hop" and the genre's fundamental elements (rapping, deejaying, breakdancing, graffiti) as opposed to the slick, crossover-minded fare on MTV.

Just as there was independent rock music in the '80s that didn't fit into "indie rock" as defined by Pavement and Sonic Youth, not all under-the-radar rappers were backpackers. Memphis horrorcore greats Three 6 Mafia's 1995 debut album, *Mystic Stylez*, is a cult classic on an independent label, but it's about as far from backpack rap as you can get. Yet for many, "underground rap" became synonymous with "backpack rap" or "conscious rap," in part because that community defined itself in opposition to hip-hop's most successful commercial ventures.

As with indie rock, a critique of the mainstream was inherent to the culture of underground hip-hop. Chicago emcee Common's 1994 classic "I Used to Love H.E.R." told the story of a strained lifelong romance as a metaphor for the sad state of commercial rap music. Bay Area producer DJ Shadow's 1996 masterpiece *Endtroducing. . . . .* has an interlude called "Why Hip-Hop Sucks in '96" in which a voice-over reveals, "It's the money!" The same year, Philly's live-band hip-hop pioneers the Roots parodied the excess of the rap mainstream in their "What They Do" video, set at a mansion strewn with champagne bottles and women in bikinis. These kinds of statements were manifold in the underground. Being a backpacker meant taking a stand against the encroaching impurities threatening the sacred art of hip-hop.

In the late '90s, as indie rock retreated from the post-grunge mainstream and backpack rap reacted against the rise of Puff Daddy, the two insular subcultures rarely intersected. There was surely listener overlap between those worlds, and they shared some ideals, but it's not like Belle & Sebastian were going on tour with Pharoahe Monch. Due to both natural human tribalism and institutionalized racism—such as narrowcasted radio stations that largely split Black and white performers into separate formats—the divide between the two scenes had an unmistakable racial dimension, one that became ever clearer as they began to messily intersect.

In the early '90s, alt-rock and hip-hop converged on Lollapalooza lineups and on curios like the *Judgment Night* soundtrack. Later in the decade, as grunge curdled into butt rock and indie music retreated into the esoteric and twee, there was no indie equivalent to that collision, which maybe isn't surprising; the aggro rap rock that emerged from Lolla's petri dish was exactly the kind of hypermasculine grunge aftershock the indie scene was trying to distance itself from at that time. Old *CMJ* charts suggest the only hip-hop artists getting regular spins at college radio in 1997 were DJ Shadow—a white guy making trippy instrumentals, cited as an influence by Radiohead—and the Roots, whose live-band approach to rap appealed to rockist biases.

Pitchfork rarely reviewed rap albums in the '90s, and when they began tentatively exploring the genre near the turn of the millennium, some of the writing was so embarrassing/offensive that it has since been deleted. "Man, about five years ago I was so damn white," begins a 2000 review of Common's *Like Water for Chocolate* that no longer includes a byline. "Not that my skin color actually deepened at some point in time, but I had a serious soul deficit." Not everyone who wrote about rap for Pitchfork in the early aughts was white—one exception was a Black Canadian named Rollie Pemberton, who built his own underground rap career under the name Cadence Weapon—but the site was bringing an outsider's perspective to the genre most of the time.

By the early 2000s, the indie rock audience was becoming conversant with certain corners of the underground rap world—sometimes by cultural osmosis, but sometimes thanks to the same kind of Pitchfork canonization that made stars out of Sufjan Stevens and Broken Social Scene. A subset of hipster-friendly indie rap artists came to underground prominence, adjacent to the backpackers but with sensibilities that catered to fans of quirky underground rock. A lot of the artists who ushered in these mini-scenes were white or white-passing: El-P, Aesop Rock, Atmosphere, most of Anticon.

Viewed charitably, the indie rock audience was more comfortable embracing hip-hop from outside the genre's center because they were outsiders themselves who sought art-damaged sensibilities in all kinds of music. But at least some of them were rejecting mainstream rap wholesale based on a caricature, one that aligned with backpacker critiques but had more of a foul stink to it coming from people outside the culture. The Roots and Common could be self-righteous sometimes, but when they turned their noses up at what they saw as vapid, materialist rap, they did so with great care and reverence for hip-hop as a way of life. Whereas the writer of Pitchfork's *Like Water for Chocolate* review often resembles an out-of-touch uncle ranting on Facebook—making tired points about "real" music, dismissing artists who've long since earned their legendary status, and spouting rhetoric that might fairly be labeled as racist dog whistles:

> Organics in hip-hop were replaced with electronic skitter and weak rhymes. Heart and soul were supplanted by speed freaks like Bone Thugs N' Harmony. Machismo and money superseded authenticity and love for music. "Entrepreneurs" like Master P began serving records like hamburgers, inundating the industry with clone rappers whose most impressive attributes were their ice and gold teeth. The outlook was bleak.

Woof. In articles like that one, Pitchfork clumsily championed the Soulquarian scene—a loose collective specializing in earthy, jazzy conscious rap and neo soul—which put them in step with most critics at the time. It was a rare instance of early Pitchfork seeing eye-to-eye with publications like *Rolling Stone* and a sign of the cloistered indie world taking an interest in hip-hop. But it's not like people think of Soulquarian staples like the Roots and Common as Pitchfork rap. The first true example of Pitchfork rap was Definitive Jux.

I'm sure El-P would reject that distinction. A rapper and producer from the group Company Flow specializing in hardscrabble shit talk over dystopian beats, El-P co-founded the Def Jux label in 1999. His own solo albums like 2002's *Fantastic Damage* were full of snarling, clattering beats that matched his harsh vocal delivery, and he brought a similar approach to his production for other Def Jux releases like *The Cold Vein*, a 2001 classic from the duo Cannibal Ox. Pitchfork compared the album's sound to "a musical negative, an inverse reflection of hip-hop history, full of everything DJs cast aside, from Sega sound effects to electro-industrialism, gear-work grooves malfunctioning, synthesizers belching, a menagerie of digitalia." Def Jux tends to bring that kind of language out of nerdy music writers.

Though some of the Pitchfork critics who loved Def Jux were new to rap, El-P was far from a hip-hop interloper. Company Flow were signed to the definitive backpacker label, Rawkus Records, and El's music was rooted in the grizzled New York tradition—a tradition he revered but also subverted with daring, off-kilter creativity. Def Jux acts like Murs and Mr. Lif were beloved far beyond the sphere of Pitchfork's influence. But within the website's little kingdom, Def Jux was *the* vanguard rap label—"the epicenter of post-millennial hip-hop," as reads Pitchfork's 2002 review of RJD2's *Deadringer*—never mind that Timbaland, the Neptunes, and Missy Elliott had been bringing boundary-pushing, brain-reorganizing hip-hop production to the radio and MTV for years.

Meanwhile, Rhymesayers was emerging out of Minnesota, connecting with an even broader coalition by building their ethos not on post-apocalyptic soundscapes but emotional bloodletting. Rhymesayers centered on Atmosphere, the duo of rapper Slug and DJ/producer Ant, who brought the spirit of self-loathing Midwest emo into backpacker-friendly boom bap—an intoxicating combination for certain listeners. Revisiting Atmosphere's

2002 breakthrough *God Loves Ugly* at *Stereogum*, my colleague Tom Breihan wrote, "At the time, I regarded Slug and Conor Oberst, two Midwestern self-starters who wrote poetically about their own anxieties and failings, as peers."

Pitchfork didn't endorse Rhymesayers with the same vigor they reserved for Def Jux, and they actively derided *God Loves Ugly* for the same reasons they hated on Dashboard Confessional. In a 5.7 review, the site declared Atmosphere's debut "a whiny, heavily affected mess that tries oh so hard, yet ultimately seems as empty and manipulative as the latest Ruff Ryders or Bad Boy album." But Pitchfork's ambivalence didn't stop Rhymesayers artists from building a large audience that included significant chunks of the underground rock world.

And then there was Anticon, a collective that pushed avant-garde hip-hop to obtuse extremes. Whereas Def Jux and Rhymesayers kept one foot in backpack-rap culture, Anticon contorted hip-hop until it sounded like experimental rock—abstract, psychedelic, and twee. Some of this stuff was inspired, but it definitely scanned as rap for people who don't like rap. Anticon artists weren't defying hip-hop convention so much as disregarding it, and the results tended to be irrepressibly weird. In the midst of trends like dance punk, freak folk, and poppy *O.C.*-ready indie rock, it was unsurprising that Anticon remained in the margins of the underground. It was even less surprising when many of the collective's core artists moved on from hip-hop eventually. But the crew played a part in indie music's slow embrace of rap, helping people who never thought of themselves as hip-hop fans to alter their self-perception.

A lot was happening in the early aughts to warm indie rock listeners up to rap. It wasn't just indie-rap labels like Def Jux, Rhymesayers, and Anticon priming the pump. File sharing was opening listeners up to whole new sonic frontiers. Eclectic projects like UNKLE and Gorillaz started mixing in rap verses and hip-hop beats alongside Britpop singers, and mashup projects like Danger Mouse's Beatles-meet-Jay-Z extravaganza *The Grey Album* were making similar juxtapositions. OutKast, then the biggest rap group in the world, began toying around with genre in exhilarating ways, at blockbuster scale. (I'll never forget the first time I saw the "B.O.B." video.) Figures from the gritty, mercurial MF Doom to the nerdcore pioneer MC Frontalot were inventing new indie-friendly iterations of the genre and building massive followings in the process. Grime, a new form of British rap that grew out of pirate radio and the UK garage dance music, was beginning to make its way over from England.

Music that collided the world's many vibrant strains of hip-hop and dance music was especially appealing to the hipster mindset. Diplo's mixtapes and mashups were Trojan-horsing sounds from across the globe into the burgeoning internet cool-kid zeitgeist, from raw Southern rap to Brazilian baile funk. Teaming with Diplo on the 2004 mixtape *Piracy Funds Terrorism Volume 1*, the British-Sri Lankan rapper M.I.A. emerged as a vital force and a true original—an indie-world celebrity with pop crossover potential, spouting revolutionary rhetoric about oppressed people groups. As Pitchfork's Scott Plagenhoef wrote, "[*Piracy Funds Terrorism*] highlighted her big-tent approach to global rhythms and Now Sounds, an M.O. that was cemented when she professed her love for hip-hop crew the Diplomats and rap's spiritual cousins, grime, baile funk, dancehall, and reggaeton in *The New York Times*. Faster than you can say 'galang-alang-alang,' M.I.A. became the one-woman embodiment of what to some is great about the contemporary pop music landscape."

M.I.A.'s impact was huge, but like Anticon or grime star Dizzee Rascal, she was an insurgent force coming from outside the mainstream rap establishment. These artists represented an alternative, an analog to underground rock for an audience that liked the idea of a world of sound percolating just outside the spotlight. The music was exciting, but championing it could also be a way to feel superior to the people bumping Ludacris. Getting the hipsters into rap was one thing; getting them into mainstream rap was another. But another true original was gaining traction at the same time, a figure who would transform hip-hop's mainstream from the inside out.

* * *

Kanye West would be the first to tell you that he changed everything, and he wouldn't be wrong. Except perhaps his nemesis Taylor Swift, it's hard to think of someone with more influence on the arc of twenty-first-century popular music. His impact rippled out into the indie rock world, but it started within his home turf of hip-hop, where he altered the course of the genre multiple times, starting with a debut album that pulled together the underground and the mainstream.

Kanye came up in '90s Chicago, mentored by No I.D., the producer behind Common's backpacker sacred text "I Used to Love H.E.R." He moved to New York and got his foot in the door as an in-house producer for Roc-A-Fella Records, developing his early "chipmunk soul" style on hits like Jay-Z's "Izzo (H.O.V.A.)." Kanye believed he was meant to be a recording artist, not a behind-the-scenes figure, but record labels were skeptical that a thirsty Native Tongues devotee who rocked pink polo shirts would sell. Ultimately, Roc-A-Fella's Damon Dash reluctantly signed him as an artist, partially to maintain access to his beats for other rappers on the label.

Despite rolling with the Roc, Kanye had underground bona fides, a tension he leaned into in a brilliant feat of self-branding. On *The College Dropout*, he framed himself as the bridge between those worlds, touting himself as the "first n**** with a Benz and a backpack" and putting conscious rap standard-bearer Mos Def on the same song as radio-friendly Roc-A-Fella star Freeway. The album was full of hits like "Through the Wire," "Jesus Walks," and "All Falls Down," but production-wise it could have just as easily come out on Rhymesayers. Artists like the Roots and Talib Kweli (the latter with the Kanye-produced "Get By") had been building a beachhead for backpackers within the mainstream, but they'd never achieved success on this scale.

The College Dropout was a massive hit, debuting at No. 2 on the *Billboard* album chart and spawning a No. 1 single in "Slow Jamz." Beyond stats, its impact was comparable to the effect *Nevermind* had on hair metal: Not only did its success prove there was room for a different kind of rap star, Kanye's hipster-friendly approach spawned countless imitators and made rugged gangster rap feel increasingly like a relic.

The album also attracted the attention of indie rock listeners, many of whom sensed a kindred spirit in Kanye. He recruited Jon Brion (fresh off scoring the hipster favorite *Eternal Sunshine of the Spotless Mind*) to lace 2005's *Late Registration* with epic string arrangements. He sampled Daft Punk (fresh off their iconic Coachella set) on a chart-topping hit from 2007's *Graduation*. He framed himself as a revolutionary sophisticate shaking up the mainstream—which was true enough, and which resonated with an audience primed to scoff at the supposed assembly-line qualities of radio rap. And if his rapping could be clunky, corny, and self-impressed, well, indie rock was littered with singers who couldn't conventionally sing and were celebrated as geniuses anyway.

Around the time Kanye showed up, Pitchfork started publishing more critics who took mainstream rap seriously, including my future *Stereogum* coworker Tom Breihan, who was then writing his essential *Village Voice* blog *Status Ain't Hood*. Hip-hop was already woven into other hipster fiefdoms like *Vice* and *The Fader*, but Pitchfork opening up to rap in a bigger way meant a lot of (mostly white) newcomers flooding into the genre. The site's audience would flock to anything it recommended, and in the mid-aughts, it started recommending Cam'ron and Lil Wayne alongside Sleater-Kinney and the New Pornographers. Indie rock was still overwhelmingly white enough that Black-fronted bands like TV On The Radio and Bloc Party stood out as exceptions to the rule, but the genre's audience was warming up to a kind of Black music it once scoffed at.

The Pitchfork effect was so powerful that it transformed the fan base of Clipse, made up of the Thornton brothers, Malice and Pusha T, who were close collaborators with fellow Virginians the Neptunes, the hit-making production duo of Pharrell Williams and Chad Hugo. Clipse enjoyed mainstream success with their 2002 debut, *Lord Willin'*. Its hit "Grindin'" was classic Neptunes, turning off-kilter percussion and negative space into hard-edged radio bait. Clipse allowed the Neptunes to fill their follow-up, *Hell Hath No Fury*, with some of their strangest, most forward-thinking beats, ending up with a batch of auteurist experimental coke rap that remains exhilarating to this day.

Jive Records wanted Clipse to record some crossover bids, but they refused to alter the record, which ended up in label purgatory for years. In the meantime, Clipse caught Pitchfork's attention with a mixtape series called *We Got It 4 Cheap*, released while their album sat on the shelf. "Bigger than just that new shit you cop from Canal St., these demonstrate that mixtapes, like albums, can be an art form," Sean Fennessey wrote in Pitchfork's rave review.

By the time *Hell Hath No Fury* finally dropped in November 2006, there was more enthusiasm for Clipse within Pitchfork world than at rap radio. Singles "Mr. Me Too" and "Wamp Wamp (What It Do)" didn't even crack *Billboard*'s Hot Rap Songs chart, but a 9.1 Best New Music exaltation ensured that Clipse became every white hipster's favorite rap group, me included. When I was a young reporter covering the Columbus music scene, J. Rawls, a legendary local producer who contributed to *Mos Def & Talib Kweli Are Black Star*, once asked me about my favorite rap albums of all time. I still remember his amused befuddlement when I mentioned *Hell Hath No Fury*.

Soon Clipse crowds started to look a lot whiter. They rolled with it. "The writeups were so good," Pusha T later recalled in the *Vice* video series *Autobiographies*. "The blogs were clamoring about the Clipse. We just found our niche with that album—we found out who exactly our fans was. We started off solely in the streets, and then we sort of just found these college, white, internet monsters. We even had a name: They were called the Clipsters. Like hipsters . . . And they were all about us. We embraced 'em as well."

* * *

At the same time indie rock bloggers were expanding their interest in hip-hop, an ecosystem of rap blogs was beginning to flourish.

In the mid-2000s, as more hip-hop fans got online, the discourse made its way from magazines, message boards, and MTV into MP3 blogs and MySpace pages, just as with indie rock. Within the petri dish of the 2000s rap internet, many superstars set their careers in motion. Collectively, they started something so big that it spilled over into indie rock, too.

Arguably the most important hip-hop blog was *Nah Right*. Ahsmi Rawlins, an IT worker from Yonkers, started the site in 2005, blogging under the name Eskay, which derived from his graffiti tag SK. *Nah Right* started out as a hobby for Eskay, something he did on nights and weekends or during downtime at his day job. But by mostly posting links to new music—leaked MP3s, MySpace pages, whatever piqued his interest—Eskay became a tastemaker. At the peak of *Nah Right*'s power, rap fans constantly refreshed the site for new jams, upstart artists like Drake dreamed of having their music posted there, and the comment section evolved into its own civilization. "To us, Nah Right was always the sun to this universe," ItsTheReal's Jeff Rosenthal told *The New York Times* while promoting *The Blog Era*, a highly recommended documentary podcast that goes deep into rap-blog history.

Many more hip-hop blogs such as *2DopeBoyz*, *The Smoking Section*, and *Miss Info* sprung up around the same time. They all had their own areas of focus, but together, they launched a generation of new stars into orbit. Some blogger favorites never made it beyond cult fame, and some were more like one-hit wonders in the public eye: Think Asher Roth's "I Love College." But the blogs also nurtured many of the biggest success stories of the late 2000s and early 2010s, names such as Wiz Khalifa, Wale, Big Sean, Mac Miller, Kid Cudi, A$AP Rocky, Childish Gambino, J. Cole, Nicki Minaj, Drake, and Kendrick Lamar.

These were artists who came up online, largely outside the boundaries of established rap media, though a lot of them ended up entrenched there eventually. Many of them existed in a space carved out by Kanye West, where crowd-pleasing accessibility meets cool-kid eclecticism—a mixture that lent itself to the MySpace era, with its convergence of genres and potential for viral spread. Some were hard-working DIY upstarts hustling to get their music out however they could, who discovered an audience online outside the standard distribution systems. Some were white guys sidestepping fealty to hip-hop elders. Some were Black hipsters, eager to break out of stereotypical rapper molds and simply be themselves. In a 2008 AllHipHop article about the hipster rap wave, many of the rap-blog darlings gave credit where it was due.

"Kanye, Pharrell, and Lupe [Fiasco] opened up doors because they were among the first successful artists that made it okay for black guys to be different," Sir Michael Rocks of the Cool Kids told AllHipHop. "Before them it wasn't okay to be an eclectic black guy. You couldn't wear different clothes or address certain subject matter. These dudes opened up a whole new door for black artists to be who they are and I really appreciate that. They allowed the public to see that there are black artists that aren't on the same old hip-hop thug shit. It's become more acceptable to be able to tell your own stories, you don't have to tell this pre-made rap story." In the same piece, Double O from Kidz In The Hall expressed similar sentiments about Big Boi and André 3000: "OutKast made it cool to be who you want to be and also made it viable. They were able to evolve and they were the first to say, 'The way I feel now is not the way I felt two years ago and I'll represent that.'"

Percolating below the mainstream and then exploding onto

the radio with a stylish and approachable sound, the breakthrough blog-rap stars were not unlike the indie scene that built up its infrastructure underground and then rocketed to unforeseen levels of exposure when *The O.C.* came along. It's not like they wiped out T.I., Young Jeezy, Gucci Mane, and the Atlanta trap music that reigned over rap radio in the mid-2000s. And as proved by MySpace success story Soulja Boy, hipster rap wasn't the only kind of hip-hop to go viral online. But the blog rappers surged into the public eye so forcefully and abundantly that they transformed the sound of the genre.

Inevitably, indie rockers who'd made Kanye, Clipse, and Lil Wayne part of their pantheon started snooping around this new class of hip-hop artists. It helped that a lot of those rappers were sampling indie songs, often lifting the music wholesale as was common on mixtapes. In this case the practice was somewhere between a validation of indie rock's cultural clout and a secret handshake pandering to the kids cool enough to recognize the source material. Former *Degrassi* actor Drake's 2009 breakthrough mixtape *So Far Gone*, the most successful release of the blog era, built upon the chilly Auto-Tuned rap-singing of Kanye's *808s & Heartbreak*, a divisive left turn that would become Kanye's most influential work (largely because of how much it influenced Drake). Drake also shared Kanye's taste for indie music; *So Far Gone* sampled Santigold, Swedish indie-pop singer Lykke Li, and her countrymen Peter Bjorn & John. "Me doing them shows gettin' everyone nervous," he rapped, "'Cause them hipsters gon' have to get along with them hood n****s."

Drake was far from the only emcee rapping over indie samples. Kid Cudi, who'd been a crucial architect of *808s & Heartbreak*, excerpted St. Vincent, LCD Soundsystem, Vampire Weekend, and Band of Horses and collaborated with MGMT and Ratatat. Childish Gambino, then known as the rap side project of *Community* actor Donald Glover, compiled samples by the likes of Sleigh Bells, Animal Collective, and Grizzly Bear for his *I Am Just a Rapper* mixtape series. "Opposite of Adults," a song by the duo Chiddy Bang, aggressively sourced MGMT's "Kids."

The list could go on, but in terms of making the rap and indie worlds overlap, nothing compares to Kanye bringing Bon Iver into his inner circle. Justin Vernon's voice is all over *My Beautiful Dark Twisted Fantasy*, the IMAX-scale 2010 album Kanye released to get back in the public's good graces after stage-crashing Taylor Swift's VMAs acceptance speech. Finale "Lost in the World," in particular, was built around "Woods," an a cappella Bon Iver song on which Vernon layered and digitally altered his voice, turning himself into a robot choir.

MBDTF is a staggering listen, and Pitchfork received it as such, granting the album the site's last perfect 10 rating for a decade. If you're trying to pinpoint a moment when rap was fully annexed into the indie media ecosystem, that's one solid contender. From then on, hip-hop event albums like the Kanye/Jay-Z team-up *Watch the Throne*, Drake's *Take Care*, and Kendrick Lamar's *good kid, m.A.A.d. city* (featuring a Beach House sample on "Money Trees") became appointment-listening within the indie world. These albums were titanic in their scope and ambition, and for a bloc of listeners including me, they overshadowed much of the great indie rock that was still being produced at the time.

Why did some of us shift our focus from the former indie underdogs to hip-hop's new behemoths? Maybe it was because, with Arcade Fire winning Grammys, Best Coast invading Urban Outfitters, and a slew of indie imitators on the pop charts, the genre no longer seemed cutting-edge. Maybe these rap albums were catering to the same critic-friendly sensibilities that drew some listeners to indie rock in the first place. Maybe hip-hop was forging into exciting new frontiers at a time when even the best rock bands were mostly recycling well-worn tropes. Maybe, in the long tail of poptimism, the cream was simply rising to the top. Whatever the reasons, in the early 2010s, a lot more rap was shoehorned into the universe of "indie" music by virtue of that audience's burgeoning interest in the genre.

It wasn't only hip-hop's auteurs hogging hipsters' attention. I might have rated Deerhunter's *Halcyon Digest* ahead of *MBDTF* on my personal 2010 list, but soon enough I was spending at least as much time listening to Rick Ross, 2 Chainz, and Future as exciting young guitar bands like Cloud Nothings. Eventually I found myself downloading street-rap mixtapes from DatPiff that I never would have had a context for a decade earlier, by artists who would never think of sampling Fleet Foxes. And then there were the many hipster-friendly hip-hop artists emerging from entirely different corners of the underground.

As their power and influence grew, rap blogs became a new kind of establishment, an institution to be revered or rebelled against. Early on, Odd Future adopted the latter posture. Peep the beginning of *Bastard*, Tyler, The Creator's breakthrough mixtape: "Yo, yo, fuck 2DopeBoyz and fuck Nah Right and any other fuck-n****-ass blog that can't put an 18-year-old n**** making his own fucking beats, covers, videos, and all that shit." Young Tyler really was doing it all, but his queasy, inflammatory horrorcore didn't fit into the blog-rap mold—never mind that he was pulling inspiration from a lot of the same guiding lights, such as Kanye and Pharrell. Rejection from music industry gatekeepers didn't stop him from assembling a coalition and crashing the gates.

As an elder millennial, aged twenty-seven when the hype around the group began to accelerate in late 2010, Odd Future was one of the first instances of a viral youth phenomenon that convinced me I was getting old. Here were kids a decade younger than me building an organic movement online, challenging the mores of polite society and my concepts of what rap music could be. Before they were endorsed by established media entities, they attracted an intensely devoted audience by posting DIY music videos on YouTube and a flurry of free albums and curated photo dumps on Tumblr. Odd Future were skateboarders, streetwear enthusiasts, and, above all, edgelords, prone to anti-gay slurs and teenage grandstanding about rape and murder. But at times their music also tapped into deep pain as Tyler vented his anger at his absent father. That pathos probably spoke to disaffected teens at least as much as the button-pushing.

The existence of Odd Future as a crew was central to their appeal. They were sometimes compared to the Wu-Tang Clan due to their collective energy and carefully curated aesthetic, but they had arguably more in common with the Insane Clown Posse's Juggalos. Odd Future had a worldview to rally behind—loving Supreme, hating Steve Harvey—but more importantly, it was a family. You were either in or out, for or against. Their chaotic live shows coursed with electricity, and they provided a sense of belonging for anyone willing to chant along. On top of that, there was an enticing mythology surrounding the group thanks to the disappearance of one of its brightest talents, Earl Sweatshirt.

Earl, born Thebe Kgositsile, was the group's most gifted lyricist, twisting language with ease, and his depraved fantasies were startlingly vivid. Concerned, his mother sent him to boarding school in Samoa just before Odd Future blew up. His location wasn't public knowledge, and the rest of Odd Future framed him as a prisoner, turning "Free Earl!" into a rallying cry right alongside "Wolf Gang!"

By fall 2010, the adults were catching on. In October, Fennessey published a Pitchfork primer on "Odd Future and the Swag Generation." In November, the group gave its first New York performance, earning spins on Hot 97 and a report from *New York Times* hip-hop trend-watcher Jon Caramanica. In December, Pitchfork canonized *Bastard* among the year's best albums as the Odd Future explainers kept piling up. The whole media apparatus was swarming toward the Wolf Gang, afraid of being left out.

The stage was set for February 10, 2011, when Tyler dropped his instant-classic self-directed video for "Yonkers," the lead single from his album *Goblin*. "I'm a fuckin' walkin' paradox/ No I'm not," he began, before threatening to "stab Bruno Mars in his goddamn esophagus" and promising, "I'm stabbing any blogging f***** hipster with a pitchfork." The clip showed off his prowess both in front of the camera and behind it: a mesmerizing one-man performance in black-and-white in which Tyler eats a roach, pukes, strips off his shirt, has his eyes turn black, and ultimately hangs himself. Paired with one of the nastiest beats of his career, the provocative video affirmed Odd Future was going places. Soon Tyler was jumping on Jimmy Fallon's back, appearing on the cover of *Billboard*, accepting awards live on MTV, and signing as a solo artist to the prestigious XL Recordings.

Very quickly, Odd Future became enmeshed in the music industry—including the indie media establishment, who appreciated Tyler's shout-outs to Liars and Stereolab and viewed the group as the most obvious example of an organic punk phenomenon in some time. Not everyone was thrilled about the mass acceptance. In May 2011, the Gay and Lesbian Alliance Against Defamation (GLAAD) issued a statement condemning Tyler's language. A few days earlier, so did Sara Quin of indie-pop duo Tegan and Sara. "While an artist who can barely get a sentence fragment out without using homophobic slurs is celebrated on the cover of every magazine, blog and newspaper, I'm disheartened that any self-respecting human being could stand in support with a message so vile," Quin wrote in a statement on the band's website. She continued:

> If any of the bands whose records are held in similar esteem as *Goblin* had lyrics littered with rape fantasies and slurs, would they be labeled hate mongers? I realize I could ask that question of DOZENS of other artists, but is Tyler exempt because people are afraid of the backlash? . . . In this case I don't think race or class actually has anything to do with his hateful message but has EVERYTHING to do with why everyone refuses to admonish him for that message.

It was a sticky subject, one that touched on the intersectionality that was spreading through progressive circles. White indie rockers were quick to glorify Odd Future's raw, vibrant music and DIY success, but even some who did not wave away Tyler's hate speech as a bit were uncomfortable being the wet blanket who holds an exciting young Black talent accountable. It's a subject that only became more complicated in the ensuing years as more members of Odd Future came out as queer, including Tyler himself.

In addition to the outrage about the group's language, there were also some raised eyebrows about the way they were received. In 2011 Cord Jefferson wrote at The Root about the fact that white-centered media institutions were the ones rushing to anoint Odd Future. The ones with largely Black audiences—be that *Nah Right* or the magazine *XXL*, known for its annual Freshman Class cover story on the best new rappers—largely ignored the group.

"As I've followed Odd Future for nearly half a year now, it's been strange to watch hip white America wholly embrace a bunch of African-American punks whose leader once tweeted, 'I want to scare the fuck out of old white people that live in middle fucking America,'" Jefferson wrote. "Not that Odd Future doesn't have any black fans, of course—hip-hop heavyweights Questlove and Mos Def are both major supporters—but the disparity of buzz for Tyler et al. between the black press and the white press has been interesting, to say the least."

Jefferson theorized that Odd Future was the latest chapter in a history of white audiences fetishizing Black male rage. Nitsuh Abebe pushed back against that interpretation at Vulture: "Maybe [Jefferson] assumes that any black man rapping about anger or violence still represents, to white people, some kind of underclass or Other. But that isn't quite the case with Odd Future . . . Tyler raps about teen angst, therapy, resenting his family, hating college, unsuccessfully wooing girls, cartoonish violence and misogyny, ADHD and suicide threats, and sitting in front of his computer compulsively masturbating. To a maladjusted middle-class white kid in a suburban basement, this isn't the Other. This is just home." Abebe's take goes a long way toward explaining what white hipsters and suburban teens saw in Odd Future. But the group was hardly the only example of a rap act that built up more of a following within traditional indie rock strongholds than with hip-hop gatekeepers.

Long before Odd Future, spillover from the bloghouse scene was fueling indie-world interest in rap music, too. From the mid-aughts onward, the canon developed in tandem with waves of trendy and eclectic dance music. Spank Rock, a Baltimore native who'd grown up on the city's Baltimore Club scene, developed a millennial version of 2 Live Crew's hypersexual party rap and worked with umpteen hip electronic producers. In 2007 he leaned into the 2 Live Crew thing with *Bangers & Cash*, a whole EP built around samples from Uncle Luke's salacious group, produced by future pop hit-maker Benny Blanco.

Spank Rock tourmates Diplo and M.I.A.'s work together was crucial in developing the hipster rap lane. On M.I.A.'s 2007 sophomore album, *Kala*, they took that style all the way to the mainstream with a song satirizing Americans' perception of immigrants. More than a year after the album's release, after appearing in the *Pineapple Express* trailer, "Paper Planes," the sing-songy, Clash-sampling closing track with the cash register and gunshot sounds, floated all the way to No. 4 on the *Billboard* Hot 100. That's one spot higher than "Swagga Like Us," the 2008 T.I./Jay-Z/Kanye West/Lil Wayne single that sampled "Paper Planes."

Diplo's electronic-focused Mad Decent label made room for off-kilter rap releases like 2010's *Sit Down, Man*, a shot of surreal, cerebral slapstick from Das Racist. The group—which comprised Punjabi-American rapper Heems, Afro-Cuban-American rapper Kool A.D., and Indian-American hypeman Dapwell—first achieved online notoriety with the novelty hit "Combination Pizza Hut and Taco Bell." But before their 2012 breakup, they became critical sensations with a savvy media presence and brilliantly assembled rap songs about life as a brown person in America.

Das Racist always kept one foot in the indie world. *Sit Down, Man* had beats from acts like Chairlift and Teengirl Fantasy, and it was peppered with indie-savvy lines like Kool A.D.'s reference to Grizzly Bear's "Two Weeks" in the album's waning moments. They played the part of intellectual jesters, rapping lyrics that seemed to be strewn with hyperlinks, keeping their tongues at least partially in cheek. As explained by the chorus on one of their best songs: "We're not joking, just joking, we are joking/ Just joking, we're not joking." Stephen Malkmus could relate.

Like Mad Decent, Fool's Gold Records, founded by DJ-producers A-Trak and Nick Catchdubs, was a bloghouse offshoot that would have a massive influence on the indie rock audience's hip-hop listening habits. Like so much in this milieu, it was connected to Kanye West: A-Trak spent years as Kanye's tour DJ, Kanye teamed with early Fool's Gold rapper Kid Sister on the single "Pro Nails," and the Fool's Gold mixtape *A Kid Named Cudi* led directly to Kid Cudi working on *808s*. When Crookers' club-friendly 2009 remix of Cudi's "Day 'n' Nite" climbed to No. 3 on the Hot 100, Fool's Gold had its first massive hit. But to me, the most iconic Fool's Gold rap record is Danny Brown's *XXX*, released as a free download through the label's website in 2011.

Brown was a weirdo from Detroit with an asymmetrical haircut, skinny jeans, and a chipped front tooth. He'd previously recorded with Tony Yayo, a member of 50 Cent's G-Unit, but lost out on a deal because 50 thought his look didn't jibe with the group. "50 was with it," Brown told MTV, "he just didn't sign me because of my jeans." Instead, Brown broke through at age thirty, rapping about excessive drug intake in an unhinged hyena yap.

Over the years, he'd get his dental situation fixed, cut his hair, tone down the vocal eccentricities, and embrace sobriety. In life and on record, he has left behind the party monster image exemplified by song titles like "Die Like a Rockstar," "Adderall Admiral," "Blunt After Blunt," and "Party All the Time." But at the time, those songs, that persona, and Brown's aggressively nasal snarl proved extremely popular with both festival audiences and critics. Indie rock listeners embraced Brown as one of their own, partially because he really was. His music only occasionally intersected with the genre—a collab with Purity Ring here, an album named after a Joy Division song there—but Brown constantly tweeted about the many indie releases he kept in rotation.

On an opposite wavelength from Brown's livewire chaotic energy, the rap underground also dovetailed with indie rock's chillwave moment via a vibed-out subgenre called cloud rap, full of atmospheric synth sounds, trippy dub effects, and drums that ranged from skittering trap to crawling trip-hop. Lil B, the self-proclaimed Based God, is widely credited for coining the term: To describe the kind of music he wanted to make, he showed the brilliant rap journalist Andrew Nosnitsky a CGI image of a castle in the clouds.

The Based God's music indeed had cumulonimbus qualities, and he rapped like his brain was cloudy, too. Lil B tackled typical rap themes like his own sexual prowess in a surreal, sometimes nonsensical stream of consciousness that drove technique-focused rap fans mad but won the hearts of an army of hyper-online meme lords. He built his cult online, with a steady stream of content: sharing ultra-positive #based platitudes on Twitter, posting a tutorial about his "cooking dance" on YouTube, and, oh yeah, releasing about one mixtape per month in the early 2010s. In a 2010 *New York Times* live review, a delighted Caramanica recorded the Based God shouting out "all my hipsters, all my nerds, all my losers, all my rebels," and rapping, "Recording freestyles every day alone in my home/ I feel like a blogger."

Hipsters and bloggers were certainly among those who made Lil B a folk hero, and they gravitated toward other cloud-rap practitioners like Main Attrakionz, G-Side, and SpaceGhostPurrp as the trend coalesced. Clams Casino, a producer from New Jersey, became the subgenre's premier auteur, crafting grandly swelling downtempo beats like DJ Shadow lost in a cinematic fog. He worked with a number of cloud rap's core artists, including the Based God himself, and his production was crucial to the aesthetic of rising rap fashionista A$AP Rocky.

Even more ultra-online than Lil B were Death Grips. The band matched blunt shout-along vocals from Stefan Burnett, aka MC Ride, with avant-garde noise-rock production by drummer Zach Hill and keyboardist Andy Morin. Despite signing to the major label Epic after their 2011 debut, *Exmilitary*, they existed far from any kind of mainstream. Instead, their caustic music—and art stunts like the erect penis on the cover of 2012's *No Love Deep Web*—appealed to listeners raised on Reddit, Rate Your Music, and The Needle Drop.

Death Grips were a common reference point when Kanye West released his blown-out and confrontational *Yeezus* in 2013. The album's deconstructed noisescapes marked Kanye's break with radio ubiquity, but they made him even more of an indie hero. Though *Yeezus* was Kanye's least commercially successful album to date, it was a sensation within the indie media sphere, inspiring a breathless 9.5 Best New Music review from Pitchfork and getting cited so often on *Stereogum* that dropping *Yeezus* references in unrelated posts became somewhat of a meme in the comment section.

The album was raw in many senses. The music pulled from dark, mechanistic corners of Kanye's Chicago hometown, from house to the drill music that was blowing up at the time. After fast-paced recording sessions in a Paris hotel, Kanye rushed to finish his lyrics at producer Rick Rubin's Malibu studio and filled his verses with violent psychosexual freakouts. He could be both funny and absurd, like when the song called "I Am a God" climaxes with the line, "In a French-ass restaurant/ Hurry up with my damn croissants!" He could be prescient and pointedly crude, as when the striking, minimal "New Slaves" capped its critique of institutional racism with a graphic sequence about ejaculation.

Despite retreating into abrasive, anti-commercial fare, Kanye was more famous than ever. He was dating Kim Kardashian, the platonic ideal of twenty-first-century celebrity, who gave birth to their first child in the days between *Yeezus*'s leak and its official release. In interviews, on social media, and onstage he was serving up ever more ostentatious pull quotes about his own genius, society's attempts to undermine him, and his vision for everything from utopian housing to water bottle design. He was a perfect storm: an aggravating, incendiary artist, undeniably talented but also undeniably a blowhard, who intuitively understood how to keep attention trained on himself at all times.

With streaming about to overtake radio, popular music was moving toward a phase where culture-saturating hits mattered less than cultivating a devoted fan base, and Kanye boasted a cult that included large portions of the indie blog readership. The thought of someone at the center of the media universe making an album like *Yeezus*—working with avant-garde producers like Hudson Mohawke and Arca, bringing the ugliest out of Daft Punk, once again summoning ghostly Bon Iver vocals—was intriguing for the hipster contingent. This isn't a perfect parallel because Kanye's perspective was informed by gratuitous wealth and a self-deifying strain of egotism, but in some ways he echoed fellow Chicagoan Steve Albini: making flagrantly offensive music under the guise of high art and running his mouth at every opportunity, spouting a mix of righteous truth-telling and extreme self-regard. He might have been an asshole, but he was *our* asshole. And at the time, his grandiose self-absorption struck me as fun, kooky provocation, a conclusion I'd have to revise in the coming years as it became clear something darker and sadder was going on with Kanye.

While Kanye was going full supervillain, a feel-good hip-hop story was bubbling up from below. Under the guidance of a hip exec named Jason DeMarco, Comedy Central's Adult Swim programming block had become enmeshed with indie rap, rock, and electronic music, even developing a record label called Williams Street. In 2012, Williams Street released *R.A.P. Music*, an album by Killer Mike, a rapper from OutKast's circle who'd spent much of the 2000s wandering in the mixtape wilderness. Mike wanted to make an album that called back to Ice Cube's aggressive, politically charged work with Public Enemy producers the Bomb Squad. DeMarco had the bright idea to pair him with El-P, who had shuttered Definitive Jux but was still thriving creatively. The result was a bold, explosive record that featured the previously unthinkable combination of Atlanta superstar T.I. rapping on an El-P beat.

R.A.P. Music was a critical smash, as was *Cancer for Cure*, El-P's 2012 album with a Killer Mike feature. Recognizing their powerful chemistry, Mike and El-P formed a group called Run The Jewels, releasing their self-titled debut as a free download via Fool's Gold and Britain's Big Dada in 2013, just weeks after *Yeezus*. The album was full of clattering beats and virtuoso shit talk, and music fans across the internet ate it up. The group quickly blew up much bigger than either artist's solo career. El-P's production and the duo's blustery vocal presence was in step with the forward-thinking noise-rap Kanye was making at the time, but they were a lot easier to root for. Both were tough, accomplished lyricists, and their partnership represented an underdog pairing of two figures from radically different corners of hip-hop: white and Black, Northern and Southern, the avant-garde underground and the mainstream-adjacent.

For Killer Mike and El-P, Run The Jewels represented a career renaissance and a creative breakthrough. It was also the birth of a genuine friendship. When I spent time with Run The Jewels for a *Stereogum* cover story ahead of 2014's *Run The Jewels 2*, the bond between both members was apparent. "I like his beats, period," Mike said of El-P. "He's just a dope-ass fucking rapper, to second it. And then tertiary, man, he's just one of the best fucking human beings I've ever met in my life in terms of his kindness and generosity to people around him." El responded in kind: "It's been the most productive time of my life, and the reason is because it's been fulfilling on a personal level as well as on a musical level. You don't meet your brother 35 years into your life, usually. I didn't have a brother when I grew up. And I feel like I got one now. And that's a fact."

That connection continued to yield incredible music, too. Released on Nas's Mass Appeal label, *Run The Jewels 2* was even harder than the duo's debut. With a ceaseless flow of magnificent flexing and production that wrangled visionary rupture into festival-friendly anthems, the album appealed to many kinds of hip-hop fans. It also paired the first record's braggadocio with a return to the social commentary that had always colored both rappers' music. Though recorded before the string of police killings that sparked the Black Lives Matter movement, *RTJ2*'s songs about injustice spoke to the spirit of the times, allowing fans to feel like the album was not only great but important.

Both Pitchfork and *Stereogum* named it the No. 1 album of 2014—an exclamation point on the era when rap became the new indie rock.

OK, it wasn't *just* rap. In the early 2010s, pop, R&B, and electronic dance music were the new indie rock, too. In those days, it seemed like hipsters were checking for anything *but* guitar-based indie rock.

Chapter 11 Soundtrack

Annie, "Chewing Gum" (2004)
Lykke Li, "Little Bit" (2007)
Dirty Projectors, "Stillness Is the Move" (2009)
How To Dress Well, "Ready for the World" (2010)
Sleigh Bells, "Crown on the Ground" (2010)
Robyn, "Dancing on My Own" (2010)
The Weeknd, "House of Balloons/Glass Table Girls" (2011)
Lana Del Rey, "Video Games" (2011)
Grimes, "Oblivion" (2012)
Purity Ring, "Fireshrine" (2012)
Frank Ocean, "Pyramids" (2012)
Solange, "Losing You" (2012)
Sky Ferreira, "Everything Is Embarrassing" (2012)
Blood Orange, "You're Not Good Enough" (2013)
Charli XCX, "You (Ha Ha Ha)" (2013)
Vampire Weekend, "Step" (2013)
Lorde, "Royals" (2013)
Chvrches, "The Mother We Share" (2013)
Haim, "The Wire" (2013)
Carly Rae Jepsen, "Run Away With Me" (2015)

11

Art Angels

Indie-rock poptimism reaches its peak.

When I came on staff at *Stereogum* in September 2013, one of my first tasks was to develop a weekly pop column. At the time, an indie music blog devoting regular space to mainstream pop was a natural step but still a touchy subject. So at the dawn of 2014, my inaugural installment of The Week in Pop included a defense of the concept. "In the internet era," I wrote, "the idea of a musical guilty pleasure has been rendered irrelevant, rightly dismissed as the product of racism, sexism, and convoluted concepts of authenticity. This is truer than ever in an era when the boundaries between genres are disintegrating before our eyes."

To my coworkers and me, the rationale for such a franchise was self-evident, most recently exemplified by Queen Bey herself. A month before my column launched, Beyoncé surprise-released her self-titled LP—the "visual album" with music videos for every song, including hits like "Drunk in Love" and "Flawless." To use a phrase that hadn't yet curdled into cliché, *Beyoncé* broke the internet. The multimedia opus popularized visual albums and surprise drops in one fell swoop. It crashed iTunes, and it launched Beyoncé into a new tier of prestige pop stardom, a deified state she has occupied ever since.

Beyoncé sent the general public into a frenzy as well as critics and bloggers. "The album is brassy but elegant, its post-coital breath smelling faintly of cheap liquor sipped from a crystal flute," wrote Carrie Battan in Pitchfork's 8.8 Best New Music review. "It finds Beyoncé shifting gears to pull off her most explicit and sonically experimental music to date, exploring sounds and ideas at the grittier margins of popular music." Tom Breihan's assessment at *Stereogum* began, "There's some chance that Beyoncé's new self-titled album is the best album that anyone has released in 2013." This reverent attitude was mirrored by myriad cool kids in urban enclaves around the world. Hipsters had been warming up to Beyoncé for years, but from here on out, she had Radiohead-level cachet.

Such was the spirit of the times. In the early 2010s, indie rock poptimism came home to roost. It wasn't the fact that the indie audience and its gatekeepers were paying more attention to the biggest stars in music, though they certainly were. It was that many of the hottest new indie artists at the time were also pop stars of a sort, or else they aspired to be. Meanwhile, established favorites were working hard to nudge their music away from traditional rock archetypes.

A decade on from the rise of the Best New Music star-making pipeline, there was a tangible shift in the kinds of artists who were building buzz. As indie culture had sprinted away from post-grunge slop in the late '90s, it was now racing to get away from the sounds of Mumford & Sons and Foster The People. The lines further blurred between indie and pop, a flood of new alternative pop stars became a central component of the indie media sphere, and rock bands were largely marginalized within the very subculture that used to center them. It got to the point where many indie fans who still favored live drums, distorted guitars, and DIY grit turned to emo, a genre that had long been a punch line among indie fans. Meanwhile, veteran bands like the National, Spoon, the Hold Steady, and the War On Drugs started to feel more like a new kind of classic rock—less a part of youth culture than kindred spirits with Wilco's alleged "dad-rock."

As someone who was hitting thirty and would become a dad myself before too long, I found a lot to love about that cohort, but I knew those bands did not represent the zeitgeist. We were witnessing the rise of Grimes and Haim, of Lana and Lorde, of Chvrches and Charli. Within half a decade, the baseline of "indie pop" rapidly progressed from Sleigh Bells to Purity Ring to Sky Ferreira to . . . Carly Rae Jepsen? It was a transformational era, one that saw the word "indie" finally obliterated beyond all meaning. For a minute there, hipsters fully gave themselves over to pop music. And a crucial dimension to that devotion was a newfound fixation on R&B.

* * *

The mystery was half the appeal. When *House of Balloons* hit the internet, not much was publicly known about the artist who made it, which made alluring, disturbing music that much more alluring and disturbing. Who was the bleary-eyed falsetto behind this haunting, art-damaged R&B? How real were its tales of nihilistic debauchery? Whose idea was it to sample Beach House and Siouxsie And The Banshees and to make the cover art look, to quote Pitchfork's 8.5 Best New Music review, "like Spiritualized crossed with Tumblr art-porn"?

Anonymity was a popular promotional tactic in the early 2010s. At a time when it was easier than ever to flood the internet with information about yourself, nothing could be more gauche than a band photo. Even better than an absence of identity was a lack of context altogether, allowing the imagination to run wild and creating the illusion of exclusivity: This artist is so new that nobody knows anything about them, but *you*, plugged-in listener, are in on the ground floor. Sometimes powerful forces were at work, ensuring that these clandestine projects made their way to an army of tastemakers and trend-chroniclers. Other times artists really did emerge from obscurity by a fluke of fate, because the right person clicked on their SoundCloud page. By the time everyone on your timeline was posting about the same mixtape, it wasn't always obvious how the buzz began.

In the days after March 21, 2011, when *House of Balloons* first went online as a free download, the Weeknd was the mysterious new entity of the moment. Many were enraptured (and some were repulsed) by all the sordid drugs and sex in the songs, presented with a darkly stylish palette that stood out from the R&B norm. By the time Pitchfork's review ran eight days later, it had come out that the singer was a guy from Toronto named Abel Tesfaye. Newly minted Toronto royalty Drake had offered his endorsement. Think pieces at newspapers like *The Guardian* and *The Village Voice* were starting to flow.

The occasion for those articles was a sudden abundance of R&B that appealed to an indie rock audience. The two worlds, which traditionally had not overlapped, were colliding often enough that the critic Eric Harvey jokingly tweeted about "PBR&B." He was slightly mortified to see his quip cited in the *Village Voice* feature on the emerging trend and lots of subsequent press, enough so that he half apologized for coining the term in a Pitchfork feature two years later. (And now "PBR&B" is immortalized in a book! To quote *Uncut Gems*, a movie in which The Weeknd plays himself: That's history right there, you understand?)

As 2011 progressed, Tesfaye released two more mixtapes, began playing live shows, and contributed to Drake's tour de force *Take Care*. But he wasn't the only underground R&B supernova to storm into the public eye with a fresh, boundary-busting sound. On a much different wavelength, Janelle Monáe, an Atlanta-based singer with an eccentric theater-kid vision of soul music, had earned widespread accolades for her 2010 debut *The ArchAndroid*. An eclectic concept album about a time-traveling android named Cindi Mayweather, it drew comparisons to titans like David Bowie, Prince, Janet Jackson, and OutKast, whose Big Boi guested on the Pitchfork-endorsed single "Tightrope." A spectrum of alternative R&B that included both Monáe and Tesfaye was already quite broad, and it grew more variegated all the time.

In the winter of 2011, a few weeks before *House of Balloons* dropped, the Odd Future Tumblr account posted *Nostalgia, Ultra*, the debut mixtape from Frank Ocean. It was not your average Odd Future release. Whereas Tyler, The Creator and associates were making grimy lo-fi hip-hop, the man known to his family as Christopher "Lonny" Breaux had been working as a songwriter for Justin Bieber, Brandy, and John Legend. He understood the art of pop songwriting. He had a classic R&B voice too, smooth yet gritty in that manner derived from gospel, and he was using it to sing about drugs, sex, and heartbreak in bursts of bright, clear melody—an artisanal millennial Stevie Wonder.

Nostalgia, Ultra was the poppiest thing an Odd Future affiliate had released, but it also catered even more directly to hipsters. On the project's big single "Novacane," Ocean sang about a druggy sexual encounter initiated at Coachella, an alternative institution that was not yet viewed as a mainstream gathering for celebrities and influencers. A snippet of Radiohead's "Optimistic" drifted through one interlude. Ocean sang over tracks by Coldplay, MGMT, and, uh, the Eagles. For me and countless others, it was love at first listen.

Overnight, Frank Ocean became a huge deal. There was critical acclaim, but this was bigger than blog hype or even Pitchfork love. He was in the studio with Beyoncé within weeks. By August he'd logged multiple guest spots on Jay-Z and Kanye West's megalithic *Watch the Throne* and appeared on the cover of *The Fader*. Ocean signed to Def Jam before *Nostalgia, Ultra* dropped, but the label had been letting him collect dust. Now it seemed like the whole world wanted a piece of him, so the corporate machine kicked into gear.

In the summer of 2012, Ocean released his official debut LP, *Channel Orange*. The album was wildly ambitious, featuring elegant, off-kilter pop songs like "Thinkin Bout You" and bold experiments like the ten-minute epic "Pyramids." The only Odd Future member to appear was Earl Sweatshirt, freshly returned from Samoa. OutKast's André 3000 was on the album too, as was John Mayer of all people, fresh off vocal cord surgery and a move to Montana. And on the ballad "Bad Religion," performed on *Fallon* with a string section the night the album dropped, Ocean sang passionately about unrequited love: "I can never make him love me!"

A week ahead of release, after journalists with advance copies of *Channel Orange* started pointing out the male pronouns in some of Ocean's songs, he posted a letter to his Tumblr revealing that although he'd dated women, his first love was a man.

As NPR's Ann Powers put it, "Instead of embracing an identity, Ocean shared a set of memories and explored complex feelings, just as he does in his songs." His coming out was historically significant—a buzzy rising star in a performatively heterosexual genre announcing to the world that he was queer—and it contributed to the sense that Ocean was an important figure.

A few months later, Miguel Pimentel entered the alternative R&B conversation. Known simply as Miguel, the Black Mexican-American singer-songwriter became an urban radio fixture with 2010 debut, *All I Want Is You*, via hits like "Sure Thing" and "Quickie." There were subtle psychedelic elements in his debut, but 2012's *Kaleidoscope Dream* brought them to the forefront. Though the album's opening track and hit single, "Adorn," brilliantly revived the warm, synthesized vibes of Marvin Gaye's "Sexual Healing," most of the tracklist was a pan-genre hallucinatory experience, laced with rock guitars and lyrics like "Do you like drugs? Well, me too."

By the time that wave of rising stars was planted at the mainstream-underground divide, white hipsters were embracing R&B with the same fervor they'd brought to the new titans of hip-hop. That shift occurred in part because these compelling figures were emerging—R&B auteurs with arthouse taste but blockbuster talent. But it was also because new experimental forms of R&B were bubbling up from the realm of indie blogs and labels.

"Stillness Is the Move" was the prologue. Brooklyn's Dirty Projectors were led by Dave Longstreth, a former Yale music student who had an uncanny ability to make knotty melodies, unorthodox chord changes, and abstract lyrics hit like classic rock. The band built its reputation with high-concept releases like 2005's *The Getty Address*, a choral and orchestral rock opera about the Eagles' Don Henley, and 2007's *Rise Above*, on which they reimagined Black Flag's *Damaged* without relistening to it first. By then, a number of women were sharing lead vocal duties with Longstreth, including Amber Coffman, his girlfriend at the time.

Coffman was the voice that breathed "Stillness Is the Move" to life. The lead single from Dirty Projectors' 2009 breakthrough *Bitte Orca* was straightforward and minimalist, with Coffman sometimes backed by nothing but drums and an African guitar riff. It was almost a blank slate for her powerhouse vocals: fluttery, acrobatic, and prone to high-pitched stabs of melody that drew comparisons to Mariah Carey from Pitchfork, *Paste*, and many others. It was unlike any other Dirty Projectors song, or really any other indie rock song at the time, and it may have opened the floodgates for R&B experimentation in the genre.

Arriving concurrently were the xx, a young British band whose low-key music blended whispery guitar-based indie-pop with traces of R&B and electronic dance music. If "Stillness Is the Move" was a virtuoso tempest, the xx's 2009 debut was a twee quiet storm, a triumph of vibes and production over traditional star power and technique. The group name-checked Mariah, Beyoncé, and Aaliyah (even covering the latter's "Hot like Fire") alongside the gods of goth, post-punk, and new wave. But Romy Madley Croft and Oliver Sim of the xx were far from divas, instead cooing and sighing about sex with an amateurish intimacy. Their sound was strikingly original, and it would prove to be massively influential.

Pretty soon, every third indie band was trying to play R&B. This was when cultural appropriation was becoming a more familiar talking point in critical circles—recall the Vampire Weekend takedown "Appropriation, Vacation"—which may be why, despite going nuts for rap, the white hipster audience didn't overwhelmingly start rapping. Hip-hop production methods proliferated within trendy microgenres, such as occult-themed "witch house" acts like Salem blending Atlanta trap drums and chopped-and-screwed Texas lurch with industrial noise and shoegaze. The duo Purity Ring laced their eerie electronic pop with cutting-edge hip-hop beats. Celebrated experimental electronic producers like Hudson Mohawke and Evian Christ drew from rap and were refracted back into the genre when Kanye West recruited them to help with *Yeezus*.

Yet despite the many ways hip-hop seeped into the instrumental dimension of indie music, vocalists from the indie world were way more likely to take a stab at R&B than rap. Maybe it felt like less of a reach—often, the main factor determining whether an artist was "pop" or "R&B" was skin color—or maybe people were trying to avoid becoming a caricature like Andy Samberg's dreadlocked trustafarian Ras Trent. Tune-Yards grappled with similar tensions on their genre-jumbling, explosively energetic *whokill*, the winner of the 2011 Pazz & Jop critics poll. "What's a boy to do if he'll never be a gangsta?" Merrill Garbus sang, reflecting on the long history of white people who romanticize the minority experience. "What's a girl to do if she'll never be a rasta?"

That lyric seemed to apply to Garbus, a former puppeteer who'd moved from New England to Oakland and was drawing from a number of cultures in her music. In the moment, not many people accused her of appropriation, but years later her high-energy shtick started to feel cringe. On *whokill*, Garbus sang songs about gentrification and police violence from the perspective of Black people in her neighborhood—noble in intent but awkward in execution. In terms of visual presentation, she wore face paint and danced passionately to polyrhythms. She was the definition of the well-meaning white hippie lady, but within a few years, she had dismissed some of her own work as problematic.

A lot of white indie musicians, even the ones who shared Garbus's earnestness, sought out subtler ways to incorporate Black musical influences, perhaps intuiting that to plunge into that realm wholesale would be culturally messy. Even the arguable go-to example of indie R&B approached the genre from a distance, through the veil of memory. Tom Krell was a philosophy PhD student splitting time between Brooklyn and Cologne when he dropped How to Dress Well's debut album, *Love Remains*, in 2010. Culled from a wealth of EPs he'd distributed through his blog, the record sounded like the ghost of R&B from around the time *Ghost* was dominating at the box office.

Krell was not a powerhouse vocalist, but a brave one, spinning fragile falsetto melodies against amorphous, mirage-like music. Pitchfork compared his voice to both Justin Vernon and Justin Timberlake, while The A.V. Club's review declared, "This is R&B minus the rhythm." One track interpolated "Crazy in Love"; the best song was named after '80s hit-makers Ready For The World, transforming their 1986 Top 10 single "Love You Down" into a bleary, indecipherable reverb cloud. It was both a genuine loving expression of late twentieth-century soul music and a high-concept experimental treatise. "I really love '90s R&B," Krell told *The Guardian*. "It's not a joke to me." Yet he was also, in a way that mirrored what had been happening with chillwave, channeling his own deeply personal childhood experience of this music.

Notably, Krell started making R&B after spending years performing rock music, as he explained in a Pitchfork profile that outlined the impetus for this project: "I've always loved singing but the only way I could ever sing in high school and college was to scream in rock bands—there aren't, like, a lot of venues to be a pop singer when you're 16. I switched to doing stuff like How to Dress Well a year ago when I stopped playing the guitar." In the same interview, Krell expressed the difference between how he was approaching R&B and the way Kanye West had approached it on *808s & Heartbreak*:

> I don't want How to Dress Well to be about me in the way that Kanye wants it to be about Kanye. For Kanye, music is a vehicle for personality and self-expression. But music allows me to depersonalize. It's a lot more about sound design than my personality. Kanye is really self-advancing. That's not what How to Dress Well is about—it's more about delivering a feeling . . . I don't want to be the tall lanky white dude trying to be Robin Thicke.

If the indie R&B scene tended to be split between Black superstars on major labels and white underground figures on independent labels, some artists were complicating that distinction. Solange Knowles, Beyoncé's younger sister, had been a major-label casualty but a minor success, commercially and critically, in the 2000s. She went independent in 2010, finding her way to Terrible Records, the label founded by Chris Taylor of Grizzly Bear. (Recall that Solange took Bey and Jay to see Grizzly Bear in Brooklyn in 2009.)

On *True*, her 2012 EP for Terrible, Solange teamed with Dev Hynes, a Black American who'd grown up in London. Hynes had played in the English dance-punk band Test Icicles and his own indie-folk project Lightspeed Champion before rebranding as Blood Orange and becoming one of the most in-demand producers of the early 2010s. Together, he and Solange concocted a dancy, new-wavey version of '80s-throwback R&B exemplified by *True*'s brilliant single "Losing You," at once joyously rhythmic and deeply melancholy. The EP made Solange indie royalty, and it contributed to Hynes's burgeoning stature as one of the most visionary talents in left-of-center pop.

Hynes's own music as Blood Orange was exploring similar vibes. After delving into funk and new wave sounds on the project's 2011 debut, *Coastal Grooves*, he blurred his '80s touchpoints into a misty mirage on 2013 breakthrough *Cupid Deluxe*, recipient of an 8.5 Best New Music review. Pulling inspiration from a range of '80s pop, rap, and R&B, as well as the queer ballroom culture that had inspired Madonna and Lady Gaga, Hynes dotted the album with drum machines, popping bass lines, warm synths, weary sax, and tightly percolating guitars. He assembled those nostalgic elements into an emotional and aesthetic masterstroke, littered with rhythms, textures, moods—and *voices*, including indie-world stars like Dirty Projectors' Dave Longstreth and Chairlift's Caroline Polachek.

Cupid Deluxe, an album that had more to do with Prince than Pavement, was both an indie sensation and further proof that no one seemed to know what indie meant anymore. That shift was culminated by a new wave of "indie" pop stars who emerged after a decade of genre-jumbling, poptimism, and the development of new mainstreams rooted in online communities rather than top-down mass media. Some of those artists had ample experience with the old system, though.

* * *

Robin Carlsson—you know her as Robyn—signed with RCA at fifteen and scored her first hit in her native Sweden at sixteen. By eighteen, she had two US Top 10 singles, "Do You Know (What It Takes)" and "Show Me Love." Robyn worked on the R&B-tinged dance-pop tracks with Denniz Pop, the songwriter and producer who helped establish Sweden as a globally dominant force in pop, and his protege Max Martin, who went on to make smash after smash, from "It's Gonna Be Me" and ". . . Baby One More Time" to "Blank Space" and "Blinding Lights." (Only John Lennon and Paul McCartney have written more American No. 1 hits.)

Her 1995 debut was called *Robyn Is Here*, and sure enough, there she was at the epicenter of teen pop as it was about to explode. But Robyn's 1999 album *My Truth* was not released in America, partially because it included songs referencing an abortion she had as a teenager. She left BMG after that, but circa 2002's *Don't Stop the Music* she was disappointed with her new label Jive's attempts to market her as the next Christina Aguilera. Robyn's star was fading fast. But in 2004, after discovering Swedish synth-pop visionaries the Knife and having a dance music awakening at New York club the Shelter, she reinvented her music and persona, shifting away from pop-R&B toward gleaming electronic beats. She also left the majors to start her own label, Konichiwa Records.

The resulting album, 2005's *Robyn*, made her the favored pop star of the Pitchfork set. The Robyn of *Robyn* had a commanding personality, and she had range: The playful, rap-infused electro-pop track "Konichiwa Bitches" was halfway between M.I.A. and Lily Allen, while "With Every Heartbeat" was a string-laden electronic tearjerker that practically invented LCD Soundsystem's brand of balladry. The site had been building a small canon of under-the-radar pop artists, particularly the Norwegian singer Annie. The 8.2 review of *Robyn* scoffed at the idea that Robyn was "this year's Annie," which proved prescient when Annie mostly disappeared into history while Robyn became the godmother of indie-leaning pop stars.

As the 2000s wore on, pop kept creeping into the indie sphere. Hipsters threw their enthusiastic support behind superstars like Justin Timberlake. Synth bands like MGMT and Passion Pit came to the forefront. Figures like Robyn's fellow Swede Lykke Li, who worked on her 2008 debut, *Youth Novels*, with Björn Yttling of Peter Bjorn and John, further popularized the archetype of the indie pop star. When Robyn finally returned in 2010 with *Body Talk*, a series of EPs leading up to an album of the same name, she was received as a conquering hero by basically the whole music media apparatus.

Pitchfork Music Festival even booked her that summer, slotting her right between Liars and Broken Social Scene. Before the fest I had dismissed Robyn as Pitchfork's token pop star, but as her performance wore on, I warmed up to her. Based on the timestamps of my old tweets, I bought in right after hearing "Dancing on My Own," the towering, triumphantly melancholic *Body Talk* opener that would go down as one of history's most iconic pop songs. Though it never charted on the Hot 100, "Dancing on My Own" was a hit across the media landscape, from old guard print rags to the new webzine hegemony. The rippling synth anthem kept growing in stature along with Robyn herself, becoming a not-so-secret handshake for cool kids worldwide. At the end of the 2010s, it topped several lists of the decade's best songs.

By that point so many more pop stars with an indie sensibility had sprung up in Robyn's wake. The same year *Body Talk* dropped, Claire Boucher released her first two albums under the name Grimes, which she took from MySpace's grime genre tag without knowing what grime was. A Vancouver native studying at Montréal's McGill University, Grimes was prone to flights of fancy like sailing down the Mississippi River in a DIY houseboat with her then-boyfriend and a bunch of chickens. (They didn't get far.) Her *Dune*-themed debut album, *Geidi Primes*, and its follow-up, *Halfaxa*, sounded like noisy, trippy, experimental fare half the time, and even its synth songs were too weird to pass for pop. But by 2011's *Darkbloom* EP, her still-eccentric music was starting to become more accessible, like Kate Bush high on grandiose ideas and a whole lot of drugs.

With 2012's *Visions*, released through the venerable indie rock label 4AD and awarded Best New Music in an 8.5 Pitchfork review, Grimes's eerie electronic pop came into focus. "*Visions* fused traditional pop and new jack swing structures with the pointedly nontraditional forms of IDM, noise and punk," critic Jenn Pelly wrote in a 2018 NPR feature. "The voraciously curious spirit of post-punk was alive in Grimes as a pop language. She took the independence and oddity of bedroom pop and rendered it big screen." Lead single "Oblivion" blended crisp drum programming, a squelching low-end synth riff, and well-placed samples with Grimes's eerie high-pitched vocals—a chaotic mixture, but one that cohered into something addictively catchy and unique.

"Oblivion" is about surviving sexual assault: "See you on a dark night," Grimes repeats on the deceptively chipper chorus, while the first verse is about how she never goes walking after dark because "someone could break your neck, coming up behind you." In the unforgettable music video, Grimes sings and dances to the song in hypermasculine spaces like a football game, a motocross rally, and a group of shirtless dudes. As she told Pitchfork, it was a way of "asserting this abstract female power in these male-dominated arenas," and it foretold an era in which women telling stories about harassment, assault, and trauma became normalized—as well as one in which women came to the forefront of traditionally male-dominated indie music like never before.

Visions was still an outré album, especially compared with Robyn's *Body Talk*. But if it was only *sort of* pop music, Grimes was definitely playing the part of the auteurist pop star. A multidisciplinary creative with no shortage of big ideas, she was building an immersive visual world to go along with her music—the "Genesis" video, co-starring rapper/stripper Brooke Candy and an albino python, was even more striking than "Oblivion"—and her unapologetically strange, confident, messy persona made her a lightning rod. Some saw her as a gifted visionary and women's rights icon (in 2013, the progressive women's blog Jezebel praised one of her Tumblr posts as an "epic feminist manifesto"). Others dismissed her as a pretentious fool whose music didn't hold up to scrutiny, though the latter stance became harder to defend when she released her masterpiece *Art Angels* in 2015, leaping to a new tier of pop dynamism without forgoing her idiosyncrasies.

Whatever they thought of her, blog readers couldn't stop clicking every time she opened her mouth—or, more often, typed into Twitter or Tumblr—which led to a lot of posts about Grimes and a lot of friction between her and the bloggers mining her social media accounts for content. Grimes framed her music as "post-internet," but her persona was, too. Like Kanye West and Best Coast's Bethany Cosentino, she was a prolific poster with seemingly no filters, someone who funneled both her stream-of-consciousness takes and her carefully reasoned theses onto her social media accounts. She seemed to have a love-hate relationship with the attention that came along with that robust online presence, which could be a distraction from her creative output but contributed to her status as an indie celebrity.

After a Pitchfork article quoted one of Grimes's posts about feminism, she temporarily deleted her Tumblr in 2013, writing that her account was "not a news source." But because her opinions about subjects like technology, culture, and her own music got such a rise out of people, the blogosphere couldn't resist amplifying her polarizing takes and watching the traffic roll in. Grimes expressed her discontent with this arrangement in many ways, be it through her music (she told SiriusXM that "California" from *Art Angels* is "a hate track for Pitchfork") or social media ("Fuck you," she tweeted at *Stereogum* after a 2019 post about an interview in which she called *Art Angels* "a piece of crap.") She later revealed to *Vanity Fair* that in 2012 she coordinated a DDoS attack on *Hipster Runoff* that temporarily shut down the site and damaged its servers. The intent was to blackmail Carles into deleting a "super wack" "Grimes gone wild" story with a photo of her kissing another woman. *Hipster Runoff* removed the post and left Grimes alone.

One figure *Hipster Runoff* definitely did not leave alone, and one of the only artists who rivaled the extreme reactions Grimes elicited from comment sections, was Lana Del Rey. Lizzy Grant grew up in upstate New York and moved to NYC for college in 2004. While studying metaphysics at Fordham, she began gigging and recording. By the time she graduated, she was working with veteran producer David Kahne, who helped her create her 2008 EP *Kill Kill* and her 2010 album *Lana Del Ray aka Lizzy Grant*. Though the album has a cult following now, it didn't move the needle at the time, and Grant bought the rights back from her small indie label to take it off the market ahead of a rebrand.

Her breakthrough would come the following year with "Video Games," released under the new full-time guise of Lana Del Rey.

The Lizzy Grant material had introduced some of LDR's foundational principles, but here they were on full display: the retro glamor; the extreme melodrama; the ability to mash together high and low culture of the past and present, transplanting slices of twentieth-century Americana into an early twenty-first-century dream state. Inspiring not-quite-congruent comparisons to Fiona Apple and Cat Power, she masterfully framed herself as the "gangster Nancy Sinatra." Describing her own vibe to *The Guardian* as "Lolita got lost in the hood," she sang "Hollywood sad core" in a husky low register and fluttering falsetto.

On "Video Games," against maudlin piano chords and swooning strings, Del Rey professed her undying love for a real man's man who drinks beer, throws darts, and plays Xbox. In the single art, she rocked a flower crown, one of many looks that would be profoundly influential. The video collaged together webcam closeups of Lana dolled up like Priscilla Presley with paparazzi footage, home movies, lo-fi Hollywood iconography, skateboarding videos, and more. At Pitchfork, Nitsuh Abebe described its appeal: "It has a little of that dolorous haze to it, and it draws nice connections between the middle of the 20th century—this era that now seems, like paste jewelry, equal parts tacky and glamorous—and the present moment, which manages to combine tackiness and glamor in its own new and special ways."

In the media, everything about Del Rey was controversial. At *The Village Voice*, Maura Johnston compared her to Kreayshawn, the white female novelty rapper who'd scored ironic buzz with her single "Gucci Gucci." Some, such as former Titus Andronicus bassist Amy Klein, raised concerns about the Del Rey persona's retrograde, anti-feminist qualities, blogging that she "has conquered America with plastic surgery, video games, a regression to nostalgia, and an appeal to the sex drive of every male music critic on the planet." *Hipster Runoff*, which fixated on Del Rey so much that it half-jokingly rebranded as a 24/7 LDR news source, ran exposés on her backstory and speculated that she got lip injections, while culture site The Awl pushed back against critiques of her invented persona by pointing out that figures from Bob Dylan to Lady Gaga had done the same. Everyone had to get their take in.

Eventually it came out that Del Rey had signed to Interscope, and she started making high-profile TV performances, including a disastrous turn on *Saturday Night Live*. The discourse got more and more negative, culminating in widespread pans of her 2012 re-debut, *Born to Die*. But as the media establishment prepared to dispose of her, teens on Tumblr embraced Del Rey as their new queen. In that realm, the endless scrutinizing about authenticity was beside the point. For a class of alt-leaning young women, she was a style icon with beguiling complexity. "The character at the center of *Born To Die* is the Gen Z female fantasy of a woman, an early example of the unhinged female protagonist," my *Stereogum* colleague Danielle Chelosky wrote years later, drawing connections to Gillian Flynn's *Gone Girl* and Ottessa Moshfegh's *My Year of Rest and Relaxation*. "It was the beginning of an era of reconstructing girlhood, of wanting to be villains instead of victims."

On Tumblr, a new class of alternative pop stars flourished. Some, like the London club kid Charli XCX, were critically acclaimed by Pitchfork and the hipster media apparatus. Marc Hogan's Best New Music review of Charli's debut *True Romance* praised her as a descendant of Robyn and Santigold and enthused about her "evident pop ambition, an overriding sense of an imagined mass audience for music that's radio-ready yet outsider-friendly." Others, like Marina and the Diamonds, the project of Greek-Welsh singer Marina Diamandis, were dismissed as frauds. Laura Snapes's 5.9 takedown dismissed Marina's *Electra Heart* for "trying to dress up the high-gloss record that she had made with Katy Perry's collaborators (seemingly at the behest of her major label) in layers of philosophy, mythology, artifice, and blonde wigs."

Those distinctions didn't matter on Tumblr, where indie cred was less important than a smart sense of style and a captivating persona. The community that developed there was almost like an alt-leaning evolution of teen magazines, where bands like Arctic Monkeys, who'd been embraced by the media establishment, were peers with upstarts like Manchester pop-rockers the 1975, at first widely dismissed as the boy band version of an indie band. It was the perfect space for a singer like Sky Ferreira, who blurred the borderlines between rock and pop, between music and fashion.

As a teen, Ferreira was discovered on MySpace by Bloodshy & Avant, the Swedes who produced Britney Spears's "Toxic." After teaming with them on some forgettable electropop songs, Ferreira found her footing with 2012's *Ghost* EP, a hip and eclectic five-song set that ranged from hard-charging grunge and synth pop to more stripped-down singer-songwriter fare.

Ghost was headlined by "Everything Is Embarrassing," which Ferreira wrote with Blood Orange's Dev Hynes and Ariel Rechtshaid, another guy who was reinventing himself as one of the coolest producers in the world. (In the 2000s, he was best known as the producer of "Hey There Delilah.") Crisp and smoothly gliding yet heavy with melancholy, "Everything Is Embarrassing" was an expertly crafted '80s nostalgia bomb that felt like the freshest pop song in the world. It put Ferreira on the map, in part thanks to a black-and-white music video from director Grant Singer that made the most of Ferreira's style and charisma.

Ferreira had worked as a model—Hedi Slimane, the new creative director of Saint Laurent, shot her *Ghost* cover art among other portraits—and as her music career blew up, she became a fashion icon. When MySpace gave way to Tumblr in the 2010s, the indie sleaze look morphed into a new iteration known as soft grunge, in which women accented their American Apparel tennis skirts and babydoll dresses with fishnets, chokers, leather, combat boots, smudged makeup, and bleached-blond hair with the dark roots showing. Ferreira, and the "Everything Is Embarrassing" video in particular, have been widely cited as inspo for this movement.

Ferreira was closely tied to the indie rock world, in part through her romance with Zachary Cole Smith, the frontman of the dreamy, trendy Brooklyn band DIIV. The relationship added to the sense of chaos that always seemed to swirl around her, particularly in September 2013 when the couple was arrested in upstate New York for having forty-two decks of heroin in their truck. (Smith and Ferreira have always maintained that the drugs were his and that Ferreira was clean; the charges against her were eventually dropped.) The arrest complicated Ferreira's life, but it also raised her profile ahead of debut album *Night Time, My Time*, which came out about a month later. It deserved all the attention it could get.

Night Time, My Time was a perfect test case for the marriage of pop and indie. Working mainly with Ariel Rechtshaid and another young producer riding the pop-indie divide, Justin Raisen, Ferreira came away with a sound Pitchfork praised for "bridging the gaps between '80s pop sparkle and full-bodied '90s grunge in a streamlined way." The album brilliantly swirled together its nostalgic reference points into a sound that felt fresh and alive.

Huge walls of distorted guitar, John Hughes movie synths, the occasional rippling electronic beat—it added up to a powerful, stylish backdrop for Ferreira's bright neon narration about the travails of young love and the struggles of life as a fashion plate and record-label refugee. To give a sense of her headspace, this is an album where "Nobody Asked Me (If I Was Okay)" appears consecutively with "I Blame Myself," yet the songs feel brisk and vibrant as they convey Ferreira's rough-and-tumble experience. *Night Time, My Time* was well-received in the moment, and in hindsight, few albums from the era hold up better.

At the same time Ferreira was becoming an indie sensation, an even younger alternative pop star in the major-label system was blowing up even bigger. Ella Yelich-O'Connor had just turned sixteen when she released 2012's *The Love Club*, her first EP as Lorde. The New Zealand teen had been discovered by Universal at age twelve and eventually paired with producer Joel Little. Together they developed a stripped-down, synth-forward aesthetic that fit squarely into the indie zeitgeist yet undeniably scanned as pop. That sound would take Lorde all the way to the top of the charts.

The standout single on *The Love Club* was "Royals," a sparse track built from little more than a basic programmed beat, finger snaps, and layers upon layers of Lorde's voice. In a captivating melody, she sang about her life apart from the glitz and glamor of wealth, critiquing a pop cultural fixation on "Cristal, Maybach, diamonds on your timepiece" while concluding, "That kind of luxe just ain't for us/ We crave a different kind of buzz." It was a sentiment that matched with traditional underground ethics but also spoke to many who felt like a luxurious existence was out of reach, delivered via music so fluid and minimal that it seemed to exist at the crossroads of genre.

Despite the broad-based appeal, the message rubbed at least a few listeners the wrong way, including Veronica Bayetti Flores, a writer at the blog *Feministing*, who declared "Royals" racist: "Because we all know who she's thinking when we're talking gold teeth, Cristal, and Maybachs. So why shit on black folks? Why shit on rappers?" Flores's uncharitable, but not unreasonable, interpretation incited debate at other outlets like *Complex*, *The Guardian*, and even cnn.com, but the backlash was nowhere near widespread enough to stop Lorde's rise to the top.

By the time "Royals" reappeared on *Pure Heroine*, Lorde's 2013 debut album, the song was making a rapid ascent to No. 1 on the *Billboard* Hot 100, where it remained for nine weeks. Alternative rock stations were playing it. Pop stations added it. Eventually I heard it on rap radio, too. Everyone in the world wanted a piece of Lorde's little anti-materialist anthem, including the Grammys, who named "Royals" Song of the Year in 2014, making Lorde the youngest songwriter to ever win the award. But the love affair ran deepest in the indie sphere. Despite the fact that Lorde's rise happened apart from the indie music infrastructure, she became a beloved figure within indie circles, a quirky pop prodigy whom alt-leaning listeners recognized as one of their own.

As the indie pop star archetype became more prevalent, the limits on who could be an indie pop star kept evolving, sometimes in counterintuitive ways. At the same time figures like Grimes and Lana Del Rey were emerging online, former *Canadian Idol* contestant Carly Rae Jepsen was lighting up the charts with "Call Me Maybe," a goofy, lighthearted tune about instant attraction that got a huge boost when Justin Bieber enthusiastically cosigned it and his manager Scooter Braun threw his promo muscle behind it. "Call Me Maybe" was nobody's idea of an indie pop song; though there were some charmingly amateur qualities about it, it wasn't hip or artsy in any way. It would not have sounded out of place on Radio Disney. Yet within a few years, Jepsen would become more beloved within the indie sphere than the pop mainstream.

After her "Call Me Maybe" moment concluded, Jepsen followed the usual trajectory of a pop singer with a fluke hit. In the afterglow, she released a cloying track with Owl City that kept her voice on the radio. She dropped more singles from her own album *Kiss*, but none stuck. Without a proper mainstream foothold, she embarked on a period of reinvention. By 2015, she was ready to launch herself back into the limelight, but the public had minimal interest in "I Really Like You," a solid but obvious attempt to recapture the chaste, headspun "Call Me Maybe" magic. Instead, something surprising happened: While radio washed its hands of CRJ, hipsters went all-in.

In the leadup to Jepsen's 2015 album *Emotion*, Braun told *The New York Times*, "This time we wanted to stop worrying about singles and focus on having a critically acclaimed album." Truthfully, they didn't stop chasing a hit until it clearly wasn't going to happen, but they definitely came through on the critically acclaimed front, pursuing a status dubbed by outlets like *The Fader* and *The New Yorker* as "mindie"—"a major artist with indie bonafides." Jepsen was obsessed with songs like Solange's "Losing You" and Sky Ferreira's "You're Not the One," which led her to work with figures like Dev Hynes, Ariel Rechtshaid, and Vampire Weekend's Rostam Batmanglij alongside more mainstream figures like Sia, Greg Kurstin, and Shellback. The personnel list was sprawling, yet Jepsen had a consistent vision in mind: a sparkling '80s throwback in which synths, guitars, and blaring saxophone collided in service of songs about crushes, passion, and heartbreak.

As more tracks from *Emotion* trickled out and promo copies

found their way to journalists, buzz began to build. Writers like my former *Stereogum* colleagues James Rettig and Claire Lobenfeld started spreading the word that the "Call Me Maybe" girl had recorded a pop masterpiece—a sentiment backed up by singles like "Run Away with Me," a throbbing, sax-blasted burst of euphoria that brought the weaponized nostalgia of M83's "Midnight City" out into the light of day. The album traversed the divide between the chipper approachability of '80s teen idols like Debbie Gibson and Tiffany and the mature sophistication of Robyn, whose trajectory from mainstream fixture to underground darling Jepsen was following.

When *Emotion* dropped after many months of buildup, we named it Album of the Week at *Stereogum*, and at year's end we voted it the third-best album of 2015. Other influential indie hubs like The A.V. Club, Consequence, and Drowned in Sound published raves as well. Pitchfork, while stopping short of Best New Music, called it "as solid and spotless a pop album as you're likely to hear this year." By the next summer, Jepsen was on the mainstage at Pitchfork Music Festival. Somehow, a pop singer with the demeanor of a hapless rom-com protagonist was now at the center of the hipster zeitgeist.

* * *

How did "indie" music get from Pavement to Carly Rae? After retracing that path—the softened Hollywood version of "indie" that emerged after *The O.C.*, the eclectic influence of MP3-era technology, the way a thrift-store fashion sense and the hipster archetype worked their way into mass culture—what sticks out most are issues of social class and self-definition. It helps to remember Mark Greif's definition of the hipster as one "who in fact aligns himself both with rebel subculture and with the dominant class, and thus opens up a poisonous conduit between the two," as well as Nitsuh Abebe's concept of The Game, in which bourgeois people compete to critique "anything that smacks of being bourgeois" in a race to set themselves apart. It's a narrative I cannot exclude myself from.

Middle-class people like me—who saw ourselves in Seth Cohen more than any archetypical punk character, whose fandom was rooted online rather than in a local scene, who didn't have staunch ideological reasons for embracing underground music—gravitated toward scalable middlebrow versions of indie rock. When that music got a mainstream foothold and it became clear there was an audience for it, money flowed in, and the baseline understanding of indie was reshaped in our image. Hipster became a lifestyle brand, which in turn was gentrified into the baseline of millennial yuppie culture, soundtracked by a defanged version of indie rock that sounds nice at Chipotle—music that was, as Zachary Lipez described it in a 2014 *Vice* screed, "about being really reasonable and maintaining your lawn; metaphorical and literal."

In its 2013 report "Youth Mode," the trend forecasting collective K-Hole discussed "Mass Indie" culture, which "mixes weirdness with normalness until it levels out. This is the dogma of: old jean jacket over an evening dress, expensive leisure activity in an industrial space, one party animal per party." When normies adopted "Mass Indie" culture as their own, it led to the proliferation of hazy IPAs and the Grammy-friendly version of indie rock that ultimately yielded Mumford & Sons. Hipsters who defined themselves as different and cutting-edge rushed away from all that because, as "Youth Mode" explained, "There's a limited amount of difference in the world, and the mainstreaming of its pursuit has only made difference all the scarcer. The anxiety that there is no new terrain is always a catalyst for change."

Many of those reacting against bougie whitebread indie rock reasoned that the opposite of a group of solemn guys with guitars is a solo woman backed by keyboards and drum machines. Yet there were some non-reactionary sentiments behind the rise of the "indie" pop star, too. The shift toward pop dovetailed with an earnest desire to center women, minorities, and queer performers after years of indie-world discourse about the old rockist biases. The indie media establishment, which had always been more straight, white, and male than the actual indie music scene, was making efforts to diversify its perspectives, too. This included Pitchfork, which—even after a 2015 sale to legacy media giant Condé Nast, who prized the webzine's "very passionate audience of millennial males"—tried to expand beyond that audience by publishing a more diverse cast of writers and hiring a woman of color, Puja Patel, to lead the site in 2018.

The drive to be more inclusive was in step with the broader spirit of the 2010s, a decade of massive social upheaval that saw gay marriage legalized, the launch of the #MeToo and Black Lives Matter movements, unprecedented visibility for transgender people, and an ultra-politicized environment in the wake of Donald Trump's first ascent to the presidency. These issues were constantly seeping into the indie music discourse at the time. The idea that listening to certain artists reflected your progressive bona fides—even that it constituted political action—gained currency in some circles. But aside from this kind of thinking, which could be both noble and deranged at times, there was a more simple, visceral response at play: that of noticing how much Fleet Foxes had in common with the Lumineers and thinking, "Ew."

By and large, indie rock bands reckoned with those cultural

currents by doing their best to keep up with the pop stars. Not every band participated in this dance. Some new faces on the scene, such as DIIV, Japandroids, and Cloud Nothings, kept their guitars steadily whirring throughout the whole ordeal. Many of the breakthrough bands of the late 2000s—Grizzly Bear, Dirty Projectors, Animal Collective—retreated into knotty experimentalism rather than attempt to cross over further. (Yeah Yeah Yeahs' *Mosquito* album cover was definitely self-sabotage, right?) But some of the biggest names in indie pointedly altered their DNA to become less like a conventional rock band.

Bon Iver started messing around with Auto-Tune on 2009's *Blood Bank* EP, ended 2011's *Bon Iver, Bon Iver* with an adult contemporary power ballad centered on electric piano, and delved deep into abstract electronics on 2016's *22, A Million*. Arcade Fire—whose lack of syncopated rhythm was once held up by critic Sasha Frere-Jones as evidence that indie rock had become sexless, soulless, and oppressively white—teamed with LCD Soundsystem's James Murphy on 2013's *Reflektor*, an album that gave their hulking arena rock a dance music exoskeleton. Tegan and Sara, whose sound had evolved over the years to encompass layers of folk, punk, and indie rock, went all-in on sparkling synth pop for 2013's *Heartthrob* and ended up touring with Katy Perry. So many established bands were moving away from a traditional indie rock sound. And for a while, the hottest new indie bands of the moment were becoming less and less identifiably "rock" with each passing year.

In a smart 2013 Grantland article about the changing nature of "indie pop," Ian Cohen noted that when Sleigh Bells broke through in 2009 with the violently loud and noisy "Crown on the Ground," it passed for pop thanks to Alexis Krauss's sugary sweet melodies and cheerleader chants. Yet four years later, the same band's rock elements stood out more compared with newer bands pursuing an increasingly poptimized sound. One prime example was the Glasgow trio Chvrches, whose members had done time in guitar-centric indie bands before pivoting to sparkling, surging synth pop at festival scale. In Lauren Mayberry, the band had not just a laser-beam vocalist but a compelling, outspoken rising star out front. Their debut, *The Bones of What You Believe*, was stacked with anthems that put an indie singer-songwriter slant on gargantuan EDM. I loved that album *so much*. It struck me as proof that indie rock's metamorphosis into pop music did not have to be a bad thing.

So did *Days Are Gone*, the first full-length album from the SoCal sister trio known as Haim, though that one was more contentious. Danielle, Este, and Alana Haim had played music together in their family band Rockinhaim growing up, and as teens two of them were in a teeny-bopping rock group called the Valli Girls. As Haim, they were marketed to an indie audience despite a major-label deal and basically no aesthetic connection to the historical lineage of indie rock. Instead, they proudly mixed up '90s pop, '70s California soft rock, and more into an effervescent, shape-shifting sound.

Haim wrote their own songs, but they were songs that evoked the Eagles, Wilson Phillips, and Sheryl Crow. They played guitars, but they were just as likely to set them down and bust out some choreography. Within two years of *Days Are Gone*, they'd be part of Taylor Swift's "squad." You can see why people who were looking for an alternative to the hearty bros-with-guitars version of indie rock saw Haim as a breath of fresh air—especially when they were making records as impeccable as "The Wire," my favorite song of 2013. But it's just as easy to understand why a band like Haim would cause consternation in comment sections filled with Spoon fans and inspire think pieces about the death of indie rock.

In one such article at Grantland, the critic Steven Hyden praised Haim but also insightfully compared the state of indie rock in 2013 to the end of "alternative rock" as an actual alternative circa 1997 via bands like Sugar Ray, Smash Mouth, and Third Eye Blind. Highlighting Haim's cross-pollinated, genre-agnostic approach, he continued:

> Haim represents something of a platonic ideal for critics who have spent the past decade systematically deconstructing the pop canon and stripping away the remnants of "rockism" . . . In the process, any suggestion that musicians committed to the standard guitar-bass-drums configuration could represent "the future" has come to be seen as old-fashioned, if not ignorant of the cultural and technological vanguard. Haim might resemble a traditional band, but they don't always sound (or act) like one. And while classic rock forms the crux of its sound, *Days Are Gone* is a record that could exist only right now.

Haim recorded most of *Days Are Gone* with the Sky Ferreira/Blood Orange collaborator Ariel Rechtshaid, who was emerging in 2013 as one of the most stylish architects of indie's pop metamorphosis—"the only person on the planet who's worked with both Cass McCombs and Usher," my colleague Tom Breihan wrote at the time. Also contributing to that reputation was his work on Vampire Weekend's third album, the masterful *Modern Vampires of the City*. Vampire Weekend had begun adding electronic elements on 2010's *Contra*, but on *MVOTC*, their music became even more graceful and fluid. It was an album about millennials reckoning with mortality and growing disillusioned with their youth slipping away, and it found Ezra Koenig and Rostam Batmanglij growing into some of the most mature musical visionaries of their cohort.

Arriving months before my thirtieth birthday, *MVOTC* became one of the most important albums of my lifetime, a milestone in my own transition to full-fledged adulthood. Musically, it embodied that role by achieving new levels of streamlined sophistication, incorporating the influence of pop in a more tasteful and natural way than many of VW's peers. In a 9.3 Best New Music review, *Pitchfork*—which would go on to name *MVOTC* the best album of 2013—praised Koenig's "omnivorous" taste and his ability to smoothly weave together disparate reference points. Chief among the examples was "Step," a melancholy midtempo track that blended classical harpsichord flourishes with elements of an old Souls of Mischief hip-hop track and lyrical references to Modest Mouse. "Wisdom's a gift, but you'd trade it for youth," Koenig sang. "Age is an honor/ It's still not the truth."

In a 2015 appearance on the *No Effects* podcast, Koenig articulated the philosophy that allowed Vampire Weekend to so skillfully navigate the changing pop and indie landscape. It involved rejecting the rock band configuration as passé, a form to be subverted rather than embraced. "Call us pretentious, but we wanted to think of [Vampire Weekend] more as a project or something rather than a band," he said, expressing the pervasive but sometimes unspoken idea that "the concept of a band has become even less relevant." He continued, "The band concept eventually just became associated with a kind of old-school white rock mentality, so it's ultimately no surprise that people have found that a bit dated."

With these kinds of sentiments proliferating, the race to transform "indie" pop into just plain pop was playing out rapidly before our ears. The electronic duo Purity Ring's 2012 debut *Shrines* was dark and eerie, but by 2015's *Another Eternity* I had a friend mistake their glittering new songs for Taylor Swift. Some acts like these found more commercial success than others, but many of them never quite made it over the hump to become mainstream hit-makers. Competing against the likes of Beyoncé revealed some of the artists attempting a crossover to be amateurs cosplaying as pop stars, while others simply didn't have the industry support to make the leap to Top 40 radio and other strongholds of sustainable pop stardom.

Eventually, indie's evolution into pop music ran up against a dead end. The handful of indie-branded pop artists who did graduate to household name status, like Lana Del Rey, could do so because of the changing nature of pop stardom, as streaming and social media loosened radio's grip on the pop charts and altered the dynamics of fandom. Concurrently, those same technological changes were wreaking havoc on the old indie infrastructures, widening the gulf between the haves and have-nots and sending most independent acts back underground whether they wanted to be there or not. Ultimately, indie rock's biggest impact on the pop charts would be its influence on pop's 1 percent.

Chapter 12 Soundtrack

Parquet Courts, "Stoned and Starving" (2013)

Waxahatchee, "Peace and Quiet" (2013)

The War On Drugs, "Red Eyes" (2014)

Alex G, "Harvey" (2014)

Courtney Barnett, "Pedestrian at Best" (2015)

Speedy Ortiz, "Raising the Skate" (2015)

Pinegrove, "Old Friends" (2016)

Angel Olsen, "Shut Up Kiss Me" (2016)

Car Seat Headrest, "Drunk Drivers/Killers Whales (Single Version)" (2016)

St. Vincent, "Los Ageless" (2017)

Lorde, "Green Light" (2017)

Mitski, "Washing Machine Heart" (2018)

Soccer Mommy, "Your Dog" (2018)

Snail Mail, "Pristine" (2018)

The 1975, "Love It if We Made It" (2018)

boygenius, "Me & My Dog" (2018)

Caroline Polachek, "So Hot You're Hurting My Feelings" (2019)

Clairo, "Bags" (2019)

Lana Del Rey, "Venice Bitch" (2019)

Taylor Swift, "Cardigan" (2020)

12

Love It If We Made It

The end is here.

The first time I heard "Chocolate," it awoke something within me. It was *so* slick and *so* catchy, but in ways I hadn't heard in years, let alone from an ostensible indie band. Whatever extent to which these guys were cribbing from, say, Phoenix, it was overshadowed by their callbacks to that extra-glossy runoff from the '80s that seeped into the early '90s—real "King of Wishful Thinking"-core. Indie bands had been toying with adult contemporary sounds, sometimes ironically, sometimes not. But the 1975 sounded like a band I might've actually heard on VH1 in 1992.

Matty Healy and friends hailed from Manchester, home of alt-rock titans like Joy Division, the Stone Roses, and Oasis. Yet their music had no clear connection to that lineage. Despite their Mancunian roots, it's more accurate to say the 1975 came of age on MySpace, where genres were jumbled and shameless self-promotion was the game, and blew up on Tumblr, where teenage enthusiasm melted away the boundary between indie rock and pop fandom. "We kind of excluded ourselves from any kind of tribe or predetermined idea of what we should sound like," Healy told KROQ, "and just made a record that sounds more like Whitney Houston than the Smiths."

At a time when many indie bands were lumbering into pop music, the 1975 embodied it intuitively. Representing an extremely online generation that harbored none of Gen X's concerns about selling out, they carried themselves with a stylized glamor that resembled One Direction and none of the self-effacement that once prevented indie bands from embracing their world-conquering destiny. Many indie fans, even ones who were cozying up to Charli XCX and Sky Ferreira, saw the 1975 as teenyboppers not to be taken seriously. Even some admirers were skeptical. This is what I wrote about them the week their debut dropped: "These guys are pure radio bait—U2 without the post-punk backstory, Coldplay without U2 to look up to, Take That with a Duran Duran makeover."

The 1975 were also molded by an era when Kanye West, with all his ego and ambition, felt like the most exciting thing going in popular music. Healy took after Kanye's first-thought-best-thought megalomania: the heartfelt belief in his own greatness; the tendency to put his foot in his mouth; the tireless ability to delight and infuriate people. He could be insufferable, but his band also shared Kanye's ability to balance commercial appeal with restless adventurousness.

I started to truly take them seriously with 2016's *I like it when you sleep, for you are so beautiful yet so unaware of it*, an album every bit as precious and audacious as its title suggests. The strutting plastic funk of lead single "Love Me" channeled

INXS, while the fizzing, hiccupping, tightly wound groove of "UGH!" evoked other arty '80s pop acts like Scritti Politti. The bloghouse throwback "The Sound" and the misty, bass-powered new wave ballad "Somebody Else" pulled off two significantly different approaches to synth pop. There was an agnostic gospel song, a Sigur Rós–style post-rock track called "Please Be Naked," and a dreamy ballad about Healy's grandmother. Veering from a fragile whimper to a commanding roar, Healy's vocals worked as a portrait of the modern male condition at a time when phrases like "toxic masculinity" and #notallmen were in circulation. Lyrically, he was coming into his own as a social critic, mapping out his generation's relational politics one interaction at a time.

The band leaned even further into Too Much-ness on 2018's *A Brief Inquiry into Online Relationships*, the album that finally caused Pitchfork to buy in. *Inquiry* is best known for "Love It If We Made It," widely hailed as a millennial "We Didn't Start the Fire" for the way it piled up rapid-fire references to everything from Donald Trump to Lil Peep, like a news feed scrolling past faster than you can comprehend it. The band wraps up all those trending topics in music that builds up pressure until it bursts—a social-conscience soundtrack that would have killed on MTV.

Like the best anthems of its ilk, "Love It If We Made It" is powerful enough to transcend its heavy-handedness. Pitchfork named it the best song of 2018, with writer Sam Sodomsky declaring, "Unpacking every reference becomes less entertaining than just standing back and watching the fireworks, as one headline explodes into the next." This kind of topicality was standard practice during the first Trump administration, when every pop culture artifact was expected to address Big Important Subjects. Healy wrote about current events well enough, but he was at his best when he was dialing it down a notch, weaving subtle social commentary into immaculate pop-rock tunes like "It's Not Living (If It's Not with You)."

The title *A Brief Inquiry into Online Relationships* underlines Healy's proclivity for writing about online life, a theme he'd keep hammering on subsequent releases. Perhaps only addiction, a struggle Healy dealt with personally, is a more prominent thread in his work—OK, sure, sex too. On that note, the 1975 dealt with internet culture most directly on "If You're Too Shy (Let Me Know)," a brass-blasted ditty about infatuation via video chat that touches on voyeurism, pornography, and the potential for intimacy through a screen.

With that song's parent album, 2020's *Notes on a Conditional Form*, the 1975 reached unsustainable levels of intentional bloat, hopping from genre to genre and cramming in just about every theme in the discourse: climate change, mental health, queer coming of age. On "The Birthday Party" Healy even grazed the conversation around consent, accountability, and cancel culture via mention of Pinegrove, a rootsy, emotive, hyper-literate indie band who were becoming one of the defining acts of their generation until an opaque misconduct scandal derailed their momentum.

Very little about the 1975 was "indie" in a way that would have computed in 1992. They were signed to a major label, released chart-topping albums, enjoyed pop radio airplay, and eventually toured arenas. They started out as pinups with a female-skewing fan base and did not obscure their emotions or their ambitions with performative shrugs. They pulled influence from across the stylistic map, but especially from soft-rock cheese. Even before he briefly dated Taylor Swift, their singer was a celebrity—and indeed was the child of television actors, not some scrappy outsider working his way up through the DIY circuit. By the 2010s, none of that seemed incongruous with the vague public understanding of indie music.

* * *

What happened to indie rock in the early twenty-first century? It blew up. It spread out. It transformed, little by little, into pop music. It infiltrated festival lineups and iPods. It became enmeshed in lifestyle marketing campaigns. It soundtracked shopping, scrolling, snorting lines, and tripping balls. It crashed the awards shows but couldn't fully conquer the Hot 100. And while all that was happening, many in the underground continued undeterred, keeping the flame for an assortment of subcultures that had little to do with whatever "indie" had come to mean in the marketplace.

Sociologically, there are many ways to understand the genre's public-facing transformation, some of which seem to contradict each other. One way to think about it: As boardroom-approved, playlist-friendly versions of indie music rose to prominence, the genre went from the province of freaks, geeks, and outsiders to normies with pedestrian taste.

The more your average Greek life participants and Foo Fighters fans bought into indie rock, the more the elitist zine-scrawling segment of the genre's audience—which came to be represented by the likes of Pitchfork, *Vice*, and assorted edgelord message boards in the 2000s—reacted against being lumped in with Chad and Becky. Artists who wanted to be on the cutting edge wanted nothing to do with corny *Grey's Anatomy*–core, at least until Alex Patsavas came calling with a check in hand. A decade earlier, Nirvana famously responded to widespread adulation by trying to scare away the casuals with the extremely abrasive *In*

Utero. But in a community where the mainstream had always been anathema, another way to be transgressive was to ditch the well-worn guys-with-guitars configuration in favor of sounds you might hear in the club or on Top 40 radio.

For some artsy kids in urban enclaves, getting way into pop was another way of performing an exotic identity, not so different from early aughts hipsters embracing the signifiers of the white working class or "green" hipsters cosplaying as shamans. For others, like me, it was a retrenchment into the comfortable and familiar under the guise of progressive sophistication—a way to reconnect with a childhood forged by the radio and MTV while still basking in the glow of prestige. Across the board, opening yourself up to a broader range of sounds was a natural consequence of file sharing, iPods, and MySpace, and the evolution in listening habits was mirrored by rock bands eager to prove they were chic, worldly, and not hung up on old underground biases.

But if dabbling in pop was a reaction against smooth and cuddly Zach Braff rock, it only led to even poppier forms of indie music, which progressively felt more disconnected from the post–Velvet Underground lineage that once defined the genre. As the rock band archetype fell out of fashion, some indie listeners gravitated toward exciting new rap and R&B artists who built their careers through blogs and MySpace, just like their favorite indie bands once had. Eventually all the genre-jumbling yielded a new generation of indie-leaning pop stars, like Charli XCX, forged in the flames of bloghouse, and Lorde, who referenced Broken Social Scene on her debut album. Concurrently, a handful of pop artists with no underground bona fides, like Carly Rae Jepsen, recognized the increasingly mainstream-adjacent indie world as a niche they could thrive in.

As the boundaries blurred, some music was lumped into the "indie" sphere not because of any sonic connection but because it was championed by the same gatekeepers and celebrated by the same audience. "Indie" became a fluid term, like "pop" as defined by Top 40 radio: less a defined musical style than a container for a particular audience's evolving tastes. Further complicating things, the word came to stand for the preferences of *multiple* audiences, from trend-conscious Pitchfork readers to comfort-seeking SiriusXMU listeners to the people booking DIY house shows to the people rocking flower crowns at Coachella to, I guess, Hozier fans at the brewpub? Indie meant so many things that it came to mean nothing.

Thanks to the rise of poptimism—the philosophy that rejected many of the old rock-critic truisms as the product of racist, sexist, and homophobic biases—leaning into sounds traditionally beloved by women, minorities, and queer people became a way not only to push stuffy rock fans' buttons, but to show off your progressive credentials. Whatever virtue signaling might have sometimes been involved, this line of thinking led to genuine efforts by multiple institutions, including record labels like Sub Pop and Merge, to acknowledge a world beyond the white male perspective.

As this was happening, some listeners who'd fallen in love with Deerhunter and Japandroids felt abandoned by the indie media sphere as it raced to herald anything *but* old-school indie rock. There was noticeable backlash—in, say, the *Stereogum* comments section—whenever Pitchfork and similar outlets were perceived to be betraying their roots. For those of us who were just doing our best to reflect where culture was going, it was easy to wave off these disgruntled readers as trolls or incels or whatever.

But sometimes it was tough to tell whether this kind of criticism stemmed from Gamergate-style bad-faith discourse or earnest disappointment about feeling left behind.

When indie artists struggling to go pop became a cliché in its own right, guitar-driven indie rock with no obvious crossover ambitions regained its cool factor. Yet it wasn't as if all this history was simply undone. Tastemakers who'd internalized poptimism's inclusive ethos made concerted efforts to champion women, minorities, and queer artists to a far greater extent than ever before. Indie music certainly did not become a utopia, as evidenced by articles like Martin Douglas's "The Only Black Guy at the Indie Rock Show" at *MTV Hive* and Sarah Sahim's "The Unbearable Whiteness of Indie" at Pitchfork. But by the late 2010s, LGBTQ+ and minority artists were more visible in the scene than ever before, and most of the hottest new indie acts were solo women or female-fronted bands. Slowly, maybe excruciatingly, the face of the genre was changing. With that in mind, here's another social framework for understanding indie rock's metamorphosis: Rather than plucking this music from the underdogs and handing it over to the basic bitches, these changes started pulling the genre away from traditional white male power structures and toward the historical have-nots.

Multiple interpretations are valid. There's no easy, all-encompassing explanation for the transformations this book has attempted to track. I can meticulously map out those metamorphoses and pick apart the cause-and-effect of it all, but I can't make a sweeping proclamation about whether on balance the genre's evolution has been good or bad. Keeping close tabs on this corner of the music world over the course of multiple decades has been both thrilling and frustrating; it has left me rolling my eyes sometimes, but probably not as many times as it has tingled my spine.

I named this book after "Such Great Heights" because—in terms of lyrics, music, and cultural impact—the Postal Service's signature song exemplified so much about the genre's journey. "Such Great Heights" is a sleek synth-pop stunner, a gooey Hollywood romance, a subtly defiant triumph. The song was a crucial early instance of indie rock embracing accessible sounds, welcoming many more people into the tent, and soaring to ubiquity—including multiple commercial syncs. Indie music really did fly higher than I ever imagined when I first got Pitchfork-pilled.

But I just as easily could have called the book "Losing My Edge." While indie rock was gaining a more eclectic sound, a more diverse slate of artists and fans, and a lasting influence on mainstream pop culture, it was forfeiting a coherent sense of identity. Once critics like me could apply the descriptor "indie" to gargantuan pop stars without flinching, the genre had lost its center of gravity and, to some extent, its soul. Fortunately, the kids coming up from behind eventually recaptured some of that old DIY spirit.

"Losing My Edge" was prophetic in several ways. It portended a world where indie rock freely intermingled with electronic dance music. It spelled out the arch hipster desperation to stay one step ahead, which drove artistic innovation but also spurred early adopter types to reject old favorites when they got too popular. It also acknowledged plainly that trends move in cycles: "I hear that you and your band have sold your guitars and bought turntables/ I hear that you and your band have sold your turntables and bought guitars."

By the mid-2010s, that wheel was spinning again. In the underground, a reclamation of guitars was well underway. Coworkers a decade younger than me were all over Grimes and Lana Del Rey, but they were also devoted to a new generation of indie rockers. Bands like Waxahatchee and Speedy Ortiz were becoming scene leaders by digging back into '90s indie aesthetics. Guitar-focused artists like Alex G and Car Seat Headrest were building up prolific discographies and faithful followings on Bandcamp, the platform that became ground zero for 2010s independent music. After years of turning emo into a punch line, indie gatekeepers like Pitchfork and *Stereogum* even warmed up to a massive network of emo bands who'd been cultivating a vibrant community away from the media spotlight, a dynamic and diverse field of groups like the Hotelier, Joyce Manor, and The World Is a Beautiful Place & I Am No Longer Afraid to Die.

It wasn't like the trope of the "indie" pop star went away—not with pretty boys the 1975 developing begrudging critical cachet, figures like Charli XCX bouncing between the mainstream and the underground, and artists like Lana Del Rey bridging the gap between indie-pop stardom and the real thing. But for hipsters in locales like Philadelphia, Brooklyn, and upstate New York, guitars were so back. As the decade progressed, some rock acts that emerged in that moment experienced glow-ups of their own. Some, such as Mitski and Japanese Breakfast, even pioneered a new kind of pop stardom—not by leaving all vestiges of rock behind, but by arriving at a pop-rock hybrid sound on their own terms.

Yet those kinds of success stories started to feel less and less likely. For indie artists in the 2010s, breaking through to a mass audience—even making a living in music—was more of an uphill battle than it had been a decade before, in the heyday of music blogs and *The O.C.* That increased degree of difficulty had a lot to do with big tech. The online world that had paved the way for indie's ascension was starting to feel like a gentrified neighborhood where only those who'd already achieved success could thrive.

* * *

The internet giveth, and the internet taketh away.

So much of the infrastructure that brought indie music to the masses (and transformed the genre in the process) was built online. Napster and MySpace broadened listeners' stylistic horizons and opened up new pathways for people to discover music beyond the tightly controlled old-media empires of radio, TV, and glossy magazines. By eliminating the cost of printing and distribution, online publishing allowed for an instantaneous buzz-building ecosystem. Selling MP3s was like printing money for independent record labels. But if the tech advances of the 2000s were a boon for indie music, the 2010s saw many of those new strongholds destroyed by new Silicon Valley developments that seemed to benefit only music's biggest stars.

By the early 2010s, there was a robust landscape of online media dedicated to coverage of indie music, but big tech did a number on them all. As social media platforms like Twitter and Instagram became fixtures of modern life, much of the curation and conversation that once happened on blogs moved onto the timeline. Google monopolized digital ad sales, contributing to the decay of online publishing. Social networks became the dominant way for people to engage with the internet, evolving into addictive, casino-like realms designed to keep users from leaving—and wielding incredible power regarding which links would be given oxygen. Repeatedly, entire media business plans hinged on driving traffic from Facebook, and then Facebook changed its algorithm, and the clicks dried up.

Admittedly, other avenues for music discovery arose. With his pioneering YouTube channel The Needle Drop, Anthony Fantano became a one-man Pitchfork for a new generation. Forums like Rate Your Music and the r/indieheads subreddit built up their own canons of modern classics. Some artists figured out how to promote themselves in the changing landscape, without endorsements from gatekeepers. Still, blowing up in a post-streaming environment often had more to do with chance. TikTok functioned like a roulette wheel, launching songs new and old to virality at random. Celebrity influencers flexed their promo muscle from time to time, too; as *Fader* editor Naomi Zeichner said in a 2017 *Bloomberg* feature, "Kylie Jenner can blow up a song by posting it on Snapchat." Mostly, though, people started finding their music on Spotify.

Streaming changed the music industry, and those changes were generally not great for indie music, commercially speaking. For many listeners, platforms like Spotify eliminated the need for critics and music journalists: With a seemingly infinite library of music available on demand, what was the point of the album reviews that used to dictate whether you spent $17 on a CD? (I disagree with this stance, but it definitely proliferated.) These platforms developed their own editorial arms and built up a robust menu of playlists, which wielded hit-making power—to say nothing of the personalized playlists created by algorithms based on your listening habits. Streaming platforms were also social networks, where you could peruse the tunes your friends were hearing. As with Facebook, Spotify was designed to be a self-contained universe.

Streaming is not the only reason the music press withered away—the journalism infrastructure was crumbling, including the alt-weeklies that used to boost local scenes and highlight acts touring through town—but Spotify contributed to that demise. As the 2010s rolled on, a crowded field of outlets covering new music shrunk to a handful with meager budgets and barebones staffs. *The Fader* went out of print. *Vice* declared bankruptcy. *Stereogum* would have been folded into *Billboard* or sold to private equity vampires if founder Scott Lapatine hadn't raised funds to buy it back himself.

Where there once were countless avenues for artists to get the word out about their music, as the 2010s rolled on, the options became depressingly limited—and many of the most effective were controlled by Silicon Valley execs, not people with their ear to the ground. Pitchfork still had the power to drive fans mad with a 5.9 album review, but the site went out of its way to broaden its coverage beyond indie music, which led to some fantastic journalism but also loosened its grip on its original audience. Bands could still pop off randomly, but indie music felt less and less like it had a center of gravity.

An even bigger problem for indie bands was streaming's impact on their money. Even at its peak of popularity, indie rock wasn't exactly lucrative. Remember how Grizzly Bear had to license their music to make ends meet? They weren't the only ones. Jessica Hopper's 2013 Buzzfeed feature "How Selling Out Saved Indie Rock" is about how a generation of hip execs, many of whom found work in advertising after being laid off from record labels, created a bulwark for indie music on Madison Avenue. The story starts with Tegan and Sara playing songs for the staff at Chicago's Leo Burnett ad office under fluorescent lights, seeking a sync. "A tiny sliver of bands are doing well," the band's

Sara Quin told Hopper. "The rest of us are just middle class, looking for a way to break through that glass ceiling."

That was the situation in 2013, when streaming was still catching on and paid MP3 downloads were just starting to fall off. As the public got on board with the idea of infinite music for a small monthly fee and the user base for streaming services grew exponentially, many musicians' incomes plummeted. The convenience of streaming reduced album sales significantly. (One sales market that surged was collectible vinyl releases from big stars like Adele and Taylor Swift, which caused months-long delays at the pressing plants indie bands depend on.)

Thanks to royalty rates of half a cent per track stream at best, Spotify's payout model only works at scale. As streaming became the main way people engaged with music, bands that might have made at least a supplemental income off album sales were reduced to a few dollars per month. The idea of mounting and sustaining a music career started to feel less realistic than ever. There were exceptions like the prolific rock band Car Seat Headrest, whose Will Toledo claimed in 2017 that he was making decent money off Spotify streams of his sizable catalog—almost $30,000 over four years from the albums released *before* he signed to Matador—but that's not exactly a fortune, and not many artists command such a big fan base.

Streaming impacted the evolution of the music itself, too. In the indie world, the primacy of streaming contributed to the rise of chillout music like soft-rock prankster Mac DeMarco and the electronic psychedelia of Tame Impala's *Currents*. As passive listening became the norm, vibes supplanted explosiveness—great news for dreamy acts like Beach House, but not for anyone who was seeking to rock out. As institutions like SiriusXMU codified a frictionless aesthetic not all that different from Top 40 radio, streaming services like Spotify lent themselves to music on a smaller scale, the antithesis of the Arcade Fire–style bombast that caught the world's attention a decade earlier—especially once Frank Ocean's *Blonde* arrived in 2016 and deconstructed minimalism came into fashion.

Bedroom pop, intimate DIY music that gained traction as a lo-fi underground alternative to commercialized indie, eventually saw its own breakout stars like Alex G and Clairo evolve their sounds in algorithmically friendly directions. That scene ended up professionalized, too, exemplified by Spotify's Lorem playlist, dubbed "Gen Z's *TRL*" by *W Magazine*. A similar process played out with hyperpop, an uncanny experimental electronic subgenre pioneered by British artists like Sophie and the PC Music crew: What began as a radical, boundary-pushing sound popular on indie blogs evolved into a trendy buzzword with its own easily digestible Spotify playlist.

These trajectories are not so different from what happened with the hippies and punks or when MTV had its way with grunge. This time the process of musical commodification was mediated by apps and devices. The internet that fostered the indie explosion of the Bush era had been a wild frontier, but by the end of the Obama years it was becoming a sanitized corporate realm. So perhaps it's natural that the dominant strains of indie music followed suit—at least if you buy the common critique of the producer who did more than anyone to blur the lines between indie and pop.

* * *

If the five words that transformed indie rock in the 2000s were, "Welcome to the O.C., bitch," two more forever altered its trajectory in the 2010s: Jack Antonoff. Mere mention of his name is enough to start an argument. The bespectacled dude who first crashed the mainstream as the guitarist for Fun went on to become one of the most influential and contentious figures in popular music, in part for the way he collapsed the distance between pop blockbusters and prestige indie.

Antonoff was in a unique position. Fun had broken through to a radical extent for a twenty-first-century rock band. They reached No. 1 on the Hot 100 with "We Are Young," landed another Top 10 single with "Some Nights," and won Best New Artist at the Grammys, all thanks to an album that infused theatrical indie-ish rock songs with the brash maximalist production that defined the era's rap and pop. They worked their way to the center of the music industry, and like most rock bands that managed to crack the pop charts, they were patently uncool. Not trashed-by-Pitchfork uncool, but definitely ignored-by-Pitchfork uncool.

Yet Antonoff had hipster bona fides. He and his bandmates came from an underground circuit full of bands hauling gear and merch across the country in vans. He was dating Lena Dunham, a fellow lightning rod whose HBO series *Girls* defined pretentious young New York living in the 2010s. His pre-fame open-hearted '80s-informed rock band Steel Train toured with Tegan and Sara, and his post-fame open-hearted '80s-informed rock band Bleachers had Grimes and Yoko Ono on their debut album. He understood how to move through the space where the underground and the mainstream intersected, and he rapidly claimed it as his own.

Before the afterglow of Fun's breakthrough had faded, Antonoff had risen to prominence as a behind-the-scenes figure. His first hit as a hired gun was as a co-writer on "Brave," a chipper and resolute 2013 single by Sara Bareilles often confused for Katy Perry's "Roar." When "Brave" climbed to No. 23, Antonoff officially had his foot in the door. But his real big break came when he entered the inner circle of the young woman who was becoming the center of the music industry.

Antonoff met Taylor Swift at industry events in 2012. Supposedly they bonded over their love of Yazoo's 1982 synth-pop hit "Only You." Within a year, they'd teamed up on a one-off single called "Sweeter than Fiction" that bore some of that Yazoo influence. It foretold a plunge into larger-than-life '80s pop aesthetics on *1989*, the 2014 release the former teenage country star billed as her "very first documented official pop album."

For *1989*, Swift mostly worked with super-producer Max Martin. But a handful of *1989* tracks involved people outside his crew, including two she wrote with Antonoff, who kept that shiny, synthy energy flowing. "Out of the Woods," in particular, hit the '80s button with a sledgehammer. It's built around a loop of Antonoff's voice doing a big Springsteen/U2 "oh-oh-oh." The keyboard notes are large and blocky, the drums booming and gated as if by Phil Collins himself. It all coheres into a monolithic wall of sound that wasn't all too different from what indie synth bands like Chvrches were doing.

From then on, Antonoff remained one of Swift's closest friends and collaborators. He provided more "oh-oh-oh" action for 2016's "I Don't Wanna Live Forever," a Zayn Malik duet from the *Fifty Shades Darker* soundtrack that climbed to No. 2. By her next album, 2017's heel-turn-but-not-really, *Reputation*, the tracklist was nearly split 50/50 between Max Martin and Jack Antonoff productions. Crucially, Antonoff worked on the chart-topping lead single "Look What You Made Me Do," a thinly veiled dig at

Kanye West, who'd reignited the tabloid mega-feud between the two artists. Swift wasn't just turning to Antonoff for artsy deep cuts anymore.

"Sometimes he sits at the piano and we both just start ad-libbing and the song seems to create itself," Swift said of Antonoff in a 2017 *New York Times* feature. "His excitement and exuberance about writing songs is contagious." The story emphasized how much artists enjoyed his deeply personal mode of collaboration, a therapy-like process he described as "excavating." Writer Joe Coscarelli asserted that "empathy is Mr. Antonoff's songwriting superpower," framing him as an artisanal alternative to the major-label assembly line. "Mr. Antonoff has broken out as one of the most in-demand architects of modern hits," Coscarelli wrote, "an insider's outsider who has used his punk essence and idiosyncratic approach to forge a distinct lane of his own."

At the same time Antonoff was becoming a permanent fixture of Taylor Swift's world, an ever-increasing number of indie-leaning artists worked with him on statement albums of their own. A few years down the line from the advent of the indie pop star, artists from that sphere had not taken over the pop charts. Instead, they'd settled in alongside critically acclaimed rock bands and rappers into a prestige quasi-mainstream stature comparable to what HBO has often been for TV, often commanding a healthy audience but soaking up disproportionate amounts of media attention compared with whichever *CSI* spinoff was actually the most-watched series in America at the moment. (In this analogy *CSI: Vegas* is, I guess, Imagine Dragons?) Antonoff wasn't the only producer working in this space—others included Justin Raisen, Ariel Rechtshaid, and Vampire Weekend's Rostam Batmanglij—but he owned it to the extent that I once wrote a

Stereogum pop column headlined "In the Future, All Music Will Be Produced by Jack Antonoff."

Lorde, a major-label artist with an indie disposition, teamed with Antonoff on 2017's *Melodrama*, the long-awaited follow-up to her blockbuster debut, *Pure Heroine*. It didn't come close to a "Royals"-level hit, but within the prestige pop lane, it was a smash. Pitchfork gave it an 8.8 Best New Music review. *Stereogum* named it the best album of 2017. Lorde toured arenas with Run The Jewels and Mitski: the ultimate hipster's night out.

St. Vincent—Lorde's inverse in that she came from the indie world but carried herself more like a celebrity with each passing album cycle—hopped on the Antonoff train the same year, tapping him to produce her own arthouse hit, *MASSEDUCTION*. Pitchfork compared the album to key influence David Bowie's big mainstream swing, *Let's Dance*, noting the involvement of Antonoff as well as Kendrick Lamar producer Sounwave and St. Vincent's supermodel ex-girlfriend Cara Delevingne: "All of which, in 2017, looks an awful lot like a pop album."

The more projects Antonoff took on, the more his initial '80s fixation faded, giving way to an adaptable style that let artists take the lead but smoothed out their rough edges. As *Stereogum*'s Gabriela Tully Claymore wrote in her own *MASSEDUCTION* review, "the guy has proven himself to be very good at working with women who have a strong point of view, who will always sound like themselves regardless of who's assisting them." By 2019, he had supplanted Martin as Swift's main collaborator, and he continued to work with indie-world stars on some of the most acclaimed releases of their careers, such as *Norman Fucking Rockwell!*, the album that completed Lana Del Rey's arc from critical punching bag to universally revered soothsayer.

The more pervasive Antonoff became, the more backlash

against him persisted. "Jack Antonoff Makes a Lot of Music and None of It Is Good" read one 2019 headline from *Vice*'s Noisey vertical, over an article that accused him of trafficking in dull filler and diluted nostalgia. A 2021 Pitchfork piece wondered whether, "as the designated steward of Tasteful Pop, maybe his omnipresence has flattened the sound of that niche between mainstream pop and indie music." The harshest critique came in a widely circulated 2023 takedown from *The Drift*, which dismissed Antonoff—who by then had won the second of three straight Grammys for Producer of the Year, Non-Classical—as "pop music's blandest prophet." Writer Mitch Therieau lamented, "Antonoff hasn't taken over the landscape of contemporary pop so much as diffused across it, leaving behind a faintly perceptible vapor of understated good taste."

The common refrain was that big-ticket indie had finally converged with pop, resulting not in glorious elevated pop but in not-especially-dynamic easy listening indie. It was mood music, dinner party music, the kind of sonic wallpaper that flourishes on Spotify—and Jack Antonoff was its architect. There was some truth to the idea that Antonoff had helped the supposedly tasteful intersection of indie and pop to become increasingly flavorless, but it's hard for me to feel a lot of contempt for someone who played a crucial role in songs like Swift's electrifying "Cruel Summer" or Del Rey's enchanting "Venice Bitch." He has credits on way too many amazing records for me to write him off as the boogeyman. And anyhow, plenty of the biggest success stories in his chosen lane had nothing to do with him.

* * *

There were many kinds of breakout indie stars in the latter half of the 2010s: from the dad-friendly dream state heartland rock of the

War On Drugs to the daring, explicitly queer art rock of Perfume Genius; from bands that perfected an aesthetic, like Alvvays, to bands that brilliantly rambled across the stylistic map, like Big Thief. Of all the storylines that defined indie in that era, the most prominent was the centering of women-led projects that might have been marginalized or tokenized in the past. I'm not naive enough to argue that sexism in indie rock went away, but women were in the spotlight more and more, and as the baseline of the genre, not in the context of patronizing "women in rock" magazine articles (though occasionally you'd still encounter those).

So many of the most celebrated artists of those years were female singer-songwriters, sometimes presenting as solo artists (Angel Olsen, Courtney Barnett, Maggie Rogers, Clairo, Jessica Pratt) and sometimes as bands that were de facto solo projects (Waxahatchee, Snail Mail, Soccer Mommy, Weyes Blood, Japanese Breakfast, Jay Som). These artists did not all sound the same, but collectively, they represented a changing gender dynamic in indie rock. They also helped usher the genre into a new phase of mainstream infiltration. Some began in a rock or folk context and evolved their sound and/or image in a poppier direction over time. Some, as they morphed into prestige pop stars, even developed the same kinds of parasocial fan armies that congealed around the biggest names in music.

A few watched their songs become TikTok hits, too, but as radio spins and MP3 downloads gave way to the seemingly infinite libraries of on-demand platforms like YouTube and Spotify, the institution of pop stardom depended less on hits. Instead, being a pop star required a compelling persona, perhaps cultivated on social media, and a deep catalog to be purchased on vinyl and streamed relentlessly. These were elements many of the pop stars from the indie world could readily provide. Top 40 radio was the final frontier most indie artists never conquered; by the late 2010s, they didn't need to. Pop stardom was less about getting past industry gatekeepers and more about building your own nation-state of ride-or-die superfans who worship your every move and maybe become the bane of your existence.

One indie star whose career followed that trajectory was Mitsuki Miyawaki. The artist known as Mitski majored in studio composition at SUNY Purchase, and her first couple of albums are full of jazzy ballads. But she began building her legend with 2014's cult classic *Bury Me at Makeout Creek*, which translated her outwardly poised, inwardly tumultuous performance style into raw, confessional indie rock. Mitski had a highly mannered way of singing, but behind that prim-and-proper veneer was a cauldron of barely contained emotions. The contrast created an intoxicating tension in her music: her voice soaring and trembling, performing death-defying feats with the graceful poise of a gymnast in flight. As a writer, she excelled at startling melodies with lyrics to match: "I want a love that falls as fast as a body from the balcony, and I wanna kiss like my heart is chasing me down."

By 2016 Mitski had signed to Dead Oceans, part of a powerhouse trio of sister labels with Secretly Canadian and Jagjaguwar, and released another tour de force called *Puberty 2*. It's a stylistically intrepid album, but its signature hit, the fuzzed-out alt-rock stunner "Your Best American Girl," shoots down the middle by design. It's a song about Mitski, a Japanese-American woman, "wanting so badly to fit into this very American person's life, and simply not being able to," she once told NPR. So of course it's delivered in a format any Weezer bro could comprehend.

The Best New Music–anointed *Puberty 2* made Mitski one of the biggest things going in indie rock. She followed it in 2018 with an even more genre-defiant LP called *Be the Cowboy* that conquered the indie world completely. In declaring it the No. 1 album of the year, Pitchfork's Stacey Anderson wrote, "*Be the Cowboy* finds her ready for the arena, with nimble, airtight songs full of broad pop choruses and big, irrepressible emotions presented as candidly as dry-cleaning receipts."

No one knew how ready for the arena Mitski really was. Although her body of work had grown more expansive with each LP, her live show had mostly been standard rock-band fare, with Mitski either behind a guitar or stalking the stage with a mic. On her second tour supporting *Be the Cowboy*, she introduced choreography inspired by butoh, a form of post-war Japanese dance theater "in which performers draw on chaotic internal emotions but depict them with precise, repetitive gestures," as *The New Yorker* explained it. Instantly, a Mitski show became one of the great spectacles on the indie–pop divide. Just as her albums played out on her own terms, her live show was an exercise in pageantry far removed from the scrappy bombast of early indie rock, but also way more artsy-fartsy than your average pop-star production.

Mitski was never fully comfortable with the pressures of fame or the non-creative work responsibilities that come with it, especially as she witnessed her fan base curdling into the kind of stan army that teams up to attack anyone online who dares criticize their hero. "I'm terrified of crowds," she told *The New Yorker* in 2019. "I've always been someone who's outside of crowds and either at the mercy of crowds or just observing them." In the same feature, she lamented, "What really just eats at my soul is that I'm actively being consumed as a person—it's not just my music that's being consumed."

In summer 2019, Mitski announced an indefinite hiatus from touring and shut down her Twitter account. She told interviewers she would have retired from music altogether except she still owed another album to Dead Oceans. So it was with much ambivalence when, in 2021, she ratcheted up to new levels of fame as two of her songs from *Be the Cowboy*, the jazzy disco jam "Nobody" and the pulsing synth-rocker "Washing Machine Heart," went viral on TikTok. It didn't matter that 2022's more expressly poppy *Laurel Hell* yielded more lukewarm reviews. When she returned to the road post-COVID, the venues got bigger, the tickets harder to come by, the streaming numbers ever more impressive. Semi-reluctantly, she had become a prestige superstar, not with blatant crossover attempts but by playing her own game.

One of the only indie artists to rival Mitski's success was her Dead Oceans labelmate Phoebe Bridgers. Bridgers emerged from Pasadena in the mid-2010s with an indie-folk template that would prove to be deeply influential. Songs like "Smoke Signals" and "Funeral" were downcast, whispery narratives dressed up in stylish cinematic production not so far from the breathy balladry of Sufjan Stevens's *Carrie & Lowell*—a sound that became as appealing to Hollywood music supervisors in the 2010s as radio-friendly indie rock had been in the 2000s. (How many of the millennials who discovered Death Cab through *The O.C.* grew up to watch *This Is Us*?)

Bridgers's music became shorthand for depression at a time when depression was a more widespread cultural talking point than ever; note the scene in the TV show *Shrinking* in which Jason Segel's character weeps on a bicycle listening to "This Is the End" and shouting, "Fuck you, Phoebe Bridgers!" But occasionally, amidst the abject sadness, Bridgers showed flashes of the blunt, irreverent humor she regularly served up on Twitter. Her songs were littered with little knife-twist lyrics that doubled as straight-faced punch lines. This duality, the sadgirl confessionals matched with the deadpan wit, was central to Bridgers's appeal. She was a gifted songwriter and a magnetic personality with awkward charisma and no apparent filter. In the years after her 2017 debut, *Stranger in the Alps*, her career went into overdrive.

Whereas Mitski's music about loneliness was largely a solitary endeavor, Bridgers collaborated with countless figures. She was first associated with Ryan Adams, who she later accused of misconduct, and Bright Eyes' Conor Oberst, who went on to make a whole album with Bridgers in the band Better Oblivion Community Center. She was featured on songs by *so many* artists: Lord Huron, Manchester Orchestra, Joyce Manor, Noah Gunderson, Storefront Church, Mercury Rev, Fiona Apple, the 1975, the National's Matt Berninger, Paramore's Hayley Williams. But nothing elevated her stature like the supergroup she formed with two of indie's other masters of devastation.

In 2018, Bridgers started boygenius with Lucy Dacus, an alto whose meticulously crafted rock songs framed her as wise beyond her years, and Julien Baker, a soprano whose emo-tinted guitar balladry was so mystical and expansive it could almost pass for post-rock. The band name was a pointed commentary on the way gender affects public perception and presentation of creative work. For the cover of their debut EP, the trio re-created the pose from a famous photo of boomer folk-rock heroes Crosby, Stills, & Nash, whose David Crosby was later called a "little bitch" by Bridgers when he criticized her attempt to smash a guitar on *Saturday Night Live*.

Each of the three artists had an incredibly distinctive approach that made them an unmistakable voice right away. Yet they had some important things in common, especially the way they bravely laid bare their struggles—with abuse and addiction, with familial alienation and suicidal ideation, with religious upbringings and queer awakenings. Crucially, the boygenius members also seemed to truly love and respect each other. They came to represent an ideal of female friendship in an era when music, and society at large, was growing more and more individualistic. Bridgers, Baker, and Dacus were a perfect match for one another, and the indie audience noticed.

Though boygenius released only one six-song EP at first, it was a zeitgeist-defining sensation. Released by indie standard-bearer Matador, which had recently added Dacus and Baker to its roster, *boygenius* crystallized the moment in indie rock (women-led, queer, singer-songwriter-oriented, addressing trauma head-on) and yielded some of the best material of each artist's career (Bridgers may never top the heartbreaking, anthemic "Me & My Dog"). They went on tour together, each artist performing their own set before coming together for a rousing finale.

All three members emerged from that brief initial boygenius moment way more famous than they went into it, Bridgers most of all. In the aftermath of *boygenius*, she moved straight into the Better Oblivion Community Center album cycle with Oberst. Through rampant collaboration and funny online exploits, she became an inescapable presence in the music media. By the time she released her sophomore solo album, *Punisher*, at the dawn of 2020's COVID summer, she was arguably the biggest star in indie.

Punisher was clearly informed by previous generations of indie music. The title track is about Bridgers's obsession with the late Elliott Smith, while the rare up-tempo songs like "Kyoto" and "This Is the End" called back to brassy blog rock. Cat Power is an obvious forebear. Yet the album's eerie, dejected balladry was decidedly of-the-moment, especially at a time when people were stuck at home feeling trapped and depressed.

Punisher was a critical smash, including an 8.7 Best New Music review at Pitchfork. It earned Bridgers major visibility boosts like an *SNL* appearance and a Grammy nomination for Best New Artist. Soon she had launched her own Dead Oceans sublabel, Saddest Factory, elevating artists like Claud and MUNA. She began dating celebrities like budding movie star Paul Mescal and the actor-comedian Bo Burnham. She even ended up on a song with the biggest pop star in the world at the height of her indie era.

*   *   *

Four months into a global pandemic that had confined most people to their homes, Taylor Swift revealed that rather than baking sourdough bread or playing hours of *Among Us*, she had spent lockdown making an album with the guitarist from the National. Swift was coming off 2019's *Lover*, a poppy, pastel-colored LP that saw her carefully plotted career trajectory give way to a seeming confusion about what to do next. Many were wondering if her grip on popular music was loosening. Instead, just when some of us counted her out, she somehow ascended to even greater heights of fame, fortune, and public adulation—and she did it by embracing the trappings of easy listening indie rock.

"Taylor Swift indie-folk quarantine album, anyone?" I wrote in a *Stereogum* post announcing *Folklore*. Based on the personnel involved, I didn't know what else to call it. When the music went live a few hours later, that perception was reinforced. Pop stars had recruited indie giants to work on their albums before; Beyoncé's "Hold Up," for instance, evolved from Diplo and Ezra Koenig interpolating Yeah Yeah Yeahs' "Maps." But *Folklore* took pop-star indie immersion to new extremes. Aaron Dessner, the National member whom Swift had approached about teaming up, later revealed that many of the tastefully solemn tracks he sent her were originally intended as songs for his main band.

"Swift has gone full NPR-core indie," my colleague Tom Breihan wrote in his review. "Eight years after clowning an ex for playing an indie record much cooler than hers, Swift has made an indie record that's not remotely worried about being cool," he continued, noting that rather than summoning someone trendy like the culture-jamming absurdists 100 gecs, Swift had dialed up the inoffensively tasteful version of indie rock that had taken over the world a decade earlier.

Although Pitchfork initially made a point of ignoring the mainstream, Pitchfork circa 2020 had evolved to the point that it would have reviewed any new Taylor Swift album. Now, though, she was meeting Pitchfork on its own turf. "*Folklore* will forever be known as Taylor Swift's 'indie' album," Jill Mapes wrote in an 8.0 review that withheld Best New Music honors, much to Swifties' consternation. (Mapes had to switch her Twitter account to private due to the harassment and doxxing she faced—these are the heights to which deranged Mitski stans aspire!) Mapes noted the comfortable familiarity of this music: "While it's true that *Folklore* pushes the limits of Swift's sound in a particular, perhaps unexpected direction, her reference points feel more like mainstream 'indie' homage than innovation, taking cues from her collaborators' work and bits of nostalgia."

Like so many millennials, Taylor Swift had developed an affinity for indie music while coming of age. Now, she was grafting it into her own catalog, reshaping it in her own storyteller/influencer/billionaire image. *Folklore* came out on Republic Records, a subsidiary of Universal, the largest record label in the world. It was released by a monolithic celebrity, a radio and tabloid superstar who remains the closest thing her generation has to the Beatles. It topped the *Billboard* 200 for weeks on end, sent all of its songs to the Hot 100, and won the Grammy for Album of the Year. Yet everyone agreed it was indie. Two decades after trading *TRL* for Radiohead, indie rock fandom had led me all the way back to the peak of pop stardom.

* * *

Everyone wants to fit in somewhere. That's how I felt in high school, when I was building my identity one band at a time. Awkward and insecure, I tried to find common ground with the popular kids via *TRL*, even if not many of those nu-metal bands really felt like *mine*. But I also kept exploring new sounds, seeking out artists that resonated on a deeper level, eventually looking for ways to define myself *against* the norm. Because feeling like you're in on the new thing, the secret thing, the *special* thing can be even more enticing than a generalized sense of belonging.

When the new, secret, special thing becomes the popular thing, you can tell yourself you're on the cutting edge without venturing out from the safety of the center. That's one way to understand indie's rise as a mainstream cultural force. It's cynical, but not entirely inaccurate, to sum all this up—the transformation of indie rock into pop, the permeation of indie aesthetics into mass culture, the stretching of the word "indie" beyond all meaning—as yet another *Conquest of Cool*, an instance of capitalism swallowing up any subculture big enough to be noticed by executives. It didn't hurt that creative and commercial maneuvers that once would have been dismissed as selling out were reframed as trendy, progressive choices.

Yet when I flash back to all the indie music I fell in love with over the years, I don't think first about the music business or the relentless pursuit of cool. I think about the thrill of discovery—of reading about a special new band, tracking down their album, and learning it lives up to the hype. I think about private moments of exhilaration, racing down the freeway with the perfect song blaring from my car speakers. I think about the people I shared the music with, who traded geeky lists with me and joined me on concert road trips. The random MP3s I downloaded, the cover art that imprinted itself on my brain, the playlists I painstakingly assembled to fit on an eighty-minute CD-R: It all comes rushing back, and I get excited about my old favorites all over again.

Within the mess of marketing campaigns, the above-it-all posturing, and the chase for the next flavor of the week, there was often music too good to stay underground forever. Some of it was nerdy, some ultra-hip. Some was powerfully intimate, while some kept listeners at a distance. Some was pristine, some slathered in noise. Taken together, this music spoke to the sensibilities of people—thoughtful, sensitive, adventurous, artsy, elitist, depressed people—who weren't being served by the narrow sliver of popular music allowed to flourish on the radio. When the structures were in place for that music to become more accessible, of course listeners flocked to it.

It is tempting to judge the faceless masses, as if most people who bought into indie music did so because it was sold to them, whereas *I* came to it honestly, connected with it organically, and had an altogether realer experience. That would certainly exemplify a classic hipster mindset. But whatever corporate pandering contributed to me embracing these artists, I fell in love with the best of them because they were great—sometimes *transcendently* great, given how far they reached beyond our little corner of the internet.

I was reminded of that greatness when I went to the inaugural Best Friends Forever festival in October 2024 and saw my beloved Dismemberment Plan reunite. The Plan were one of my first loves in indie rock, a band I'd obsessed over for more than two decades. Their lyrics were clever and poignant, their songwriting catchy and chaotic, their performances intense and incredibly fun. At eighteen, I couldn't believe a band like that existed or that they were available to see up close and personal—they even let the audience come onstage! At age forty-one, feeling those memories come flooding back while shouting along to classic after classic, the band's existence still seemed inconceivable.

By now, that old familiar rush was amplified by nostalgia. So it went at shows by other old favorites like the National and Vampire Weekend, where very few of us in the crowd were at risk of being ID'd at the bar. I was struck by not only the amount of graying hair in the audience but the scale at which these shows were operating. This music that shaped so many of us in our youth had become classic rock for millennials.

That sentiment was underlined when the Postal Service reunited for an arena tour with Death Cab for Cutie celebrating the twentieth anniversary of *Give Up* and *Transatlanticism*. At the Columbus date, from a suite full of fortysomethings, I watched a highly professional performance with production value light-years beyond Death Cab's old basement dive bar gigs down the road. That night, I ran into people I hadn't seen for years. The line about "slowly growing old together" hit different.

Yet this music is not strictly the domain of those of us who lived through it. Curious young listeners have always dug into the past, a practice that went into overdrive in the era of YouTube,

Spotify, and TikTok. In an on-demand world unbound from linear media, there's minimal difference between old and new, underground and mainstream. Sometimes songs bubble up through the algorithm for reasons unexplained, like when the obscure B-side "Harness Your Hopes" became Pavement's biggest song on Spotify. Sometimes they're attached to viral trends, like when the same Pavement track was the basis for TikTok's Utah Boy Fit Check trend. The bite-sized song snippets that proliferate on TikTok can become ends unto themselves, but they can also spark further listening. Mitski's 2021 TikTok hits elevated her to a new tier of stardom, and when her song "My Love Mine All Mine" went viral on the platform in 2023, it became her first Hot 100 hit.

Some instances of borrowed nostalgia make perfect sense. The early 2020s fascination with "indie sleaze" arrived right on time per the twenty-year nostalgia cycle, and after a lifetime mediated by devices and antiseptic apps, it was no surprise to see Gen Z romanticizing a freer, sloppier time before constant smartphone use. On the other hand, I never expected perennial underdog Charli XCX to conquer the music industry with *Brat*, an album and promo campaign steeped in indie sleaze aesthetics, designed to revive the messy aggro spirit of bloghouse for the age of hyperpop. Even more surprising was the TikTok-fueled resurgence of Duster, a relatively anonymous late-'90s space-rock band who achieved wild new levels of popularity decades after their initial run. Ditto the litany of minor shoegaze bands that found new life when shoegaze became to the early 2020s what dance-punk was to the early 2000s.

The kids are building their own canon out of the internet's infinite archive. And like my generation, they're doing it partially by tracing backward from a new wave of artists whose appreciation for the classics comes through loud and clear. How many MJ Lenderman fans have worked their way back to Silver Jews, Songs: Ohia, and Drive-By Truckers? Surely many young Momma listeners have followed the thread to the Breeders and Liz Phair. It's mystifying to consider the possibility, but some teens might have learned about Arcade Fire and Joanna Newsom because of Black Country, New Road.

I don't know if the people discovering indie music today feel like they've happened upon an alluring secret world the way I did. In an era where everything is "indie," where genre barriers mean less than ever and you can summon entire discographies with a click, maybe it all feels commonplace. Maybe with culture more fragmented than ever and Pitchfork conceding its place as the genre's primary arbiter in pursuit of more ecumenical coverage, there's no uniform way to experience indie music anymore. Maybe the indie rock I once knew is dying. Maybe it died a long time ago.

Or maybe we're getting ready for the next big surge. In the mid-2020s, artists continue to pull inspiration from the storied lineage that attracted me to indie rock in the first place, sometimes refracting those influences in stunning new ways. Countless microcommunities are flourishing on Bandcamp and in other shadowy corners of the internet. Personal newsletter platforms like Substack are reviving the spirit of blogs, and some of the savviest writers in the music sphere are even bringing back physical zines. It's harder than ever to make a living in independent music, but you don't have to poke around long to find flurries of exciting creative activity everywhere. It will be fascinating to see who achieves escape velocity and what heights they reach.

Acknowledgments

Thanks to all the musicians, journalists, and entertainment-industry types who inspired this book. Thanks to everyone who has given me a platform to enthuse about music I love and think too hard about What It All Means, and thanks to the many readers who've supported those endeavors. Endless thanks to everyone I've worked with at *Stereogum*: Scott Lapatine, Michael Nelson, Amrit Singh, Tom Breihan, Claire Lobenfeld, Miles Bowe, Gabriela Tully Claymore, James Rettig, Ryan Leas, Caitlin White, Peter Helman, Collin Robinson, Julia Gray, Rachel Brodsky, Danielle Chelosky, Abby Jones. You've all taught me so much. Thanks to my agent, Jack Gernert, for helping me make this book a reality. Thanks to my editor, Hannah Phillips, for taking a chance on me and providing so much wisdom and encouragement. Thanks to Lily Cronig and everyone else at St. Martin's for getting this project over the finish line. Thanks to my family for putting up with so many late nights writing and researching, and my friends for letting me ramble on about my progress at every opportunity. Thank you, whoever you are, for taking the time to read *Such Great Heights*.

Notes

Chapter 1: Slanted and Enchanted

6   *"an intense caste system"* Ann Powers, "The Merchants of Cool," interview by Barak Goodman and Rachel Dretzin, *Frontline*, PBS, February 27, 2001, https://www.pbs.org/wgbh/pages/frontline/shows/cool/interviews/powers.html.

12   *"a clearly defined elitist taste"* Jon Landau, "Rock and Roll Music," *Rolling Stone*, April 1, 1971.

14   *Many upgraded their signals* Michael Patrick Brady, "'Live from the Underground' details the influential world of college radio," WBUR, December 5, 2023, https://www.wbur.org/news/2023/12/05/live-from-the-underground-history-college-radio-katherine-rye-jewell.

18   *but decided not to sign* John Cook with Mac McCaughan and Laura Ballance, *Our Noise: The Story of Merge Records, the Indie Label That Got Big and Stayed Small* (Chapel Hill; Algonquin Books, 2009), 65–67.

Chapter 2: Take Me Out

27   *as he once described it* Lindsay Zoladz, "The Dismemberment Plan," Pitchfork, June 27, 2013, https://pitchfork.com/features/update/9159-the-dismemberment-plan.

31   *"the stuff of which legends are made"* Joe Levy, "Is This It," *Rolling Stone*, Oct. 11, 2001, https://www.rollingstone.com/music/music-album-reviews/is-this-it-252334/.

36 *"so six months ago"* Julia Chaplin, "NOTICED; A Hat That's Way Cool. Unless, Of Course, It's Not," *The New York Times*, May 18, 2003, https://www.nytimes.com/2003/05/18/style/noticed-a-hat-that-s-way-cool-unless-of-course-it-s-not.html.

37 *"re-consolidate in metropolitan hubs"* Keith Harris, "Did New York Kill Indie Rock?," *Journal of Popular Music Studies* 36, no. 2 (2024): 10–13, https://doi.org/10.1525/jpms.2024.36.2.10.

39 *with a supercharged chorus* Chris Willman, "Dr. Luke: The Billboard Cover Story," *Billboard*, September 3, 2010, https://www.billboard.com/music/music-news/dr-luke-the-billboard-cover-story-956518.

Chapter 3: This Song Will Change Your Life

49 *barely scraping by* Dan Ozzi, "Ben Gibbard Ranks Death Cab for Cutie's Eight Albums," *Vice*, August 9, 2018, https://www.vice.com/en/article/rank-your-records-death-cab-for-cutie-ben-gibbard.

49 *didn't have a manager* Patrick Hosken, "We've Got A File On You: Ben Gibbard," *Stereogum*, September 12, 2022, https://www.stereogum.com/2199216/ben-gibbard-death-cab-for-cutie-asphalt-meadows/interviews/weve-got-a-file-on-you.

49 *until the following year* Greg Kot, *Ripped: How the Wired Generation Revolutionized Music* (New York: Scribner, 2009), 86.

55 *The group's sales spiked* Marlow Stern, "Bands Made Popular By 'The O.C.': The Killers, Death Cab for Cutie, Rooney, More," *The Daily Beast*, August 5, 2013, https://www.thedailybeast.com/bands-made-popular-by-the-oc-the-killers-death-cab-for-cutie-rooney-more.

65 *"The Moldy Peaches"* Kimya Dawson and Adam Green, "Moldy Peaches Reunite on 'Juno' Soundtrack," interview by Alison Stewart, *The Bryant Park Project*, NPR, January 16, 2008, https://www.npr.org/2008/01/16/18137357/moldy-peaches-reunite-on-juno-soundtrack.

67 *due to their breakup* Laura Snapes, "'I was susceptible to being taken advantage of': Be Your Own Pet return after surviving sleazy indie," *The Guardian*, March 18, 2022, https://www.theguardian.com/music/2022/mar/18/be-your-own-pet-return-diy-punk-jemina-pearl.

68 *"Times New Viking"* Kevin Jagernauth, "Beck Wrote 21 Songs For 'Scott Pilgrim'; Brian O'Malley Initially Wanted Times New Viking To Pen Songs For Sex Bob-Omb," The Playlist, July 16, 2010, https://theplaylist.net/beck-wrote-21-songs-for-scott-pilgri-20100716.

Chapter 4: Best New Music

78 *Al Pacino's pitchfork tattoo* Dave Itzkoff, "The Pitchfork Effect," *Wired*, September 1, 2006, https://www.wired.com/2006/09/pitchfork.

78 *was already trademarked* Puja Patel, "Pitchfork Founder Ryan Schreiber

NOTES

on the Music of His Life," Pitchfork, January 8, 2019, https://pitchfork.com/features/5-10-15-20/pitchfork-founder-ryan-schreiber-on-the-music-of-his-life.

83 *120,000 daily readers* Greg Kot, "Pitchfork: Intonation Festival leads hit parade in an amazing year for concerts," *Chicago Tribune*, December 25, 2005, https://www.chicagotribune.com/2005/12/25/pitchfork-intonation-festival-leads-hit-parade-in-an-amazing-year-for-concerts.

83 *ballooned to 240,000* Kot, *Ripped*, 116.

Chapter 5: Music Is My Boyfriend

106 *online music market* Jacqui Cheng, "Apple owns 66% of online music market, Amazon second at 13%," Ars Technica, December 17, 2010, https://arstechnica.com/gadgets/2010/12/apple-owns-66-of-online-music-market-amazon-second-at-13.

106 *music retailer on Earth* Nathan Ingraham, "iTunes Store At 10: How Apple Built a Digital Media Juggernaut," The Verge, April 26, 2013, https://www.theverge.com/2013/4/26/4265172/itunes-store-at-10-how-apple-built-a-digital-media-juggernaut.

122 *unique monthly users* Nicholas Jackson and Alexis C. Madrigal, "The Rise and Fall of Myspace," *The Atlantic*, January 12, 2011, https://www.theatlantic.com/technology/archive/2011/01/the-rise-and-fall-of-myspace/69444/.

127 *boasted twenty-two million users* Jackson and Madrigal, "The Rise and Fall of Myspace."

128 *blocking independent labels* Scott Thill, "Is MySpace Music Deliberately Blocking Indies?," *Wired*, September 20, 2008, https://www.wired.com/2008/09/is-myspace-musi.

Chapter 6: D.A.N.C.E.

147 *faced backlash* Emma Orlow, "I Shop, Therefore I Am," *Huffpost*, June 12, 2012, https://www.huffpost.com/entry/i-shop-therefore-i-am_b_1418377.

148 *to friends and businesses* "Dov Charney on Reforming the Global Garment Industry," hosted by Reihan Salam, *The VICE Podcast Show*, produced by *Vice*, May 29, 2013, https://www.vice.com/en/article/the-vice-podcast-show-dov-charney-on-reforming-the-global-garment-industry.

148 *nearly $400 million* Andrew Ross Sorkin and Michael Barbaro, "American Apparel to Be Sold to Investment Firm," *New York Times*, December 18, 2006, https://www.nytimes.com/2006/12/18/business/18cnd-retail.html.

Chapter 7: Upward over the Mountain

169 "Freak Folk's Very Own Pied Piper," *New York Times*, December 12, 2004, https://www.nytimes.com/2004/12/12/arts/music/freak-folks-very-own-pied-piper.html.

Chapter 8: Fake Empire

184 *a giant Slip 'N Slide* Patrick Sauer, "The McCarren Park Pool Parties: An Oral History," *We'll Have to Pass*, November 9, 2020, https://have2pass.substack.com/p/the-mccarren-park-pool-parties-an.

186 *Murphy was embarrassed* James Murphy, "James Murphy and Opinions on Black Eyed Peas," interview by Greg Kot and Jim DeRogatis, *Sound Opinions*, December 3, 2010, https://www.soundopinions.org/show/262.

191 *sexual misconduct allegations* Marc Hogan, "Arcade Fire's Win Butler Accused of Sexual Misconduct by Multiple Women; Frontman Responds," Pitchfork, August 27, 2022, https://pitchfork.com/news/arcade-fires-win-butler-accused-of-sexual-misconduct-by-multiple-women-frontman-responds.

195 *a Tumblr account* https://whoisarcadefire.tumblr.com.

201 *the attention of Jeff Bhasker* Andrew Hampp, "How fun.'s 'We Are Young' Scored Chevy's 'Stunt Anthem' Super Bowl Spot," *Billboard*, February 5, 2012, https://www.billboard.com/music/music-news/how-funs-we-are-young-scored-chevys-stunt-anthem-super-bowl-spot-1099054.

Chapter 9: Terminally Chill

222 *criticism personally* Rachel Brodsky, "We've Got A File On You: Bethany Cosentino," *Stereogum*, July 27, 2023, https://www.stereogum.com/2231105/bethany-cosentino-best-coast-solo-debut-album/interviews/weve-got-a-file-on-you.

Chapter 10: Late Registration

246 *access to his beats* Mickey Hess, ed., *Icons of Hip Hop: An Encyclopedia of the Movement, Music, and Culture*, Vol. 2 (Westport: Greenwood, 2007), 555–578.

Chapter 11: Art Angels

271 *"dad-rock"* Rob Mitchum, "I Introduced the Term 'Dad-Rock' to the World. I Have Regrets.," *Esquire*, October 11, 2019, https://www.esquire.com/entertainment/music/a29419783/what-is-dad-rock.

278 *her own work as problematic* Helen Brown, "Tune-Yards interview: 'I have to sing to survive. Even as a f***** up mess of a white American,'"

The Independent, March 18, 2021, https://www.the-independent.com/arts-entertainment/music/features/tune-yards-interview-merrill-garbus-new-album-b1818979.html.

283 *They didn't get far* Lora Pabst, "This boat don't float," *The Minnesota Star Tribune*, June 26, 2009, https://www.startribune.com/this-boat-don-t-float/49134952.

295 *"millennial males"* Ravi Somaiya, "Pitchfork Media Becomes Part of Condé Nast Stable," *The New York Times*, Oct. 13, 2015, https://www.nytimes.com/2015/10/14/business/media/conde-nast-buys-pitchfork-media.html.

296 *oppressively white* Sasha Frere-Jones, "A Paler Shade of White," *The New Yorker*, Oct. 15, 2007, https://www.newyorker.com/magazine/2007/10/22/a-paler-shade-of-white.

Chapter 12: Love It If We Made It

306 *an opaque misconduct scandal* Jenn Pelly, "Reckoning With Pinegrove," Pitchfork, September 26, 2018, https://pitchfork.com/features/article/reckoning-with-pinegrove.

313 *monopolized digital ad sales* Leah Nylen and Davey Alba, "How Google Allegedly Monopolized the Ad Technology Market," *Bloomberg*, September 20, 2024, https://www.bloomberg.com/news/articles/2024-09-20/how-google-allegedly-monopolized-the-ad-technology-market.

314 *for a new generation* Joe Coscarelli, "The Only Music Critic Who Matters (if You're Under 25)," *New York Times*, September 30, 2020, https://www.nytimes.com/2020/09/30/arts/music/anthony-fantano-the-needle-drop.html.

314 *definitely proliferated* Casey Newton, "How platforms killed Pitchfork," Platformer, January 18, 2024, https://www.platformer.news/why-pitchfork-died.

316 *months-long delays* Chris Willman, "Adele's '30' Sends Vinyl Pressing Plants Into Overdrive, While LP Shortages Leave Many Artists Chasing Pavements," *Variety*, November 3, 2021, https://variety.com/2021/music/news/adele-vinyl-record-pressing-plant-lp-shortages-1235103951.

316 *only works at scale* Damon Krukowski, "Spotify made £56m profit, but has decided not to pay smaller artists like me. We need you to make some noise," *The Guardian*, November 30, 2023, https://www.theguardian.com/commentisfree/2023/nov/30/spotify-smaller-artists-wrapped-indie-musicians.

316 *claimed in 2017* Jem Aswad, "Car Seat Headrest's Will Toledo Defends Spotify's Royalty Payments," *Variety*, December 29, 2017, https://variety.com/2017/biz/news/car-seat-headrests-will-toledo-defends-spotifys-royalty-payments-1202649885.

323 *more and more* Joe Coscarelli, "Rock's Not Dead, It's Ruled By Women: The Round-Table Conversation," *New York Times*, September 1, 2017, https://www.nytimes.com/2017/09/01/arts/music/rock-bands-women.html.

330 *his main band* Neil McCormick, "How The National became the world's most influential band," *The Telegraph*, April 20, 2023, https://www.telegraph.co.uk/music/artists/the-national-influential-taylor-swift-ed-sheeran-bridgers.

334 *biggest song on Spotify* Nate Rogers, "Why Is The Obscure B-Side 'Harness Your Hopes' Pavement's Top Song On Spotify? It's Complicated," *Stereogum*, November 17, 2020, https://www.stereogum.com/2105993/pavement-harness-your-hopes-spotify/columns/sounding-board.

Index

12 Rods, 80
22, A Million (2016, Bon Iver), 296
The 1975, 288, 303–6, 312
1989 (2014, Taylor Swift), 201, 319
(500) Days of Summer (2009), 69–71
808s & Heartbreak (2008, Kanye West), 251, 279

Abebe, Nitsuh, 19–20, 99–100, 227, 257, 286, 294
Abrams, Jonathan, 118
Adams, Ryan, 327
Aim and Ignite (2009, Fun), 200
Albarn, Damon, 112
Albini, Steve, 16–17, 225, 262
Allen, Lily, 124–26, 222
Alligator (2005, The National), 188–89
All Music Guide, 20
"All My Friends" (LCD Soundsystem), 186
American Apparel, 134, 145–50, 171
Amoeba, 55
Anderson, Stacey, 325
Anderson, Tom, 118, 127, 129
Anderson, Wes, 52, 167
Andrew, Angus, 34, 39
Andrew WK, 142
Animal Collective (AnCo), 162–63, 182, 209–11
Another Eternity (2015, Purity Ring), 300
Anticon, 243
Antonoff, Jack, 200, 202, 318–22
Aoki, Steve, 144–45
Apple, 105–14
  "Get a Mac" campaign (2006), 108
  iPod Nano campaign (2007), 110, 111
  iPods, 106
  iTunes Music Store, 106, 107
Arcade Fire, 75–78, 84–85, 87, 92, 94, 182, 185, 191–95, 296, 317, 335

INDEX

The ArchAndroid (2010, Janelle Monáe), 273
Arctic Monkeys, 123–24, 126, 288
"Are You Gonna Be My Girl" (Jet), 38, 109
Ariel Pink, 196, 216–18
Ark (2003, Animal Collective), 162
"Around the World" (Daft Punk), 136
Arrested Development, 64
Art Angels (2015, Grimes), 284–85
Arular (2005, M.I.A.), 137
Atmosphere, 242–43
A-Trak, 144, 150
Augé, Gaspard, 142
A.V. Club, 86, 219, 278
Avett Brothers, 169
Axelson, Eric, 27

Badly Drawn Boy, 9
Baker, Julien, 327
Ballance, Laura, 107
Bandcamp, 128, 312, 335
Banger, Ed, 142
Banhart, Devendra, 66, 158–60, 163, 169
Based God, 260
Batmanglij, Rostam, 223, 299
Beach House, 227–29
Beam, Sam. *See* Iron & Wine
Beck, 58, 67
Before Today (2010, Ariel Pink), 217–18
Bejar, Dan, 196
Belle & Sebastian, 19, 70
Berninger, Matt, 187–90
Best Coast, 220–24, 252
Best Friends Forever, 116
Be the Cowboy (2018, Mitski), 325–26
Beyoncé, 269–70, 274, 279, 300, 329
Bhasker, Jeff, 201

Bieber, Justin, 291
Bitte Orca (2009, Dirty Projectors), 276
Blake, James, 231
Bleachers, 202, 318
Bloc Party, 38, 145, 247
Blonde (2016, Frank Ocean), 317
Blood Bank (2009, Bon Iver), 296
Blood Orange, 279–80
Bloodshy & Avant, 288
Body Talk (2010, Robyn), 282, 284
The Bones of What You Believe (2013, Chvrches), 297
Bon Iver, 173–75, 181, 195, 198, 252, 262, 296
Bon Iver, Bon Iver (2011, Bon Iver), 296
Bonnaroo, 206–10
Born to Die (2012, Lana Del Rey), 286
Boucher, Claire, 282–85
Bowie, David, 85, 87, 183–85, 321
Braff, Zach, 58–60, 159, 308
Brand New, 121
Brat (2024, Charli XCX), 334
Braun, Scooter, 291–92
"Brave" (Sara Bareilles), 318–19
Breihan, Tom, 60, 98, 243, 247, 270, 298, 330
Bridgers, Phoebe, 222, 326–28
A Brief Inquiry into Online Relationships (The 1975), 305–6
Bright Eyes, 169–70, 327
Brion, Jon, 224, 246
Broken Social Scene, 82, 110, 240, 308
Brown, Ethan, 29
Brownstein, Carrie, 171
Bunyan, Vashti, 163, 169
Burial, 143
Bury Me at Makeout Creek (2014, Mitski), 324
Busy P, 142

INDEX

Butler, Syd, 106–7
Butler, Win, 76–77, 191–94
Buzz Media, 87
Byrne, David, 205

Cadence Weapon, 240
Califone, 161
"Call Me Maybe" (Carly Rae Jepsen), 291–93
Cam'ron, 98, 247
Cancer for Cure (2012, El-P), 263
Cansei de Ser Sexy (CSS), 112
Capital Cities, 199
Carey, Mariah, 209, 276
Carles, 144, 211–12, 215, 221–22
Carlin, Andrew, 190
Carrabba, Chris, 116
Carrie & Lowell (2015, Sufjan Stevens), 326
Carter, Sean, 139
Casablancas, Julian, 21, 30–31, 156
Castaways and Cutouts (2002, The Decemberists), 155
Cat Power, 114, 328
Cera, Michael, 64–69
Chafin, Chris, 149
Chan, Franki, 144–45
Change (2001, The Dismemberment Plan), 28
Channel Orange (2012, Frank Ocean), 274
Charli XCX, 287, 304, 334
Charney, Dov, 148–49
Cherry Tree (2004, The National), 188
chillwave, 211–18, 229
ChrisMix™, 104
Christgau, Robert, 96
Chung, Alexa, 224
Chutes Too Narrow (2003, The Shins), 59
Chvrches, 297

Clap Your Hands Say Yeah (CYHSY), 87–90
Clarity (1999, Jimmy Eat World), 116
Clipse, 247–48
Coachella, 141, 157
Coastal Grooves (2011, Blood Orange), 280
Cobain, Kurt, 16, 72
Cobrasnake, 146
Coffman, Amber, 276
Cohen, Ian, 90, 215, 296
The College Dropout (2004, Kanye West), 38, 246
Collins, Evan, 168
Collision Course (2004, Jay-Z and Linkin Park), 139
Common, 239–41, 245
Condé Nast, 295
Converse, 223, 236
Corgan, Billy, 15
Corrigan, Tommy, 120
Coscarelli, Joe, 320
Cosentino, Bethany, 220–24
Crazy for You (2010, Best Coast), 221–22, 224
"Crazy in Love" (Beyoncé), 180
The Creek Drank the Cradle (2002, Iron & Wine), 158, 159, 170
Crooked Rain, Crooked Rain (1994, Pavement), 17
Cross (2007, Justice), 142–44
Cupid Deluxe (2013, Blood Orange), 280
The Cure, 14–15

Dacus, Lucy, 327–28
Daft Punk, 135–36, 141–42, 208, 246, 262
Dahlen, Chris, 83, 98
Danse Macabre (2023, Duran Duran), 34

Dashboard Confessional, 116–17, 120, 243
DatPiff, 237, 253
Dawson, Kimya, 65
Days Are Gone (2013, Haim), 297–98
Dead Oceans, 324, 326, 329
Deadringer (2002, RJD2), 242
Death Cab for Cutie, 28, 48–50, 53–54, 56, 76, 82, 333
Death Grips, 261
"The Decade in Indie" (Abebe), 19–20
The Decemberists, 76, 155–56, 166, 182
Deerhunter, 253, 309
Definitive Jux (Def Jux), 241–43
De La Soul, 113
DeMarco, Jason, 263
Dessner, Aaron, 188, 190, 330
Dessner, Bryce, 188–90
Destroyer, 196–97
Deusner, Stephen, 191
DeWolfe, Chris, 118, 127, 129
Dibb, Josh, 163
DiCrescenzo, Brent, 80, 197
Digital Ash from a Digital Urn (2005, Bright Eyes), 170
Dim Mak Records, 144–45
Diplo, 125, 137–38, 144–45, 244, 258, 334
Dirty Projectors, 209, 275, 276
Disco Demolition Night, 93
Discovery (2001, Daft Punk), 136
The Dismemberment Plan, 25–28, 82–83, 140, 333
The Dismemberment Plan Is Terrified (1997, The Dismemberment Plan), 26
DJ Shadow, 239–40, 261
Dntel. *See* Tamborello, Jimmy
Dombal, Ryan, 111

Don't Stop the Music (2002, Robyn), 281
Dost Andrew, 200
Drake, 249, 251, 273
Drew, Kevin, 82
Droste, Ed, 180, 227
dubstep, 143

Earl Sweatshirt, 254–55
Ed Banger Records, 142
Ek, Phil, 172
El-P, 241–42, 263–64
Emergency & I (1999, The Dismemberment Plan), 27–28, 82
Eminem, 5
Emotion (2015, Carly Rae Jepsen), 292–93
"Emo: Where the Girls Aren't" (Hopper), 121
Empire Of The Sun, 199–200
Eno, Brian, 12, 110
eUniverse, 118, 127
"Everything Is Embarrassing" (Sky Ferreira), 288–89
Evolution Control Committee, 139
Exile in Guyville (1993, Liz Phair), 17, 95, 97
Exmilitary (2011, Death Grips), 261

Fantano, Anthony, 314
Favela on Blast (2008), 137
Fearless (2021, Taylor Swift), 194
Feels (2005, Animal Collective), 162
Feist, 110–12
Ferdinand, Franz, 37–38, 123
Ferreira, Sky, 288–90, 304
Fever To Tell (2003, Yeah Yeah Yeahs), 33
Flaming Lips, 40, 57, 80, 205, 230
Fleet Foxes, 171–74, 253, 294

Flowers, Brandon, 38
Foo Fighters, 7, 307
Fool's Gold Records, 259
For Emma, Forever Ago (2007, Bon Iver), 173–74
Foster, Mark, 199
Foster The People, 270
Free People, 147
Freeway, 246
Frenchkiss Records, 106
Frere-Jones, Sasha, 296
Friendster, 118–19, 128
Frightened Rabbit, 190, 198
Fucking Awesome, 144–45
Fugazi, 26, 35
Fun, 200–2, 318
Funeral (2004, Arcade Fire), 75–76, 84, 87, 191

Garbus, Merrill, 277–78
Garden State (2004), 58–60, 70, 159, 167
Geidi Primes (2010, Grimes), 283
Get Up Kids, 116
Gibbard, Ben, 39, 41–44, 49–50, 54, 60, 72
Gimme Indie Rock (1991, Sebadoh), 10
Girls Can Tell (2001, Spoon), 56
Girl Talk, 26, 139–40
Give Up (2003, The Postal Service), 39, 42, 333
Goblin (2011, Tyler), 255
God Loves Ugly (2002, Atmosphere), 243
Godrich, Nigel, 67
The Golden Apples of the Sun (2004, Banhart), 159–61
González, José, 167
Goodman, Lizzy, 29, 156
Gorilla vs. Bear, 211, 216
Gossip Girl, 63
Go! Team, 136, 142

Graduation (2007, Kanye West), 133, 246
Grande, Ariana, 5
Green, Adam, 65
Green Album, 220
Greene, Ernest, 213
Greenwald, Andy, 91, 121
Greenwood, Jonny, 8
Greif, Mark, 35, 157, 211, 293–94
The Grey Album (2004, Danger Mouse), 139
Grey's Anatomy, 62, 98, 110, 167, 307
Grimes, 282–85
Grizzly Bear, 179–81, 184, 196, 209, 226–27, 315
Guero (2005, Beck), 58
Guided by Voices, 30

Haim, 297–98
Halcyon Digest (2010, Deerhunter), 253
Hansard, Glen, 167
Harmer, Nick, 49
Harrington, Tim, 76
Harris, Emmylou, 170
Harris, Keith, 37
Harrison, Andrew, 123
Harvell, Jess, 143
Harvey, Eric, 272–73
Haunted Graffiti, 196, 217
Hawk, Davye, 214
Hayne, Dick, 147
Healy, Matty, 303–6
Heartthrob (2013, Tegan and Sara), 296
Hell Hath No Fury (2006), 247–48
Her Majesty the Decemberists (2003, The Decemberists), 155
"Hey Ya!" (OutKast), 52, 154–55
High Fidelity (2000), 50, 71
High Violet (2010, The National), 190

Hill, Zach, 261
Hipster Primitive, 157
Hipster Runoff, 211–12, 221, 285, 287
Hogan, Marc, 287
Hollertronix, 137–38
Homework (1997, Daft Punk), 135–36
Hopper, Jessica, 99–100, 121, 315–16
Horn of Plenty (2004, Grizzly Bear), 180
Hot Fuss (2004, Killers), 38–39
Hot Hot Heat, 34
House of Balloons (2011, The Weeknd), 271–72
Howe, Alison, 124
How It Feels to Be Something On (1998, Sunny Day Real Estate), 116
How To Dismantle An Atomic Bomb (2004, U2), 108
How to Dress Well, 278–79
Hughes, John, 290
Hugo, Chad, 247
Hunter, Mark, 146
Hyden, Steven, 298
Hynes, Dev, 279–80
The Hype Machine, 140

"I Bet You Look Good on the Dancefloor" (2006, Arctic Monkeys), 123
I like it when you sleep, for you are so beautiful yet so unaware of it (2016, The, 1975), 304
Illegal Art, 139–40
Illinois (2005, Sufjan Stevens), 183
I'm Wide Awake, It's Morning (2005, Bright Eyes), 170
InnerSpeaker (2010, Tame Impala), 229–30
Interpol, 187–88

In the Aeroplane over the Sea (1998, Neutral Milk Hotel), 155
In Utero (1993, Nirvana), 307–8
Irglová, Markéta, 167
Iron & Wine, 43, 60, 63, 158–59, 168, 170, 174
Is This It (2001, Strokes), 29–32, 109
It's Blitz! (2009, Yeah Yeah Yeahs), 209
It's Never Been Like That (2006, Phoenix), 208
"I Used to Love H.E.R." (Common), 239, 245

Japandroids, 309
Jay-Z, 139, 179, 181, 192, 196, 199, 200, 209, 227
Jefferson, Cord, 256–57
Jepsen, Carly Rae, 291–93
Jet, 109, 110, 122
Jimmy Eat World, 116–17
Jive Records, 247–48
Jobs, Steve, 106, 109
Johnson, Calvin, 144
Jonathan Fire*Eater, 33
Jones, Norah, 111
Jonze, Tim, 89
Joy Division, 186, 260
Junior Senior, 136, 142
Juno (2007), 65
Justice, 142–44

Kala (2007, M.I.A.), 258
Kaleidoscope Dream (2012, Miguel Pimentel), 275
Kanye West, 54, 199–202, 209, 245–47, 250–52, 261–63, 279, 304, 320
Kapranos, Alex, 37–38
Kaputt (2011, Destroyer), 196–97
Karen O, 29–30, 34
KCRW: *Morning Becomes Eclectic*, 76

Kelly, Zach, 230
Kendrick Lamar, 321
Kid A (2000, Radiohead), 8, 9, 40, 80, 81, 197
Kid Cudi, 144, 223
"Kids" (MGMT), 199, 208, 209, 252
Kiewel, Tony, 41
Killer Mike, 263–64
Killers, 38–39, 57
Kill Kill (2008, Lana Del Rey), 285
Kill Rock Stars, 155
Kill the Moonlight (2002, Spoon), 56, 107
King of the Beach (2010, Wavves), 220–21
Kiss (2012, Carly Rae Jepsen), 292
Klein, Amy, 286
Knowles, Solange, 179, 279–80
Koenig, Ezra, 91, 92, 99, 299, 329
Kot, Greg, 49, 72
Krauss, Alexis, 296
Krauss, Alison, 194
K Records, 144
Krell, Tom, 278–79

Lady Sovereign, 124
Lana Del Ray aka Lizzy Grant (2010, Lana Del Rey), 285
Lana Del Rey, 285–87, 321
Lapatine, Scott, 85, 193, 315
Lateralus (2001, Tool), 81
Late Registration (2005, Kanye West), 246
LCD Soundsystem, 34, 39, 94, 135, 185–87, 281, 296
Led Zeppelin, 12, 116
Legrand, Victoria, 227–28
Leithauser, Hamilton, 33
Lennox, Noah, 162
Les Savy Fav, 27, 76, 106
Let It Die (2004, Feist), 110
Lewis, Jenny, 41, 170

Li, Lykke, 72, 251, 282
Life Is Full of Possibilities (2001, Dntel), 40
Like Water for Chocolate (2000, Common), 240–41
Lil B, 260–61
Lil Jon, 99
Lil Wayne, 98, 247
Limp Bizkit, 104
Lind, Zach, 116
Linkin Park, 139
Lipez, Zachary, 294
Lollapalooza, 15, 54, 86, 197, 206, 239
Lonerism (2012, Tame Impala), 230–31
Longstreth, Dave, 275–76
Lorde, 290–91
Lord Willin' (2002, Clipse), 247
"Losing My Edge" (LCD Soundsystem), 34–35, 39, 94, 135, 185, 186, 311
Love, Courtney, 15
The Love Club (2013, Lorde), 290
Love Remains (2010, How to Dress Well), 278
Lynch, David, 228

M83 196, 293
Mad Decent, 144
Makeoutclub, 117, 119
Make Up the Breakdown (2002, Hot Hot Heat), 34
Malik, Zayn, 319
Malkmus, Stephen, 3, 259
Mangum, Jeff, 114, 154–55, 160
Manners (2010, Passion Pit), 209
Mapes, Jill, 330
"Maps" (Yeah Yeah Yeahs), 39, 329
Mars, Thomas, 208
Martens, Todd, 229
Martin, Max, 39, 281, 319

INDEX

MASSEDUCTION (2017, St. Vincent), 321
Matador Records, 17–18, 21, 33, 95, 316, 328
Mayberry, Lauren, 297
MBDTF, 201, 252, 253
McDonald, Michael, 196
MC Frontalot, 244
MC Ride, 261
Meader, Vaughn, 194
Meet Me in the Bathroom (2022), 29, 156
Melodrama (2017, Lorde), 321
Meloy, Colin, 155–56
Mercer, James, 51, 59, 61
Merge Records, 69, 75, 84, 194
Merriweather Post Pavilion (2009, Animal Collective), 210–11
MF Doom, 244
MGMT, 43, 199, 206–9, 229–30, 251–52
M.I.A., 125, 137–38, 244–45, 258
Michigan (2003, Stevens), 82, 163
"Midnight City" (M83), 196, 293
The Milk-Eyed Mender (2004, Joanna Newsom), 161
Millard, Drew, 36–37
Mitchum, Rob, 34
Mitski Miyawaki, 324–27, 330, 334
The Modern Age (2001, The Strokes), 30
Modern Vampires of the City (2013, Vampire Weekend), 298–99
Modest Mouse, 57, 189, 299
The Moldy Peaches, 65
Molina, Jason, 63
Monáe, Janelle, 273
Moore, David, 84
Moore, Sonny, 150
Morin, Andy, 261
Morrison, Travis, 25–28, 82–84
Mos Def, 257

Mos Def & Talib Kweli Are Black Star (1998, Black Star), 248
MTV, 4–6, 15, 40, 53, 113, 117, 120, 179–80, 182, 255, 305, 317
MTV2, 107, 117
Muhly, Nico, 180
Mumford & Sons, 198, 270, 294
Murder Inc., 21–22
Murdoch, Rupert, 127–28
Murphy, James, 34, 37, 39, 94, 135, 138, 145, 185–87, 296
Music from The O.C.: Mix, 1 (2004, Warner Bros.), 56–57
My Beautiful Dark Twisted Fantasy (2010, Kanye West), 201, 252
MySpace, 113, 117–29, 206–7, 222, 249–51, 289, 308, 313
MySpace Music, 128–29
Secret Shows, 126
Mystic Stylez (1995, Three, 6 Mafia), 238
My Truth (1999, Robyn), 281

Nah Right, 249, 257
Napster, 8, 31, 103–4, 313
The National, 88, 188–90
Native Tongues, 238, 245
The Needle Drop, 314
Nelson, Ivy, 116–17
Neon Bible (2010, Arcade Fire), 191–93
Neptunes, 247
Neutral Milk Hotel (NMH), 19, 114, 154–55
Nevermind (1991, Nirvana), 15–16, 29, 246
New Rock Revolution, 31, 33, 39, 156
News Corp, 127–29
"New Slang" (The Shins), 58–60
Newsom, Joanna, 160–61, 163
New Weird America, 161

"New York, I Love You but You're Bringing Me Down" (LCD Soundsystem), 185–86
Nick & Norah's Infinite Playlist (2008), 66–67, 70
Night Ripper (2006, Girl Talk), 139–40
Night Time, My Time (2013, Sky Ferreira), 289–90
Nirvana, 11, 15, 16, 28, 29, 43, 72, 307
NME, 31, 123, 124
No Love Deep Web (2012, Death Grips), 261
Nostalgia, Ultra (2011, Frank Ocean), 273–74
Notes on a Conditional Form (2020, The, 1975), 306
Nothing Feels Good (Greenwald), 115, 121
Now Here Is Nowhere (2004, Secret Machines), 87

Oberst, Conor, 51, 169, 170, 243, 327, 328
The O.C., 47–59, 62–64, 70–72, 95, 107, 146, 167
Ocean, Frank, 273–74, 317
Odd Future, 236–37, 253–57
Oh, Inverted World (2001, The Shins), 58–59
OK Computer (1997, Radiohead), 8
Oldham, Will, 161
O'Malley, Bryan Lee, 67
One Direction, 304
The Only Place (2012, Best Coast), 224
Oracular Spectacular (2007, MGMT), 199, 205, 207
Ounsworth, Alec, 88, 89
Our Endless Numbered Days (2004, Iron & Wine), 159
Our Noise (2009), 85

OutKast, 154–55, 244, 250, 263
Owl City, 199, 292

Palomo, Alan, 214
Panda Bear, 162, 213
Parker, Kevin, 229–31
Parry, Richard Reed, 77
Passion Pit, 43, 209
Paste, 167
Patsavas, Alexandra, 55, 62, 63, 72, 307
Pavement, 17, 18, 70, 81, 238, 334
Pecknold, Robin, 171–72
Pelly, Jenn, 121, 283
Pentz, Thomas Wesley, 137
Perry, Katy, 145, 296, 319
Person Pitch (2007, Panda Bear), 162, 213
Peter Bjorn and John, 63, 282
Petrusich, Amanda, 170
Petty, Tom, 30
Phair, Liz, 17, 95–97
Phillips, Amy, 71
Phoenix, 208–9
The Photo Album (2001, Death Cab for Cutie), 49
Pimentel, Miguel, 275
Piracy Funds Terrorism, Vol. 1 (2004, Diplo and M.I.A.), 137–38, 244
Pitchfork, 9, 19–21, 39, 59–60, 109, 116, 136, 143, 159, 162, 181, 223, 228, 240–43, 255, 305, 335
  Best New Music review, 77–100, 104, 111, 138, 139, 156, 162, 172, 185, 190, 197, 217, 219, 228, 248, 261, 270, 272, 280, 283, 287, 293, 299, 321, 329–30
  Music Festival, 84, 136, 162, 166, 282, 293
Plagenhoef, Scott, 83, 244

INDEX

Plans (2005, Death Cab for Cutie), 54
Plant, Robert, 194
poptimism, 94, 97–100, 225, 309
Portlandia, 171, 213
Portman, Natalie, 58, 70
Portner, Dave, 162
The Postal Service, 39–43, 49, 60, 159, 199, 311
Powell, Mike, 100
Powers, Ann, 6, 96, 275
Prospect Hummer (2005, Animal Collective), 163
Puberty, 2 (2016, Mitski), 324–25
Punisher (2020, Phoebe Bridgers), 328–29
Pure Heroine (2013, Lorde), 291, 321
Purity Ring, 277, 300

Questlove, 257
Quin, Sara, 256, 316

Rabbit Fur Coat (2006, Jenny Lewis), 170
Rabin, Nathan, 71
Radiohead, 8, 9, 40, 48, 67, 80, 81, 104, 197, 274
Rage Against The Machine, 103
Raisen, Justin, 289, 320
Raising Sand (2007, Plant and Krauss), 194
Raphael, Sally Jessy, 157
R.A.P. Music (2012, Killer Mike), 263
The Rapture, 34, 156
Ratatat, 136
Rawkus Records, 242
Rawlins, Ahsmi, 249
Rechtshaid, Ariel, 288–89
Red Hot Chili Peppers, 54, 104
Reed, Lou, 12, 33
Reflektor (2013, Arcade Fire), 296

Rejoicing in the Hands (2004, Devendra Banhart), 159
R.E.M., 15, 20, 189
The Reminder (2007, Feist), 110, 111
Republic Records, 330–31
Reputation (2017, Taylor Swift), 319
ResponseBase, 118
Reznor, Trent, 226–27
Rhymesayers, 242–43, 246
Richardson, Mark, 197, 218
Richardson, Terry, 34, 149
Rilo Kiley, 41, 170
Ripped: How the Wired Generation Revolutionized Music (Kot), 49
RJD2, 75, 242
Robyn, 280–82, 284, 293
Robyn Is Here (1995, Robyn), 281
Roc-A-Fella Records, 245–46
Rolling Stone, 14, 16, 21, 80, 81, 172
The Roots, 239–41
Rosen, Jody, 201
Rosenfeld, Josh, 83
Rosenthal, Jeff, 249
Rosnay, Xavier de, 142
Rough Trade Records, 65
Rubin, Rick, 261
Ruess, Nate, 200–2
Run The Jewels, 263–64
Run The Jewels, 2 (2014, Run The Jewels), 264

Said the Gramophone, 85, 88
Sanneh, Kelefa, 92–95, 137
Santigold, 125–26
Saturday Night Live (SNL), 7, 8, 59, 91, 95, 170, 195, 287, 327
Savage, Stephanie, 63
Saves the Day, 115–17
Scally, Alex, 227
Schreiber, Ryan, 78–83, 217
Schwartz, Josh, 47–48, 52, 55, 57
Schwartzman, Jason, 51, 55

INDEX

Scott Pilgrim vs. the World (2010), 67–68
Sebadoh, 10
Secret Machines, 87
Segran, Elizabeth, 147
Seven Swans (2004, Sufjan Stevens), 164
Sex Bob-Omb, 67
Shazam, 109
She & Him, 69, 169
The Shepherd's Dog (2007, Iron & Wine), 170
The Shins, 58–61, 172
Shrines (2012, Purity Ring), 300
Shut Up and Play the Hits (2012), 187
Silent Alarm (2005, Bloc Party), 38, 145
Simian, 141–42
Simon, Leslie, 122
Simpson, Ashlee, 95, 98
SiriusXMU, 309, 316
Sit Down, Man (2010, Das Racis), 258–59
Sitek, Dave, 33
"Skinny Love" (Bon Iver), 174–75
Skjelset, Skyler, 171–72
Slanted and Enchanted (1992, Pavement), 17, 81
Sleater-Kinney, 155, 171
Sleigh Bells, 296
Smashing Pumpkins, 15, 116
"Smells like Teen Spirit" (Nirvana), 29, 63, 72
Smith, Daniel, 163
Smith, Elliott, 19, 114, 155, 328
Smith, Zachary Cole, 289
The Smiths, 14, 19, 70, 115
SNL. See *Saturday Night Live (SNL)*
Snow Patrol, 62
Soderberg, Brandon, 216
So Far Gone (2009, Drake), 251

Soft Cell, 138
Some Loud Thunder (2007, Clap Your Hands Say Yeah), 89
Some Nights (2012, Fun), 201–2
Songs of Innocence (2014, U2), 108–9
Sonic Youth, 14–15, 75, 225, 238
Soulja Boy, 251
Soulwax, 141
SoundCloud, 128
Sour Records, 8
South by Southwest (SXSW), 174, 216, 219, 236
Spank Rock, 258
Spector, Phil, 69, 220
Spitz, Marc, 169, 171
Spoon, 56, 71, 107
Spotify, 182, 314–17, 322, 324
Springsteen, Bruce, 76, 92, 98
SRX, 209
Steel, Sharon, 50–51
Steely Dan, 196–97, 225
Stereogum, 9, 17, 49–51, 85–88, 193, 199, 210, 213, 219, 264–65, 270, 293, 315, 321
Stevens, Sufjan, 82, 163–66, 173, 183, 191, 198, 240, 326
"Stillness Is the Move" (Dirty Projectors), 209, 275–76
Strange Desire (2014, Bleachers), 202
Stranger in the Alps (2017, Phoebe Bridgers), 327
Strawberry Jam (2007, Animal Collective), 162
Streisand, Barbra, 194
The Strokes, 29–34, 38–39, 65, 93, 109, 110, 187
St. Vincent, 183, 321
Sub Pop Records, 28, 32, 39, 41–43, 59, 158
The Suburbs (2010, Arcade Fire), 192–94

"Such Great Heights" (The Postal Service), 42–43, 60
Sun Giant, 172
Sung Tongs (2004, Animal Collective), 162
Superbad (2007), 64–65
Swank, 118
Swift, Taylor, 182–83, 194, 201, 252, 297, 319–21, 329, 330
Switch, 125
System Of A Down, 7

'Tainted Love' (Soft Cell), 138
Take Care (2011, Drake), 273
Talking Heads, 27, 185
Talk Talk, 173
Tamborello, Jimmy, 39–44
Tame Impala, 229–31, 316
Taylor, Chris, 279
Tedder, Michael, 117, 122
Teen Dream (2010, Beach House), 228
Tegan and Sara, 296, 315–16, 318
Terrible Records, 279
This Is Happening (2010, LCD Soundsystem), 187
Three, 6 Mafia, 238
Through Being Cool (1999, Saves the Day), 115
Thunder, Lightning, Strike (2004, Go! Team), 136
TikTok, 182, 314, 323, 334
Tila Tequila, 126
Timberlake, Justin, 98, 195, 278
Toro y Moi, 213
Total Request Live (TRL), 4–5, 7, 21, 29, 120, 331
Touch and Go Records, 33, 84
Transatlanticism (2003, Death Cab for Cutie), 53–54, 72, 333
Travistan (2004, Morrison), 82–84
True Romance (2013, Charli XCX), 287

True That (2014, Cera), 68
Tumblr, 128, 195, 215, 223, 254, 288, 304
Turn On the Bright Lights (2002, Interpol), 33
Twee (Spitz), 169, 171
Twitter, 128, 179, 195
Two Against Nature (2001, Steely Dan), 197
"Two Weeks" (Grizzly Bear), 181, 226
Tyler, 235–36, 253, 255–57

Untrue (2007, Burial), 143
Uproxx, 48, 52, 57
Urban Outfitters (UO), 66, 134, 146–48, 183, 215, 223–24, 226, 252
U2, 76, 85, 108–9, 116, 304

Vampire Weekend, 90–92, 99, 100, 181, 223, 276–77, 298–99
Van Etten, Sharon, 68, 190
VanWyngarden, Andrew, 199–200, 207
Veckatimest (Grizzly Bear), 180–81, 184
Velvet Underground, 30, 33, 110
Vernon, Justin, 173–75, 195–96, 252, 278
VH1, 6, 85
Vibe Generation, 215
"Video Games" (Lana Del Rey), 285–86
Visions (2012, Grimes), 283, 284
Volume One (2008, She & Him), 69

Walla, Chris, 82, 83
Walt Mink, 80
Ward, Mathew, 69
Warner Bros., 17, 56–57, 86–87
Wavves, 218–21, 223

"Way We Get By, The" (Spoon), 56, 107
"We Are Young" (Fun), 201, 318
Weezer, 7, 68, 115, 220, 324
We Got It, 4 Cheap (2004, Clipse), 248
Whatever People Say I Am, That's What I'm Not (2006, Arctic Monkeys), 123
The White Stripes, 32
Williams, Nathan, 218–21
Williams, Pharrell, 247
Williams Street, 263
Wolfgang Amadeus Phoenix (2009, Phoenix), 208–9

Xdrive, 118
xx, 276

Yankee Hotel Foxtrot (2002, Wilco), 162
Yauch, Adam, 205

Yazoo, 319
Yeah Yeah Yeahs (YYY), 29, 32–33, 39, 41, 182, 187, 209, 329
Yeezus (2013, Kanye West), 261, 262, 277
Yellow House (2006, Grizzly Bear), 180
Yo La Tengo, 145
Yoshimi Battles the Pink Robots (2002, The Flaming Lips), 40
You Forgot It in People (2002, Broken Social Scene), 82
Youth Novels (2008, Lykke Li), 282
YouTube, 128, 254

Zaireeka (1997, The Flaming Lips), 80
Zeichner, Naomi, 314
Zinner, Nick, 29
Zoladz, Lindsay, 228

About the Author

Stephanie Lehnert Photography

CHRIS DEVILLE is the managing editor at *Stereogum*, where he has written extensively about the full spectrum of indie music for the last twelve years. In 2014, he launched *The Week in Pop*, a column exploring mainstream music from an indie fan's perspective, and he has profiled bands like Tame Impala and Run The Jewels. Chris's writing has also been featured in outlets like *The Atlantic*, *The Washington Post*, *Rolling Stone*, and *The Ringer*. He lives with his family in Columbus, Ohio.